Laugh Cry
Rewind

A Memoir

JUDY HAVESON

J Press Books

For permissions contact: judy@judyhaveson.com

Cover by Laura Kicinski

Author Photo by Adam Cohen

ISBN: 979-8-9866249-1-4 (print)

Printed in United States of America

Author's Note

This memoir is based solely on my memory, and let's face it, I barely remember what I ate for breakfast. Some of the stories did not happen precisely as they are depicted, some events have been compressed, some dialogue has been recreated, and some names and identifying characteristics have been changed to protect the privacy of those involved. That said, I did my utmost to keep the story as close to reality as possible. The essence of the story, and the impact of my life's events as I know them to be, are true.

To Celia—

You'll forever be in my heart, and I hope I made you proud.

Prologue

It's fun to learn which celebrities and famous people share my birthday, for no other reason than to confirm my birthday is indeed a momentous day. Notables include Mae West, the original blonde bombshell who once said, "Good girls go to heaven, bad girls go everywhere." Also, the *Raging Bull* "You talkin' to me?" actor Robert De Niro. And my all-time favorite, *Fast Times at Ridgemont High* stoner Jeff Spicoli, played by Sean Penn, whose famous line, "I'm so wasted!" defined most of my generation. Why did he have to grow up?

Celebrities aside, the most important person I will always share a birthday with is my big sister, Celia, born on Saturday, August 17, 1957. I came along seven years later, on Monday, August 17, 1964. It's certainly not an anomaly for siblings to be born on the same day. But according to my mother, she delivered two weeks early for both births, making it even more statistically unlikely.

The seven-year age gap sometimes affected our relationship, mainly because I always wanted to play with her. Celia couldn't be bothered with my childish antics, especially after discovering boys. As I grew up, she served as my role model, confidante, moral compass, protector, and best friend.

But back to our shared birthdays. I'll be honest, I thought it sucked that our birthdays were the same day because I didn't like sharing anything.

Our parents made a big deal out of our birthdays. We'd have two cakes (which my mother almost always baked and then decorated to perfection), great gifts, and sometimes week-long celebrations. My favorite cakes included Flipper, the dolphin from the television series, and Raggedy Ann. The Flipper cake had teal-colored icing made from pure sugar, which soaked through the vanilla cake and turned it blue, along with our tongues, and the intricate decorations on Raggedy Ann made her look like she might come alive and jump off the table.

Being seven years younger meant I had my celebration in the afternoon with Pin the Tail on the Donkey, musical chairs, peanut butter and jelly or cheese sandwiches, fruit punch, and cake. Later that night, Celia had the cool-girl slumber party with hot dogs and hamburgers, brownies and soda, and dance music. Of course, being the genuinely annoying little sister, I crashed her parties; shockingly, she and her friends always kicked me out.

On my eighth birthday, Celia and her friends celebrated her fifteenth birthday with an impromptu dance party while listening to Donny Osmond and David Cassidy on her new cassette tape deck. I slipped into the room and started dancing with them.

"Hey, get out of here, Judy, or I'll tell Mama," she screamed. I ignored her and kept dancing. Soon, all her friends were also screaming at me, and my mom dragged me away.

"It's not fair," I cried. "Why can't I stay? It's my birthday, too."

My mom looked at me with sympathetic eyes and said, "Because you're the little sister."

As I got older, I found a new appreciation for sharing our birthday. I looked forward to it every year, mainly because I looked up to Celia and wanted to be like her. While August 17 represented the one day of the year that bonded the two of us forever, our connection went far beyond that date.

We no longer celebrate our birthdays in person and haven't for many years. But I will always share a birthday with Celia in my heart. I remember our last celebration together. I had wanted

August 17 to be all about her and nothing about me for just that moment. But she wouldn't have anything to do with that idea at all. She said, "We will always share a birthday, and don't you forget that!" When she spoke, I usually listened. She also told me to continue our birthday traditions even after she was gone.

Today, my heart is a bit heavier every August 17. I may not have the big fancy cakes, fun parties, or even week-long celebrations, but I remember the good times and our unique connection.

My sister's death left me so lost that I wasn't sure of my purpose. Thoughts of her not being by my side left me paralyzed with fear. We'd never see each other get married or have children. We'd never travel the world together and make new memories. But her memory forever remains a guiding force in my life.

It's been many years since my sister's passing, and honestly, I'm not sure I've ever accepted it. How could I? How could anyone? But what I have done is keep her memory alive through pictures, stories, and learning. I have, of course, made plenty of mistakes and bad choices along the way, but isn't that part of life? I think she'd agree.

The following is a collection of my life stories before and after my sister's passing, illustrating how I've carried her with me through all my experiences and kept my promise to her that I never stop living. These stories represent happiness, hope, sadness, tragedy, triumph, love, and meaning, and they show I'm a survivor who doesn't take things for granted. I also don't take myself too seriously.

I'm a self-described late bloomer who, by definition, becomes successful, attractive, etc., later in life than other people. I'd also add to the list gets married and has a child after forty. Was that my plan? Who knows? Honestly, I'm not sure we ever plan how our lives will look. As the saying goes, "Make plans, and God laughs." Intended or not, this is my life. But my story doesn't begin or end here.

To be clear, I don't believe I have an extraordinary life. Or maybe I do. Anyway, where is it written that celebrities and athletes are the only people who can share their stories? (Though

I've read my fair share of books about the rich and famous). But I have another purpose for sharing my journey. I want others who have suffered an inconceivable loss or another life-altering event to know that life goes on even if it seems unimaginable. I'm living proof of this revelation.

My mother once wisely told me, "Judy, there are many things you can't change in your life, but your hair color isn't one of them." While I took this sage wisdom and began dying my hair at age twenty-eight, I understood her advice had nothing to do with my vanity. She meant that life is constantly changing. Some days we'll laugh, other days we'll cry, but then we rewind and begin anew. In truth, I've never been a fan of change. And while life might not always seem fair, ultimately, the choice to surrender or keep living is ours.

In Celia's last days, I made her promises I vowed to keep. I promised to celebrate the good times—like birthdays—and learn to accept the bad times, even when they don't make sense, and to never stop living.

So many people in my life never got the opportunity to know my wonderful sister, Celia. I will forever keep her memory alive through my promise to live my best life, even with all the ups and downs thrown my way, because, in terms of universal time, we're only here for a moment.

Part One

Chapter 1

I grew up in Houston, Texas, during the 1970s and 1980s with my mother, Barbara; my father, Robert; and my big sister, Celia. But I entered the world at the Caney Valley Hospital in Wharton, Texas, a small town fifty miles southwest of Houston that sits along the Colorado River. This idyllic setting is where I spent many summers and holidays with my grandparents, Jack and Bertha Roth.

While best known for its agriculture, cotton fields, and friendly folks, Wharton had also been a destination for many Jewish immigrants arriving from Europe beginning in the later part of the 1800s. At that time, Joe Schwartz, a successful dry goods merchant, arranged to bring his sister, Hannah Kreitstein, brother-in-law, Isaac Kreitstein, and other relatives to America. Hannah and Isaac were my great grandparents, and they became part of Wharton's tight-knit Jewish community.

The story of Wharton and many of its characters, including Joe Schwartz and the Kreitsteins, comes to life in American playwright and Academy Award-winning screenwriter Horton Foote's 1999 book, *Farewell: A Memoir of a Texas Childhood*. Foote wrote about his memories of the many kind families and colorful people he met while growing up in Wharton, daring to paint Texas and Texans in a far more intellectual light than Hollywood or Broadway ever did.

Joe Schwartz owned a successful clothing store that shared his name. The haberdashery sat in the middle of the town's square with a grand staircase ascending to the second floor from the main level, looking like part of the *Gone with the Wind* movie set. By contrast, my great grandparents owned a less-successful small shoe repair business.

In his pages about the Schwartz and Kreitstein businesses, Foote wrote about the perceived prosperity between the two merchants. He marveled at the mystery of how the Kreitstein's shoe repair stayed in business. Foote's father explained that the Jews in town, unlike the Gentiles, were loyal and always ready to take care of each other. This was symbolic of the Jewish community of Wharton.

In 1905, shortly after my great grandparents settled in Texas, my grandmother, Bertha, was born. The family quickly became part of Wharton's Jewish fabric. When she was twenty-six years old, Bertha and her parents took a train to visit relatives in New York City. During this trip, Bertha met a handsome gentleman, Jack Roth, and was instantly smitten. She told him he should visit her in Texas because she knew he'd love it.

Jack took Bertha's advice, and not only did he fall in love with Texas, but he also fell in love with Bertha. They were married in 1933. The following year, my connection to Wharton was solidified with the birth of my mother, Barbara.

My grandfather became the sole proprietor of a liquor store called Joe's Package Store, named for my Uncle Joe, my mother's younger brother. I never understood why it wasn't called Barbara's Package Store after his firstborn. My uncle never appreciated my logic. I practically grew up at this store. "Your first words weren't Da Da or Ma Ma; they were Old Crow and Johnny Walker," my mother always joked.

The small building with metal siding had a big red neon sign, "Joe's Package Store." Behind the counter, Papa sat on my favorite wooden chair with a green vinyl cushion. This chair used to sit in my great grandfather's shoe repair store and, before that, in the shoe department of Joe Schwartz.

While small in size, the store seemed larger than life to me. Liquor bottles of all shapes and forms lined the shelves stacked from the floor to the ceiling. A front window displayed seasonal selections and promotional items to draw customers inside.

I felt so grown up sitting in his chair behind the counter, ringing up customers on the manual cash register. By today's standards, if Papa allowed a minor on the premises of a store that sold alcohol and tobacco, he'd be arrested, but things were different then. I kept both the chair and cash register from his store, and each time I see them, my memories take me back to my grandfather's store. I can still smell his cigar.

Unfortunately, my memory of my grandmother, Bertha, is limited. She passed away in 1968, shortly before my fourth birthday. I do recall her carrying me around the house and singing "Hello, Dolly." In Horton Foote's memoir, he remembered her as a jolly, friendly soul who spoke with a broad Southern accent.

My mother told me Bertha was a fiery force in town, too, and it had nothing to do with her flaming red hair. A born and bred Whartonian, Bertha knew everyone in town. "My mother never met a stranger," was always my mom's description of Bertha.

But, while taking care of everyone else, she forgot to take care of herself. She passed at the young age of sixty-three. My grandfather never remarried. When my grandmother died, I gave Papa some of my Kiddle dolls. These tiny little dolls came in different colors and faces. I placed them on top of his TV to keep him company. Many of the dolls disappeared over the years, and the only one left had fiery red hair, just like Bertha. When Papa died, I buried the trinket with him, so it could keep him company.

While living in Austin, Texas, my cousin, Fred—Joe Schwartz's grandson—told me about Mr. Foote's appearance at the Texas Book Fair, and we both wanted to meet him. Since Fred, a born and raised Whartonian, and I both had ties to Wharton, we were eager to meet Mr. Foote and tell him about our shared connection.

"Mr. Foote, I want to thank you for the nice things you wrote about my grandfather, Joe Schwartz, in your new book," Fred said upon meeting Horton Foote. Fred then turned to me and said, "She isn't thrilled about how you described her great-grandparents, Isaac and Hannah Kreitstein." Fred and his smart mouth. As I extended my hand to Mr. Foote, I felt the heat rise in my cheeks from sheer embarrassment. He cautiously looked at me while shaking my hand and said, "They were lovely people."

Fred innocently teasing me represented our close relationship. He's always been more like a big brother than a cousin. And as far as bloodlines go, we're second cousins once removed. Nonetheless, we were in the same gene pool. No matter how close or far apart the genealogy family tree spread, Fred became an integral part of my life, especially after living with my family during the summer of 1972, after he graduated from NYU business school.

My mother taught elementary school and had summers off with my sister, Celia, and me. Fred mainly spent time with his friends and did his own thing, but he still found time to hang out with us and visit the beach, see movies and go to Houston Astros baseball games, or play board games at home.

On occasion, Fred would bring his friends to our house. One evening, he showed up with his girlfriend, Paula. My mother and father were out for the evening, and Celia was at a slumber party. That meant I was home with the babysitter. Fred and Paula rang the doorbell, and the babysitter answered. "Hi," he said. "I'm Fred, the Havesons' cousin, and I'm staying here and forgot my keys. Can I please come in to get them?" he asked.

The babysitter said, "I'm sorry, but I can't let anyone in the house without permission from Mr. and Mrs. Haveson."

Fred looked down at me as I stood next to the babysitter in the doorway. "Judy, please tell the babysitter who I am so I can come in and get my keys," he said.

At the tender age of eight, I channeled my inner sarcastic self, looked up at Fred, and turned to the babysitter. "I've never seen him before in my life."

We all got a good laugh out of this memory eventually. This began a special bond between Fred and me that forever made us more than merely second cousins once removed.

Fred later married a remarkable woman named Kay, and she became a big sister to Celia and me. They had four children: Leslie, Mark, Jay, and Nancy. According to genealogy, Fred's children and I are third cousins once removed. Does that even count as family? But because of my close relationship with Fred and Kay, my cousins also forever hold a special place in my heart.

Mr. Foote said nice things in his book about my great grandmother, Hannah, describing her as a friendly soul who was always sympathetic to families who were less fortunate or experiencing tragedies.

Tzedakah is the Hebrew word for charitable giving, and this is what my grandparents always taught my mother, and in turn, she taught me. It doesn't matter whether you have a lot or very little; there's always someone less fortunate who needs help. But tzedakah isn't only about giving money.

For my grandfather, tzedakah included helping his regular customers at the liquor store. All the town folk loved Mr. Jack.

"Judy, my best piece of advice for you is always to be sincere," he'd tell me. And this is why he was so beloved.

Not only did he provide his customers the ability to purchase wine, beer, spirits, cigarettes, cigars, and gum, he provided tax and legal advice. His being neither an accountant nor a lawyer made no difference to these fine folks. He also acted as a delivery service for some regulars, especially for one customer, Miss Camille, who lived in a pink house down a long dirt road. Her home hid behind overgrown weeds, and you could barely see it from the street. Papa drove to her house every Friday evening and left a brown paper bag with a fifth of bourbon or scotch or whatever she was drinking that week on her driveway.

She'd come inside the store on occasion while I was in town. I remember she dressed in church clothes, always with a hat on her head and big pearls around her neck. And she always smelled lovely.

"Well, look at how grown-up you gittin', missy. I remember when you was just waist-high," she always said to me in her Southern twang.

"How will you get the money from Miss Camille?" I would ask Papa. "She never pays you." He would look at me and say, "I just add it to her tab." I secretly wondered if Miss Camille ever paid her tab.

My happiest Wharton memories are in Papa's cozy house. Not because it was big or grandiose with expensive decorations and fancy furniture, but because it was the exact opposite. The little white house with the vast yard sat on Avenue C and Texas Street.

Pecan, pear, and fig trees filled the space. The figs and pears were the sweetest things I ever tasted, and I would sometimes eat them right from the tree, even the ones that fell on the ground. We'd jar the pears and figs and soak them in water with lemon rinds and sugar. Once they were ready, we'd eat them straight out of the jar. And I'd gather the pecans scattered all over the yard that had fallen from the tree. When our car turned the corner onto Avenue C, I couldn't wait for my treats.

Just past the front steps of the house was the living/dining room. With its sunken sofas, high back armchairs, color television, and worn carpet with squeaky floorboards from heavy foot traffic, this room represented the heart of the home. A window air conditioner unit sat in the corner, constantly running and loudly humming, especially during the hot summer months. In the evenings, I'd often find my grandfather sitting at the dining table, counting his money from the day's sales that he would deposit in the bank the following morning.

"Papa, you are so rich," I'd always tell him when I saw the twenties, tens, fives, ones, and occasional fifties and hundreds. It was only later that I learned it was typically a couple of hundred dollars at most.

"Judy, I will give you advice related to money," he said to me one night while counting the day's sales.

"What is it, Papa?"

"Never squander your money," he said. "Don't deny yourself pleasure but give yourself limits. Independence is the best thing in the world."

I've never forgotten his words.

The kitchen was compact but functional, and my grandfather cooked many meals for himself. He is responsible for my love of Cream of Wheat, celery or mushroom soup and noodles, challah French toast, and midnight snacks although not eaten at midnight. When he got home from his store every night after 9:00 p.m., he made himself a "midnight snack." Typically he had ice cream, but on Saturday nights, his snack included chips and a cold beer, which he ate and drank while sitting in front of the TV watching wrestling matches.

Next to the window in the kitchen sat an expandable table with three chairs on top of the checkered black and white linoleum-tiled floor. The fourth chair wouldn't fit, so it rotated around the house as extra seating for company. Yellow cabinet doors lined the kitchen and often stuck as if paint had dried them shut. Built-in shelves on the wall displayed many of the tchotchkes collected from his worldwide trips.

A rotary telephone hung on the wall with a long stretchy cord, which enabled you to take the hand receiver with you while cooking or if you needed to go into the next room as if it were a portable telephone before they even existed. A small storage closet sat next to the phone they called the "broom" closet, but more than brooms filled the space. It became my ultimate hiding place.

"Has anyone seen Judy? It's time to leave," my mom would yell through the house, pretending not to know where I was hiding.

"But I don't want to go back to Houston," I'd often cry, stepping out of the closet.

"I know, but you have to go to school," she'd say.

"I hate school."

"Oh, you have to go to school, Judy. Education is so important," Papa would say. "Besides, you'll be back soon."

And I knew we would.

Before I was born, Celia got very comfortable owning the title "only grandchild." For her seventh birthday, in anticipation of my arrival, my grandparents bought her a Charmin' Chatty Cathy doll, so she'd have something special to celebrate that had nothing to do with my birth. This doll was the second most popular behind the Barbie doll, but unlike Barbie, Cathy had a string in her back you pulled, and she talked. She said phrases like, "I love you" and "I'm hungry." I'm sure Celia would have preferred she'd say, "Ignore the baby" or "Let the baby cry."

My mother always told the story of when they brought me home from the hospital. She had set up my crib in the main bedroom of my grandfather's house. It was the largest room, with a smaller room next door, where Celia slept. One evening, Papa came into the room to check on me, and out of the darkness, he heard, "Stay away from *that* baby!" Having a new baby sister was an acquired taste for Celia.

But one of my all-time favorite Celia stories is when she decided to play beauty shop with her Cathy doll and cut her hair.

"What do you mean her hair won't grow back?" she cried.

"Celia, Cathy is a doll, and once you cut her hair, it won't grow back because Cathy is not a human," my mother pointedly explained.

After my mother put me down for a nap, Celia crawled into the crib to cut my hair. She hid the hair and scissors under my blanket as if no one would ever find them. Before she escaped from the crib, my mother walked into the room and busted her.

"Celia Hannah, what are you doing in that crib with those scissors?" my mother screamed. "You could have seriously hurt your sister."

"But Judy's hair will grow back," she said. That marked the end of my sister's beauty school aspirations.

As siblings, we were an odd pair. She was always taller than me, and as adults that didn't change. She stood five foot ten to my five foot three. When we were younger, my mother loved putting us in matching outfits. In one picture, she posed us together in front of the house in handmade red dresses with a white border, two big pockets on the front, and white tights.

"You always looked so cute in the dresses Mama put us in, and I always looked like I was wearing a potato sack," Celia complained. The dress appeared stretched on her long lean body.

"Trust me, just because my dress looked shorter and less stretched than yours didn't mean I looked cuter. They were still hideous outfits," I'd tell her.

We also had different hair colors. Celia's hair was dark brown, almost black; mine was light brown, or what my mother called dishwater blonde. We even had nicknames based on our hair color: Blackie and Brownie.

We had your typical sibling rivalry where jealousy ran deep. Mainly I envied her because she was older, wiser, and taller than me. These emotions became very clear when it came to our Papa. It makes sense when you think about it since Celia had him to herself for so many years before I entered the world and ruined her life. Papa became an expert mediator between us, and no matter how angry or frustrated we got with one another, he always steered us in the right direction.

"You two are sisters, and you love each other. Stop bickering and get along."

Coming from six children, he knew the importance of family, especially siblings, and taught us the same. Life was more straightforward with him, and I'm so thankful for his wisdom.

Our seven-year age gap never seemed that significant to me when we were having good old-fashioned fun together. I always felt so fortunate to have an older sister to look up to and teach me about boys, fashion, music, make-up, and how to stay out of trouble with our parents, something I often struggled to overcome.

We would have loved having another sibling, but it wasn't in the cards. My mom didn't have fertility issues preventing her from becoming pregnant after Celia, but, as she put it, "Nature stopped me from having more children until you were born." Celia and I had the best life together as sisters regardless, and I couldn't wait to see what the future held. I never imagined we'd run out of time.

Chapter 2

If Wharton represented small-town charm, friendly folks, and a tight-knit community, you'd think the big metropolis of Houston would be the complete opposite. In some ways, it was, except at times, it felt more like Wharton, especially with the life my parents created for my sister and me, where making friends and family memories took precedent over all else.

My sister and I didn't grow up in big houses or fancy neighborhoods compared to many friends around us. We grew up in the suburbs of Sharpstown, one of the first master-planned communities in the country and the first of its kind in Houston. This neighborhood personified the primarily white working middle class. Most of the children we hung out with were latch-key kids, meaning both parents worked, and we were given keys to the front door to get into the house after school while our parents were at their jobs.

Our two-story white brick house with the bright orange front door sat in the middle of a tree-lined block. During summers, children played outside, despite the sweltering humidity, until the streetlamps turned on, indicating it was time to call it a night. The neighborhood homes were filled with the sweet smell of homemade chocolate chip cookies. Each house served as a revolving door of fun with kids coming and going all summer long.

One afternoon, a man drove down our street selling wayward trees from the back of his truck. Neighbors paid him five dollars for each misfit. His trees looked more like sticks than mature saplings. My parents bought one quirky tree for Celia and another for me. While many families measured children's height and age by notches on a door frame, we'd use the growth of our trees.

"Look, I can climb to the top," I once said to Celia on my way up her tree. For some reason, hers grew thicker and taller than mine.

"But can you get down?" she laughed. She'd eventually climb up to get me, a symbolic picture of our relationship: Celia saving me from danger and forever rescuing me from myself.

Yucca trees with their sword-shaped leaves lined the front entrance of our house, daring to stab anyone who walked through my mother's plant beds. It never seemed to stop friends who toilet-papered our house, though. A vast backyard carpeted with green grass gave us even more space to play with our friends.

Our Sharpstown home played host to many childhood memories and milestones. Birthday and holiday celebrations like my father's epic surprise fortieth birthday party and the Hanukkah latke party where my mother stood in the kitchen peeling and frying potatoes all night were just a few. "I think you've eaten a dozen latkes each," she said to my father, grandfather, and cousin Fred. A generous estimate. Like a contest of who could eat the most, the final tally well-exceeded a dozen. The house smelled of fried potatoes for at least a week afterward.

Nothing matched our first day of school rituals though, especially my first day of kindergarten. This rite of passage is usually filled with emotions and later included the tradition of staged photos such as walking out the front door holding book bags and lunch boxes, posing like we were sitting for a Sears portrait, and finally, the solo smiling photo demonstrating sheer excitement about the day.

But my first day of kindergarten included none of these theatrical scenes. I instead took emotional overload to a whole new level.

"I've got the flu, so no pictures this morning," my mother said from her sickbed, barely able to move. "Just get yourself ready, and I'll take you in the car."

Pat Neff Elementary School, my new home away from home, housed K-6 students. All the new kindergarten pupils had a split day of morning and afternoon sessions. Even though the kindergarten kids were part of the student body, the kindergarten classrooms had been relegated to shacks at the back of the school. These metal portable buildings looked like mobile homes that could move at a moment's notice.

"Are you coming in with me?" I asked my mother as we drove up to the school.

"I'll just watch you from the car; I don't want to get anyone sick," she replied.

I nervously walked into the shacks where boys and girls were wandering around, looking at big circles on the carpet. Each circle had a name next to it, our new place for the year. Big smiles flashed across teachers' faces as they chatted with the parents who didn't have the flu and could come inside. I felt overwhelmed but still very excited.

Everyone was dressed in their best clothes. The girls wore dresses with frilly socks and patent leather shoes, and the boys were dressed in shorts and pressed shirts, with knee socks and saddle loafers. We all looked like we had jumped out of the pages of a JCPenny catalog.

I wandered around the classroom, searching for my name next to the big circles on the carpet until a teacher approached me.

"Can I help you find your name?" she asked.

Unlike me, many kids didn't know how to read or recognize their names in kindergarten.

"No, thank you. I can find my name," I said.

After I circled the room several times, still searching for my name, the teacher again asked me if she could help me find my name. She took me by the hand, and we walked around the classroom.

With a puzzled look on her face as she searched, she finally walked over to her desk, with me still in tow, not dropping her hand.

She pulled out a clipboard and scanned the list. "That's strange; I don't see your name," she said. "Is your mother or father here with you?"

I felt tears form behind my eyes and a lump grow in my throat. "No," I said.

She then flipped the page, scanned it, and looked excited, as if she'd just discovered gold at the end of the rainbow. "Oh, I get it; your name isn't on the carpet because you're not in the morning class; you're in the afternoon class," she said.

I quickly dropped her hand and ran out of the classroom. I ran as fast as my little legs could take me, across two different streets, down my block, and when I got to my front door, I ran inside the house, gasping and screaming.

"Mommy, you took me to the wrong class," I said. I think my mother had just crawled back into bed when I burst through the door. "I'm never going back to school," I declared. This traumatizing moment altered my life forever, and anytime I'm someplace I don't think I should be, I'm right back to that day I was searching for my name in the circle.

When my mother brought me back to school for the afternoon session, she walked into the classroom with me, Kleenex in hand.

Fortunately, I recovered from that harrowing experience. Still, I would go on to experience different challenges, primarily being bullied. Back then, they didn't call it that; it was simply good old-fashioned name-calling. Kids are cruel, especially to each other. I don't think they intend to be mean or hurtful, or maybe they do, but the bottom line is kids can be unkind. Being on the receiving end of cruelty in the formative years of grade school meant life wasn't always fun, especially in the fourth grade when I became the target of some mean kids. That's when I started wearing glasses full-time, making matters even worse.

Unfortunately, I'll have to wear glasses forever because I didn't listen to my father. "If you keep wearing glasses when you don't need them, you'll be wearing them the rest of your life," he said. I should have listened to his sage advice. So began my glasses-wearing journey that continues through today.

Maurice, a boy in fourth grade and my first crush, had dark hair cut in a mop top like The Beatles, and to me, he may as well have been Paul McCartney. His best friend, Robbie, had orange hair. The three of us sat together in class, and since I liked Maurice, naturally, I thought that meant he liked me.

"Judy, you're a four-eyed freak, leave me alone," Maurice said one day when I tried to sit with him at lunch. I cried my four eyes out all night long.

"It just means he likes you back," Celia said, trying to comfort me. I didn't see it that way. I had also selected psychedelic frames instead of getting typical colored or metal frames for my first eyeglasses. In the 1970s, everything was groovy, so why couldn't my eyeglasses be hip, too? So there I was, in the fourth grade, with my fashionable eyeglasses—branded a four-eyed freak just like every other kid in spectacles—and we began learning about the solar system, making things worse.

Most kids growing up in Houston dreamed of becoming astronauts since we were home to the Johnson Space Center. Learning about the solar system ranked as highly as math, maybe more. We'd study a different planet each week, and the fun began for me when we got to Jupiter.

"Class, can you tell me what is special about the planet Jupiter?" the teacher asked.

Robbie with the orange hair shot his hand up to answer.

"Jupiter has a big red spot and wild, crazy colors, like Judy's ugly glasses. Here comes Judy, the jumping Jew from Jupiter." Most of the class laughed, and I remember feeling the redness form in my cheeks, thinking I looked more like Mars that day than Jupiter.

"This just means he likes you," my sister told me again, her go-to answer for why boys teased me.

While this was not as insulting as other ethnic slurs, it was still insensitive. And since I was on a tiny Jewish island by myself at the school, I didn't have many advocates to stand up for me. For all these kids knew, Jews jumped, and we all came from Jupiter.

There weren't many Jewish people in Sharpstown. Our block lit up for Christmas. I was probably one of the only Jewish kids in my fourth-grade class, maybe one of only a few in the entire school. But I wouldn't classify the people in my town as anti-Semitic or evil. I'd call them uneducated about Judaism and Jewish people in general. It made no difference because I didn't decide to be friends with someone based on whether they prayed on the same day as me or celebrated the same religious holidays. But being one of the only Jewish kids in my school was undoubtedly attention-grabbing.

In the fifth grade, I bought a new pair of eyeglass frames that made me blend in with everyone else. Still a four-eyed freak but at least no longer alone.

My school challenges didn't center on my religion alone. I struggled with schoolwork and not for lack of brilliance. No, I mainly suffered from boredom. Regardless, I gave minimal effort and my grades reflected this. Fortunately, my elementary schoolteacher mother saved me.

My mom began teaching after first attending the University of Texas and later transferring to and graduating from the University of Houston.

Being a schoolteacher in the south during the 1960s came with challenges. "I will need you to take this permission slip home with you and have your husband sign it," her school's principal had told her.

"What is this, and why do I need my husband's signature?" my mother had asked.

"It's to allow you to be able to teach little Black kids we'll be busing in from other neighborhoods," he replied.

"I don't need my husband to permit me, and you don't need to ask me," my mother said. "I will teach kids of all color."

I never considered my mom a passionate women's libber or civil rights advocate. Still, this story always helped me understand the importance of standing up for yourself.

As a beloved teacher to her students, having a mom as an educator represented a blessing and a curse. A blessing because she had access to my books and materials and could help me study—who knows how far behind I would have fallen without her aid, and a curse because it meant I couldn't hide or get away with anything like poor grades or missing assignments.

While flipping through my notebook at a sixth-grade open house, my mother noticed something was off. "Robert, do you see what I'm seeing on this paper?" she asked my father.

"That's not your signature, and your name is spelled wrong," he said.

One of the oldest tricks in a schoolteacher's bag is asking for a parent's signature on a child's assignment with a poor grade, ensuring the parent sees it. It's a tried-and-tested tactic used for generations. On the opposite side, however, is the often tried-and-failed tactic whereby the student who received the poor grade on an assignment hides said assignment from the parent and simply "signs" their name as proof. I doubt I'm the only kid in history to have tried this trickery, but I'm surely one of the few who misspelled their mother's name when forging her signature.

My father inspected the paper. "I guess she thought you were Barbra Streisand," he said.

My mom spells her name Barbara, but for whatever reason, I had spelled it Barbra, like the famous singer. When she got home, my mother confronted me. "Did you think you'd get away with it?" she asked.

"Yes, I did," I said. Why lie twice?

It's important to note that Miss Honor Society Celia never pulled any tricks of this sort. So this was uncharted territory for my parents. Celia and I couldn't have been more opposite with our school priorities if we tried. She studied hard to make good grades, and I put in minimal effort. I always knew she'd go to a top school because of her academic discipline and excellent report cards and become very successful at whatever she decided to be in life. My parents had big expectations for her, too.

Imagine my father's shock when she came home after meeting with the school guidance counselor and told my parents she wanted to attend the University of Miami.

"Why there?" my father asked.

"Because they have a great football team," she replied.

"If you think I'm going to pay out-of-state tuition so you can go to a school with a great football team, you better think again," he snapped back. It was one of the first times I ever saw my father flustered when it came to anything related to Celia and school.

"What's your second choice?" my mom asked.

"Oklahoma University," she said.

"Let me guess, they also have a good football team?" my father asked.

"Yes," she said. She loved football and believed a school with a winning team would be more exciting and fun to attend.

At least she was honest.

Celia ultimately decided to attend The University of Texas at Austin, and it turns out the Texas Longhorns also had an excellent football team to satisfy her need for such a thing.

"I want to major in Elementary Education," she told my parents. "I'd like to be a schoolteacher like Mama."

While it was a compliment, my mother hoped Celia would want to do something else with her life. A year later, my mother's wish came true. Celia spent the summer working at a children's daycare facility and, after a particularly horrendous day, she decided on a different path. "Please take me to Austin, so I can change my major," Celia said, "I no longer want to be a teacher."

"Hallelujah!" my mother said.

That day, Celia changed her major from Elementary Education to Business.

Celia set the bar high for education in our home, and I could only imagine living up to her standards. I knew she worked hard, but it seemed like it came so easy to her. Nothing felt that way to me.

The area in which I did exceed expectations—other than in my mischievous childhood antics of constantly challenging my parents—was rooted in the unconditional love of my family, particularly my sister. Ours was an extraordinary relationship. We were fiercely loyal to each other, had each other's backs, and were ready to swap places in a heartbeat to alleviate the other's pain, even though neither would allow that to happen. The relationship wasn't perfect, and we had our fair share of disagreements, but our bond was unbreakable. If I could have only been graded on this subject in school, I would have been in the honor society like Celia.

Chapter 3

The best part of my mom's chosen profession had nothing to do with helping me not flunk out of school and everything to do with summer vacation. While most working moms only got a week off here and there, my mom got the whole summer off. This meant fun family adventures to the beach, Astroworld, baseball games, movies, and memorable road trips. Sometimes these trips didn't go as planned, but we always had a good time and grew closer as a family.

In the 1970s, well before the invention of GPS for cars, we'd visit the local AAA office to map out our route before each journey. The TripTiks they gave us—essentially road maps—let us collaborate with the person at the office to highlight different ways to our ultimate destination while also marking other points of interest.

After finishing at the AAA office, my mom, sister, and I would head to the grocery store to buy our road trip essentials: soda, chips, bread, snacks, fruit, and the ever important smoked turkey sliced for sandwiches. We'd eat lunch at rest stops along the way. At the time, I didn't understand why my parents didn't stop at restaurants for lunch, since we ate breakfast and dinner at a different place every day. However, when I got older, I understood that by feasting on the road, we'd save money for more important things like staying in nicer hotels and letting my sister and me buy souvenirs at each stop. This small gesture taught me a huge life lesson about the value of money and showed my parents' selflessness when it came to my sister's and my happiness. But by day four, none of us could look at another piece of smoked turkey, so we'd stop at roadside favorites like Howard Johnson's, Stuckey's, and Denny's.

My family took a lot of road trips. We flew on airplanes, too, but something about car trips brought us closer together. Our travels included driving to Florida to visit Disney World, and to Washington, D.C. to vacation with relatives from New Jersey. Our road trips were never short journeys, but in a way, that made them even more memorable. On each trip, one thing would always happen that we'd talk and laugh about for years to come. Like on the Florida trip when my mother made me share a bed with her friend's daughter because the daughter had chickenpox.

"Judy, sleep with Cara. You'll get the chickenpox out of the way before school starts," she said.

I'm sure this would be a form of child abuse by today's standards. Like magic, I got chickenpox two weeks after we got home from Florida. On our trip to D.C., my Aunt Barbara decided to buy a big bag of candy for Celia and me to share on the ride home. I ate half the bag before we left Virginia, forcing my father to pull over so I could vomit on the side of the road.

My father traveled all over the world for his work. He marketed and sold automated pipeline systems to oil and gas companies. My sister and I never really understood what that meant. But he traveled a lot. In the summer of 1976, he decided to take us with him.

"Let's turn my business trip to California into a family vacation with the girls," my father said. "We can spend two weeks driving through California, Nevada, and Arizona." We were thrilled to go on one of his business trips. Our trip out west began on July 31, 1976, driving as far across Texas as we could since that drive alone is halfway to California.

"I finally understand the concept of mile markers," I announced as I watched the miles tick off. There's nothing between Houston and El Paso unless you count the long roads, highways, hills, mountains, tumbleweeds, and skunk smells. Driving through miles and miles of West Texas, Celia sarcastically said, "Is this it?" That one question became our mantra for the entire trip. After another day of travel through New Mexico and Arizona and lots of "Is this it?" comments, we made it to Blythe, a small town just inside California's state line.

"They should rename it Fly, California because of all the flies," my father said. There were so many flies in our hotel room, it felt like summer camp. I'm not sure anyone slept since we spent most of the night swatting the annoying creatures. We left very early the following day.

We stayed at the Marriott Hotel in Newport Beach, California. Beautiful boats and yachts and great shopping sat directly across the street from the hotel. Very few things impressed me at the age of eleven, but this place did. Walking along the pier, Celia and I felt like Ginger and Mary Anne getting ready to board the SS *Minnow* from *Gilligan's Island*. I half expected to see Mr. and Mrs. Thurston Howell III with the Skipper and Gilligan coming to greet us.

My father left us the next day for business meetings, and my mother treated us to Universal Studios in Los Angeles. As we boarded the shuttle bus to the studio, the guide took our names and asked us what kind of juice we wanted to drink. "We have apple juice, orange juice, and pineapple juice, but we don't have Chinese juice; you get those in Chinatown." Later my mother explained he meant Chinese Jews, not Chinese juice. A stupid joke then and still is today.

Growing up, I watched a lot of television, and as we drove through the back lot, I believed the houses and façades were actual settings. "On your left, you'll see a big hill in the distance," the tour guide informed us. "You'll recognize it from many of your favorite television shows and movies, including the opening credits of *The Waltons*. But it's most famous for the scene in the *Sound of Music* where Julie Andrews runs down the hill singing the theme song."

I couldn't believe it.

"Next on your right is the house used in the popular drama, *Marcus Welby, M.D.*, but you younger kids may know it as the house where the Beave lives from *Leave It to Beaver*."

What? How could this be? I never viewed television shows or movies the same after this tour. Oh, and the shark in *Jaws*—also fake—and named Bruce.

After returning to the hotel, my father met us for dinner. I ordered a hamburger and fries. When it arrived at the table, I noticed mayonnaise smeared all over the bun, and that's when the fun began. I've never been a fan of most sauces, condiments, or anything that touches my food for most of my life, and at the top of the list is mayonnaise, with mustard a close second.

An appreciative child whose parents had taken her on an incredible family vacation to California would look the other way, eat the hamburger, and call it a night. Well, I wasn't that child. Instead of just letting it go and taking maybe one or two small bites, I shoved the plate away from me, wrinkled my nose, and said, "No way will I eat this with all that mayonnaise on it."

Let's say I picked the wrong time to dig in. My father, exhausted from a long day of business meetings, gave me a death stare and raised his voice. "You will eat every last bite of that hamburger, and you will not leave the table until you do."

"Judy, just eat the hamburger before getting in more trouble," Celia said.

"I don't want to," I replied.

"It's your choice, but you're making a bad decision," she warned.

Great, everyone is against me, I thought. Celia always tried to save me from trouble during conflicts with my parents. But I rarely listened or followed her guidance, even when I knew she was right.

I ate the hamburger with all eyes around the restaurant now on our table. But as I did, I made horrible retching sounds with each bite. Eventually, my father gave up and told me to stop after the first two bites, and I ultimately apologized. To this day, I ask if the hamburger comes dry when ordering to prevent future scenes.

The next day, we packed up the car, drove to San Francisco, and continued our drive up the California coast. And I thought driving from Houston to El Paso felt long. I'm not sure I thoroughly prepared myself for the length of this road trip. California is as long as Texas is vast and probably longer.

Just looking at the TripTik and the long highlighted yellow line of our route made me freak out. The drive from Los Angeles to San Francisco looked as far or further than the trek across Texas. I thought, "Will I survive another long car ride?" and "How many times will my dad let us stop and use the bathroom?" But I decided instead of worrying, I would sit back and enjoy the ride because I had used the "obnoxious kid" card the night before with the mayonnaise incident. I ended up being glad I did because the drive up the California coast did not disappoint, and we had the best time experiencing it together.

After several stops, including visiting the Queen Mary ship, seeing the Barbie factory, driving through the Del Monte Forest, eating lunch at Pebble Beach, and the miles and miles of the Pacific Ocean, we finally arrived in San Francisco.

We stayed in the Fisherman's Wharf area, and our adventure began the next day with a walk-away salad: literally food you ate while walking away.

Living in Houston, which is relatively flat, the hills and winding streets of San Francisco overwhelmed me. And these weren't just small hills; they were steep and massive. Lombard Street amazed me. "We're not seriously going to walk up that street?" I asked my mother.

The hairpin curves and windy bends reminded me of a fairy tale. Instead of walking up the street, we took a picture of it. We visited almost every store on California Street, my favorite, and my mom let us each buy souvenirs. I'm confident this began my love affair with shopping and searching for one-of-a-kind items.

Even though the calendar said August, the temperature didn't reflect the month when we left San Francisco the following morning. "We're freezing," Celia and I complained. "Please turn on the heat." We couldn't believe we spoke those words in August.

Next stop: Las Vegas. We pulled up to the Tahiti Motel in Las Vegas, and my dad got out of the car to see if they had a room for us. Exhausted and cranky, we'd been driving all day from San Francisco. My mom, sister, and I waited in the car, and tempers flared all around us. Going for hours and being cooped up in a car can do that to people. My mom and I were at each other's throats for most of the ride.

"If you don't stop biting your fingernails, I will smear quinine over them," she screamed at me. "Look at your nails; they're practically bleeding."

I had a horrible habit of biting my fingernails down to the quick, which she hated.

Suddenly, my dad ripped open the car door and said, "Let's get out of here!"

Sheer panic filled his face.

Not understanding, I asked, "Daddy, what's wrong?"

He quickly replied, "Nothing, we just need to leave."

He gave my mother a knowing look as we sped out of the parking lot.

Soon we arrived at The Tropicana Hotel and checked into a room.

"What happened to Daddy?" I asked my mom.

"There were 'working women' in the lobby," she replied.

"You mean prostitutes?" I said.

She just stared in disbelief that her eleven-year-old understood.

"What? Do you think Celia and I thought those women were going to church dressed like that?"

The hotel sat right next door to the famed MGM Grand. I couldn't get over all the lights and sounds of the Vegas Strip. I loved all the clinks and bells of slot machines and people at the Blackjack table and roulette wheel screaming when they won.

"I wish I could play the slots in the casino," I told my dad.

"I'll play them for you," he said and winked.

My sister and I settled with buying more souvenirs from the gift shop in the hotel, including a deck of cards so we could play Blackjack. We retreated to our hotel room while my parents partied. It didn't matter to us. We liked spending this sister bonding time together and talking about anything and everything. These times were always special when Celia and I could be together away from our parents.

"Do you like being away from home?" I asked her.

"I like college, but I miss being with you and Mama and Daddy," she replied.

"But you have to admit it's pretty cool being on your own, right?" I pressed her.

"Sure, but it's also hard because Mama makes things so easy, and sometimes I like that. You'll see one day."

The relationship between Celia and my mother was so much more than that of your typical mother-daughter duo. They were excellent friends. My friendship with Celia grew during these reflective times, and our sibling rivalry diminished. I loved having her as my big sister and, in many ways, my advisor in life. Of course, we'd still have moments once we got home. We were sisters, after all.

We were determined to have as much fun as possible on our road trip. Arizona and the Grand Canyon were next up, after a stop at the Hoover Dam before leaving Nevada.

We arrived at the Grand Canyon the next day, even grander than its name, and took a train ride down to the bottom, a long way down.

"We'll be walking back up to the top," my father informed us.

He was dead serious—until he started laughing. Always a huge tease.

With the last leg of the trip upon us, we geared up for another long drive across Texas. We left Arizona and stopped in Lubbock for lunch. Lubbock is the real heart of West Texas, dry and hot, with tumbleweeds blowing across the parking lot. I couldn't grasp this being the same Texas I lived in and how the two areas could be so different.

We continued driving and finally stopped in Abilene. Commonly referred to as the "Buckle of the Bible Belt," the people in West Texas took religion and social politics very seriously. Considered a "dry" town, you couldn't buy liquor either. But, outside of Abilene, Impact was a small "wet" town where you could buy beer or other spirits. We arrived at the hotel, and Celia informed us she had just started her period. Never being one to plan, this shocked her, and she was unprepared.

My sister and I found a convenience store in Impact about six blocks from our hotel. I can only imagine what this scene must have looked like: two young girls walking into a store to buy tampons and beer—just an example of the innocence of the 1970s or the start of a bad joke. And a perfect story to end a perfect family road trip.

We didn't spend every summer taking long road trips. Some summer vacations we spent closer to home. The following year, in 1977, my dad had another business trip to Oklahoma. This time he took my mom, and they left us at home.

"Celia is in charge of you while we're gone," my mother told me. "You need to listen to her and behave yourself."

We'd never been left alone like this before; we had always stayed with my grandfather in Wharton.

"I will," I promised my mother.

My connection with Celia would soon become even deeper that summer when I experienced an unthinkable trauma. And as scared as I was from this episode, having Celia by my side made me stronger, helped me survive, and allowed me to move forward with my life, never looking back.

Chapter 4

My cousin Fred and his girlfriend Kay stopped by our house on a Sunday evening in June to announce their engagement.

"I'm so excited," I said. "Do I get to come to the wedding?"

Being a kid, I rarely got invited to family weddings. Celia and I loved Kay and thought of her as our big sister. She spent a lot of time with us playing tennis, shopping, or hanging out at home.

"Bob and I are driving to Oklahoma tomorrow, and Celia's in charge of Judy while we're away," my mother said. "Will you please check in on them from time to time?"

"Of course," said Kay. "We'll make sure they're good."

Monday, June 6, 1977, was just another Monday, or so it should have been. My parents left early that morning to drive to Oklahoma for my dad's business trip, making it a mini-vacation to get some much-needed alone time away from my sister and me.

My school was out for the summer, and Celia was home from college, having just finished her sophomore year at The University of Texas at Austin. She and I had big plans for the entire week, revolving around shopping, movies, more shopping, eating, staying up late every night, and being wild sisters away from our parents. Our seven-year age gap didn't prevent us from having fun together; in fact, we were closer than most of my friends whose siblings were one to two years apart in age.

Before getting our fun week started, I had to go to the orthodontist for a checkup. I hated going to the orthodontist, and I hated wearing braces. What beauty I possessed in my preteen years with glasses and a mouth full of metal!

"Can't I skip the orthodontist today?" I asked.

"It will just take a few minutes to get your wires tightened, and we'll go shopping directly afterward," Celia said.

Dr. McGuffy, my orthodontist, and his wife were like family. They were so lovely that they made the appointments bearable, but wearing braces was still annoying. Their office occupied the second floor of the bank building attached to Sharpstown Center, the neighborhood shopping mall. My father often dropped me off in the mornings for my appointments and either Dr. McGuffy or his wife would drive me to school. I'd sometimes walk the mall and window shop while waiting for the office to open. I loved my independence.

On this June day, the sun shined bright, and the air felt like a sauna, not too unusual for pre-summer in Houston, Texas. I wore Keds, denim cut-offs, and my favorite pink T-shirt with galloping horses printed across it. Celia dropped me at the building just before 9:00 a.m., and I went straight to their office.

"I'll pick you up in an hour and meet you upstairs, so stay put until I arrive," she said.

"Okay," I said. I got out of the car and entered the building.

I walked into the elevator and punched the number two button, but the elevator didn't stop on the second floor that day. It kept going up. Oh well, I thought. I'd always wanted to know what the top floor looked like, and this detour would not make me late for my appointment.

On the way up, the elevator stopped on the sixth floor. A man stepped on and said hello.

"Hello," I said.

My mother taught me always to be polite to others. I would never have imagined this situation as anything other than sharing an elevator with another person. My entire life changed from the time it took for that elevator to go from the sixth floor to the ninth floor.

When the man got on the elevator on the sixth floor, he hit the ninth-floor button. I thought nothing of it. The elevator doors opened on the ninth floor, and he exited the car. As I looked past him into the space, I noticed an open area with no walls, large tarps splattered with paint, wires hanging from the ceiling, paint cans everywhere, giant ladders and platforms, and tons and tons of dust—a real mess.

As he walked off the elevator, he suddenly stopped, turned around, and asked, "Where are you going?"

Without hesitation, I replied, "The orthodontist."

He smiled, and as the doors began closing, he reached in with his huge hand and grabbed me off the elevator. Once my brain registered trouble, I started screaming and kicking and trying to break free. This giant man became no competition and completely overpowered my skinny twelve-year-old body. He wrapped one of his enormous hands over my mouth and dragged me with the other one around my neck, away from the elevator.

I continued to kick and scream, so he slapped me across the face and whispered in my ear, "If you don't stop, I will kill you." I stopped.

I wish I forgot everything that happened next, but I didn't. Unfortunately, I remember every aspect: the time, the clothes I wore, the smells—of the man's cologne and breath—and the construction, what the room looked like, the dust all over the floor and my clothes, the ringing in my ears, the pounding of my heart, the pain—of him on top of me and my body crashing into the hard cold concrete floor, the throbbing and burning between my legs, the sting from the slap on my cheek, the taste of my tears and his skin, but what I remember most is how I thought I would die and never see my parents or Celia again. Twelve years old. I wanted my mommy, daddy, and sister to come and save me.

Once he stopped, he stood up, threw my clothes at me, slapped me across my face again, and said, "Now, count to fifty before you get up to leave." Through the meanest eyes I'd ever seen, he then said, "If you tell anyone, especially the police or your parents, I will find you and kill you."

I sat naked with my hands wrapped around my knees, rocking back and forth, cold, afraid, and crying. I put my clothes on, slowly counted to fifty, and ran to the elevators. I kept looking around every corner. It's a trick, I thought. The evil man is probably waiting to kill me or hurt me again. I could smell him, but I couldn't see him. I'd learn later that the smells were him all over me.

When the elevator doors finally opened on the ground floor, the first person I saw was Celia. I ran out and grabbed her and started crying and gasping for air. I could barely get the words out of my mouth, but when I finally found my voice, I screamed, "He did it to me, he did it to me!"

Considering my age—twelve—and my minimal knowledge of anything sexual, "He did it to me" meant having sex with me. Although later I understood that's not what he did to me or what happened. At the time, I didn't even know what the word rape meant.

Dr. and Mrs. McGuffy and Celia quickly hurried me into the office. Mrs. McGuffy got me a glass of water while Celia tried to calm me down. Dr. McGuffy came into the room and said, "The police are on their way."

"No, no, no, you have to call and tell them not to come. He'll kill me if I tell the police. Please tell them not to come," I pleaded.

I truly believed he'd kill me. However, once the police arrived and talked to me, I started to calm down.

"You'll need to take your sister to a doctor for an examination and then bring her downtown to the police station to file a formal complaint and look at mugshots," the officer told Celia.

We held on to each other, paralyzed with fear.

"Don't leave me, ever," I said.

"I promise I won't," she said, holding on to me tight.

How could this be happening to us? To me? Suddenly, we appreciated having Kay and Fred as our emergency contacts while our parents were traveling.

Celia called Fred while we were still at the orthodontist's office and started crying as she told him what happened. Fred immediately called Kay at her office to update her and have her meet Celia and me at the police station in downtown Houston. Celia then called our family doctor, Frank Webber. Dr. Webber was such a fatherly figure. "Dr. Webber said we need to go home and get you clean clothes and shoes, but you can't take a bath or change clothes yet," Celia explained after speaking to the doctor.

When we arrived at Dr. Webber's office, he brought me into an examination room. Celia never left my side. Even though I fully trusted Dr. Webber, embarrassment overwhelmed me as he performed the examination. The pain was unbearable. I didn't understand what happened and why it hurt so much. I hadn't even started my period yet or had an examination in my private areas. I also couldn't figure out why Dr. Webber's eyes were so sad and angry.

Before leaving his office, a nurse took all my clothes and shoes and put them in a big plastic bag.

"The contents are evidence, and you'll need to take them with you to the police station," she explained. She said I would never get them back, not that I wanted any of it back, including my favorite pink T-shirt with the galloping horses.

Because her office was in downtown Houston, Kay met us at the police station and never left our side. The cold gray concrete building had long halls with overhead lights that blinked like a light bulb that needed changing. No pictures hung on the walls, and everything echoed when people walked from office to office. It's what I thought a big police station would look like.

The three of us sat outside in the hallway on a hard, uncomfortable wooden bench. Even with the hot and humid weather outside, I couldn't stop shivering as we sat and waited. The building played Muzak, overhead piped-in music, and I remember hearing "Undercover Angel" by Alan O'Day. It's a random but popular song from 1977. Every time I listen to it, I'm immediately brought back to sitting on that hard bench at the police station with Kay and Celia.

"I'm so sorry, I'm so sorry," is all I kept telling Celia as we waited to go inside.

"I don't know why you're apologizing because this isn't your fault," she replied.

But wasn't it? I kept thinking I could have done something to prevent this, or at the very least, I should have fought harder. I knew this happened to me as a punishment for past bad behavior. I couldn't process any of what happened, and in some ways, I still have a hard time with it today. Why would something like this happen to me if I didn't deserve it?

A female police officer and a male detective led us into a small windowless room.

"We want to talk to you about what happened and need you to give us as many details as you remember," the detective said.

He had a calm voice, which put me more at ease. I did my best to answer his questions and recount every aspect, but I couldn't focus because of Celia's tears, which made me cry. I just knew she felt guilty, but she shouldn't.

"Here's a book of pictures, and we want you to look closely to see if you recognize any of these men to be the man who did this to you," the detective said.

The man who raped me was Black, so all the men in the mug shot book I looked through were Black. I couldn't get the thoughts out of my head that he might be one of the angry-looking men in the mug shot book, or what if he wasn't one of the men in the book, or did all the men in this book do the same thing to other twelve-year-old girls? I didn't recognize any of the men in the pictures.

"This was likely a random act of violence," the detective told us. "Chances of us catching him are slim, and unless he attacks again—which we fully expect him to do—and unless someone else can identify him, he'll most likely get away with this. I'm so sorry."

The news comforted no one. After what felt like the longest day of my young life, we finally got home. I wanted to take a hot bath and wash everything off me. My pain was unbearable but worse, I could still smell him on my body.

"Celia, will you please stay here while I take my bath?" I asked. I wasn't sure I'd ever feel safe alone again.

Fred called my parents at their hotel in Oklahoma to tell them what happened, and that Kay was staying at the house with Celia and me. Dr. Webber then called to give them an update on his examination. He suggested they not rush home because he felt that wouldn't allow me to fully process everything.

My parents reluctantly agreed and came home a few days later. "This was one of the hardest things I'd ever done," my mom told me. But she agreed because she trusted Dr. Webber.

Kay moved in with Celia and me for the week, and she and Fred planned their wedding while staying with us. "I guess this means I am invited to your wedding," I said, smiling.

I'm pretty sure I didn't sleep the entire week. Every time I closed my eyes, I replayed everything over and over again. But worse, the pain in my body made it difficult to sleep. In my nightmares, he followed through on his threat to kill me, and most nights, I woke up screaming as if it were real.

While my physical pains eventually subsided and the bruises healed, my emotional and mental state took much longer to mend—and probably never fully will. I could never fully grasp why something like this would happen to me or to anyone. I also couldn't believe I survived. Questions and what-if scenarios plagued me. What stopped him from following through on his promise to kill me? Was he watching me, and did he know where I lived? Would he rape me again, and could others tell what happened? What would people think of me if they knew? Would I ever have a normal relationship with a boy? Would I never be able to stop thinking of this?

The other sliding door thoughts that overwhelmed me were what if I had taken another elevator car that day? Would it have skipped the second floor, too? How could taking one elevator over another be the difference in holding on to my twelve-year-old innocence a little longer versus being raped?

I'm not sure I've ever fully processed what happened, or maybe I've suppressed the entire event, but the memory forever remains in my subconscious. I've only shared this story with my closest family and friends through the years—mainly because of the embarrassment and shame of being raped. I never wanted to be treated differently or like a victim.

Even though I've come to understand this wasn't my fault, in some ways, I will always look at it as punishment and feel as if I did something wrong. Truthfully, I found myself in the wrong place at the wrong time: a victim of a "random act of violence."

* * *

About a month later, my parents sent me to Camp Young Judea, a Jewish sleepaway camp in Wimberly, Texas. I didn't want to go to this camp, but I promised my parents I would give it a try. While I enjoyed meeting new people, I couldn't wait to get home.

The camp rules were that you couldn't call home for any reason. I broke that rule when one of the boys jumped super hard during my turn on the camp's in-ground trampoline, sending me flying. I hit the ground with my mouth, causing my braces to break. The camp counselor drove me into town to the local orthodontist.

"Mommy, I want to come home," I cried when calling from the orthodontist's office. "I'm scared something bad is going to happen to me."

Of course, the trampoline, broken braces, and swollen mouth had nothing to do with my pleas. I could hear the anguish in my mom's voice when she said, "I know, honey, but we think you should stay the two weeks. We'll be there soon to get you."

I reluctantly agreed to stay.

"Truthfully, your father and I wanted to pick you up the day after we dropped you off," she told me later. "Raising an independent teenager is hard enough without a traumatic incident hanging over you."

After I got home from camp, the nightmares continued, and I'd wake up in a pool of sweat, screaming as if the rapist was in my room attacking me again. Dr. Webber recommended a rape counselor come to the house and speak to me, with the hope that I'd start to process what happened and talk about my feelings. Good in theory until she wouldn't let my mother or Celia sit in the room with me.

"Celia and I sat in the hallway listening to your conversation," my mother told me. "We wanted to make sure you were okay and be able to run in the room if you started to cry. We didn't trust the woman, and your sister didn't like her."

Unfortunately, it didn't help, and my nightmares continued. My father also had difficulty expressing his emotions about what happened to me. He believed he let me down by not being there to protect me from the pure evil of what I experienced. Honestly, he couldn't understand the depth of my pain or fear because he couldn't get past his anger at what had happened to me. Of course, it wasn't his fault at all.

"I think it might help you both if you sit down with Daddy and tell him everything that happened from the beginning to the end so he can understand and you can discuss it with someone you trust," my mom suggested.

And that's what I did. I told him everything and held back nothing. Watching the pain in his eyes as I recounted what happened to me on that day was gut-wrenching and something I'd never be able to unsee. But that conversation helped both of us start to heal and move past the horrible events of June 6, 1977. And it helped me understand more about the man who raped me. My father taught me a valuable lesson in our conversation.

He said, "Inherently, people are good. There are bad people in the world who do bad things. But the individuals who commit these acts do not represent an entire community of people who share their skin color."

Honestly, the color of his skin made no difference to me because if he were white, green, or purple, I would hate him just the same. He would still be a rapist. He would still be *my* rapist.

Rarely a day passes when I don't think about that "random act of violence." But as time marched on, I put less blame on myself. This event forever changed me, but that's all it was—an event in a series of other events that became my life. It didn't define me.

In the days following my attack, I made my father, mother, or Celia come into my bedroom every night and check under my bed and in my closet to ensure no one was hiding. They never caught my rapist. We knew it was unlikely they would find him based on what the detectives said. And while I could have spent the rest of my life wondering why and being angry at the world, I instead decided to be grateful I was still alive.

I tried putting the experience into perspective, as much as a twelve-year-old could. "I never want to be called a victim or 'that girl who got raped'; I'm so embarrassed," I remember telling my sister.

"You'll never be a victim or that girl, Judy, but you'll always be my hero," she replied.

My life and attitude could have gone entirely different in the days, months, and years following the attack. I could have believed every Black man was a rapist and every Black person was terrible because of what happened to me. My parents taught me differently. This event gave me the clarity to know that in an imperfect world, the actions of one individual do not represent the actions of all.

I grew up fast after that experience. Fortunately, my parents didn't stop teaching me these valuable life lessons. As the years went by, I needed their sage advice more and more especially as I finished my schooling, started driving, became an adult, embarked on the working world, and faced an even more life-altering event I never saw coming.

Chapter 5

One Friday afternoon in October of 1980, after my father arrived home from work early, he found the back sliding patio door unlocked. He went upstairs and committed the first cardinal sin of the Haveson household: he entered my bedroom.

My father, Robert—Bob to his friends—stood tall at six foot four, and while he often intimidated many of my friends, and boyfriends, they all described him as a big lovable teddy bear, except when I did something to really upset him.

As an adult, I've become a huge neat freak; if there is any clutter in my sight, I throw it away. If a piece of paper or receipt sits longer than a day on a table, you better claim it or kiss it goodbye forever. However, my teenage habits were the opposite; I was a total slob and borderline hoarder. I kept everything and cleaned up nothing. And I expected everyone to clean my mess.

My father knew this and had strict instructions *never* to enter my bedroom unannounced, especially if the door was closed. He forgot. The equivalent of a bomb detonating in a small space greeted him on the other side of the door. Imagine my surprise when I came home later that day and found him sitting in the family room waiting for me to walk in the house. Shock and awe don't begin to describe the yelling and screaming coming out of his mouth.

"I can't believe the mess I found in your bedroom when I came home. You're a total slob. How do you live like this? How many times do we have to tell you to clean up your room? You are grounded for the weekend, and don't tell me you won't have anything to do because you will spend the entire weekend cleaning up that mess."

To my mother's credit, she gently said, "Now, Robert, you know when Judy's door is closed, you're not to go into her bedroom."

That didn't help matters at all. But ever the negotiator, I said, "I'm really sorry, Daddy. But is it possible for me to pick another weekend for you to ground me?"

He glared at me in disbelief that I'd even think to make such a request. He knew I had chutzpah—I got it from him—but even this boldness surprised him.

"What?" he asked with wide eyes.

"I have friends coming home from college, and I haven't seen them in months. We had so many plans," I explained. For whatever reason, he agreed my punishment would be the following weekend. I quickly learned that you'd never get anything if you didn't ask for it.

After dinner, like most evenings, my father poured himself a drink and settled in to watch television. He loved his Jack Daniels or Johnny Walker nightcaps, and while I never characterized him as a heavy drinker, he sometimes indulged more than necessary. Soon after, he started complaining of stomach pains, so he took two aspirins, called it an early evening, and went to bed.

The following day, he awoke with more than stomach pains.

"Judy, wake up and call Celia to come get you. Your father has chest pains, and I'm taking him to the hospital. Meet us there," my mother explained. After Celia started working, she rented an apartment about five minutes from my parents' house. When I called her that morning, I knew she had probably been planning to come to the house later in the day, as she frequently did.

"Daddy is having chest pains, and Mama took him to the ER. Can you please come get me so we can go to the hospital?" I asked her.

I'm not sure what part of 'Daddy is going to the hospital with chest pains' Celia registered because she responded, "I'm eating breakfast and will be there when I finish."

Oh okay. Sure, I'll wait. And then I screamed, "Come get me now!"

We arrived in the ER and pulled the curtain back to find my father hooked up to beeping machines with patches all over his chest. I had to steady myself because I didn't know what I'd see once we arrived, but I didn't expect this. Then my nervous tick of sarcasm kicked in. It's a reflex; I can't help it. I learned this defense mechanism from the master—my father—like my chutzpah. I walked up to the side of his bed, leaned in close to his ear, and the first words that flew out of my mouth were, "You see what happens when you ground me?" That ended my grounding.

We would soon learn he did not have a heart attack. Instead, he had a bleeding ulcer exasperated by that after-dinner drink and the aspirin he took for his headache. The bleeding wouldn't stop, and they couldn't figure out why. He lost a lot of blood and received blood transfusions to try and stop it. Nothing worked, even pumping him full of more blood.

Dr. Blossom Zanger walked into his room to address the emergency and, not realizing it, walked into our family's life for many years to come. A revered hematologist/oncologist in the Houston area, Dr. Zanger hailed from Eastern Europe and had one of the thickest accents I'd ever heard. At first glance, I thought she looked and sounded more like Dr. Ruth, the famous sex doctor. Because I couldn't get that image out of my head, each time she spoke, I started to giggle.

"We'll need to perform exploratory surgery to find the source of the bleeding," Dr. Zanger explained. It all sounded technical, so I zoned out, but I remember how scared we all were that my father wouldn't get better.

After a battery of tests and exploratory surgery, Dr. Zanger returned to my dad's room. "Do you know if you have any family members who have hemophilia?" she asked him.

"Not to my knowledge." he replied.

She explained, "Hemophilia is a hereditary bleeding disorder with a factor eight deficiency, making it harder for the blood to clot. While not rare, it's only present in a small percentage of people, primarily males passed down through the mother."

My dad lost his mother at just fifteen years old and his father when he was twenty-five years old. His knowledge of any genetic history was limited as even his older sister was unfamiliar.

"My only memory about excessive bleeding as a kid is when I got into a fight at school, and another boy broke my nose and jaw, and I had to get my jaw wired," he said.

"You were a real hell-raiser," I joked. Again, a nervous tick.

He spoke to some of his male first cousins on his mother's side, and they told him they were hemophiliacs, and things started to fall into place.

Sometimes referred to as a "Royal Disease," it was first introduced to the world during the reign of Queen Victoria of England, who carried the hemophilia gene, passing it onto her son, Leopold. Once a carrier of hemophilia, Leopold passed the gene to his children, many of whom married into the royal families of Russia, Spain, and Germany, extending the condition throughout the European royal bloodlines.

Years later, I took a DNA test to find more information about my bloodlines. To my shock, the test showed my mainly European ancestry included eleven percent from the British Isles. It now made sense that part of my DNA, most likely the part that came from my father, is from British ancestry.

My dad stayed in the hospital for several weeks, receiving more plasma and blood transfusions to get his bleeding under control. The nurse administering the daily transfusions told him stories with each blood bag. "Today, Robert, you're getting the blood of a fisherman, and yesterday's transfusion came from a sailor's blood, so if you start dreaming of being on the water, this is why." We didn't care whose blood he received or whether these stories were true. But we had Blossom Zanger to thank for his recovery.

* * *

The following year, a few months after my father's hemophilia diagnosis, my mother came home from a doctor's appointment and announced she had cancer. Disbelief shadowed our thoughts. "How did you get cancer?" I naïvely asked.

It wasn't breast cancer, but it was near her breastbone.

"It's lymphoma," she told us. "Cancer of the lymph nodes." She underwent surgery and then started nine long months of debilitating chemotherapy. Dr. Zanger became her oncologist.

A true rock star throughout the entire ordeal, my mom drove herself to Dr. Zanger's office every Friday afternoon after work for chemotherapy treatments. When finished, she stopped at the grocery, came home to prepare dinner for us, went to the upstairs bathroom and threw up her guts, crawled in bed, and passed out, only to wake up the next day knowing she'd do the same thing again the following Friday. And this went on for nine long rough months.

While my mom's cancer hit me hard, at sixteen years old, I displayed pretty obnoxious teenage behavior, often picking fights with her for no reason. I blocked out my fear and acted as if I didn't care.

After one particularly bad argument, she'd had enough of my attitude. "I'm not sure what your problem is, but I'm sick, and one day you might regret how you're treating me," she yelled. And then she pulled off her wig to show me how the chemotherapy had taken all her hair.

That's the moment I thought my mom might die. I felt the wind knocked from my lungs. I couldn't breathe. I couldn't even speak. I ran upstairs, leaving my mom crying in the living room, holding her wig. I immediately called the one person I knew wouldn't judge me: my friend, Melinda.

"My mom has cancer and could die," I cried into the phone.

"I'll be right over," she said. That little act of kindness made me realize what an important person Melinda was to me, and I would never take that for granted.

Melinda and I had been friends since we met in a Jewish youth group when we were fourteen years old. We connected instantly. The youngest of four children, she came from a large successful family in Houston. While we were initially in the same group, she would eventually switch chapters, but this didn't impact our friendship. She and I shared a lot of fun times, but this one particular moment forever solidified my love and respect for her and made me realize she'd always have my back. We went our separate ways for college but quickly picked up where we'd left off once she came home.

"Your mom is going to be okay," she said.

As we sat on my bed, I looked at her and cried. "But I've been so horrible to her. She'll never forgive me."

She smiled and said, "Yes, she will; she's your mom."

At this point, I feared for any of my family going to a doctor, worried they'd come home with another illness. And this fear would soon come to life the following year when Celia went for a routine chest X-ray for a lingering cough. If it had only been that simple.

Chapter 6

I graduated from Westbury High School in May 1982, and the following August, I left for Southwest Texas State University (SWTS), a small college in San Marcos, Texas, aka Texas' party school on the river. I dreamed of following in my mother's and sister's footsteps and attending The University of Texas at Austin (UT), but my grades—good but not excellent—had another plan for me, the story of my education life.

"We're just worried if you start college on probation, you'll stress about keeping up with grades," my parents said when I told them academic probation would be my only option to start school at the UT. "Why would you put the added stress on yourself when there are plenty of good colleges and universities for you?"

"I just don't want to be far from you or my friends," I said. I ultimately chose SWTS due to its proximity to home and Austin, where many of my friends would be going to school. "I'll have the best of both worlds," I said.

"Just make sure you remember to study," my mom said.

Before I left for school, I wrote my sister a note telling her how much I'd miss her and need her during my first year of college. Inside the card, I wrote: "I'm serious; it will be hard to say goodbye. You are the most important person in my life, and I love you very much. I'm going to write and call you a lot, so you better be prepared. Love, always—Judy." It was true. Celia was the one person in my life who could settle my nerves and calm my fears, and the thought of leaving her overwhelmed me even though she was busy with her own life and career.

I never considered myself someone who got homesick, but I sat, in a pool of tears, watching my parents and Celia drive away after dropping me off at school. I remember taking my sister to college and crying as we drove away. "If you fall apart every time we drop her off at school, we won't take you the next time," my mother said.

I wonder if my mom said the same to my sister when she couldn't stop crying as they drove away from me. "The ride back was quiet," Celia wrote in the letter I received a few days after classes began. "I am sorry I 'cracked up'; it's just that I will miss you so much." We indeed were two peas in a pod.

Over the following months, whenever I had a bad day or didn't think I did well on a test, my sister sent me letters offering words of encouragement to keep me going. "Just a note to cheer you up." "Hang in there; things will get better." "If you want to talk, remember I'm here." I could always count on Celia to be there for me, as I'd be there for her. We had each other's backs in this wild ride called life.

At the end of my first semester at SWTS, my mom drove over from Houston to bring me home for winter break. I couldn't wait to be lazy for several weeks. No one thoroughly prepared me for the intensity of college and how tired I'd be—from studying, not partying, of course. My friends and I hung out in the dorm, saying our goodbyes, and patiently waiting for our parents to pick us up.

A rush of excitement hit me when I saw my mom's big brown Cadillac Sedan DeVille turn into the parking lot. Back in the day, Cadillacs and Lincoln Continentals, affectionately referred to as "Jew Canoes," represented status, and almost every Jewish family had one or the other. Politically incorrect, yes, but so representative of the 1980s.

"You want to drive home from San Marcos?" my mother had asked me while we were on the phone the night before.

"Are you serious? Of course, I do."

While excited to see her, I couldn't wait for the opportunity to drive. As I watched the car drive up the hill to the parking lot, I saw my father behind the wheel. At first, I was upset because he ruined my opportunity to drive. While he sometimes let me drive us around town, he preferred to do the driving on longer trips, like the three-hour drive home to Houston. I met them in the parking lot, and as my dad got out of the car to give me a big hug, he said, "Surprise!" Deep down, I knew he'd be with my mom because he hated to be left out. Being a daddy's girl, I got over it quickly.

With the trunk loaded, I started to take my place in the back seat. My mother stopped me.

"Judy, please get in the front seat and sit between us," she said.

Bewildered, I thought, why would she want me to sit between them for more than three hours on a super uncomfortable bench seat?

"Why, Mama? It's not like all my stuff didn't fit in the huge trunk." You could fit full-sized garbage cans standing up in that trunk. "The backseat is empty," I said.

I could imagine the humiliation of getting into the front seat to sit between them with the eyes of my entire dorm watching. I finally gave in, not like I had a choice, and off we went, the three of us all in the front seat.

San Marcos is sandwiched between Austin and San Antonio. You drive through little towns and back roads to reach Interstate 10 (I-10), the main highway to Houston. When we finally got to I-10, my dad pulled over into a parking lot and stopped the car. I thought to myself, "Is he going to let me drive home?" Yes, I suffered from that narcissistic one-track mind syndrome most teenagers/young adults all suffer from: shouldn't it all be about me?

What came next had absolutely nothing to do with me and everything to do with my sister. As we pulled into a parking space and my father turned off the car, my mother said, "Celia is in the hospital and having surgery tomorrow morning."

"Oh no, she's been in a car accident, right?" I asked.

Frankly, given her driving record, it was shocking to me that she hadn't been in an accident yet.

"What happened? Is she okay? What's the car look like?"

As I continued my rapid-fire questions, my mother finally spoke.

"Just calm down, and I'll tell you everything we know, and she wasn't in a car accident."

A few months earlier, Celia had complained about a pulled muscle from a Jazzercise class. "Oh, you will use any excuse not to exercise; stop whining," we teased her. The pain only got worse.

I sat quietly as my mom explained why Celia was having surgery. "In addition to the pulled muscle she thought she got from exercise class, she developed a bad cough that wouldn't go away. I told her to go see Charlie and get a chest X-ray." Chest X-rays were my mother's go-to remedy for any ailment.

At twenty-five years old, Celia wasn't a child. She lived on her own and had a great job, but Charlie (Dr. Holmsten), our family internist, called my mom first to tell her what he saw or thought he saw on the X-rays. His dry sense of humor and non-alarmist personality endeared him to his patients, so when he believed something to be concerning, he addressed it right away. He saw a small mass close to her lungs and heart that appeared to be the size of a golf ball and thought she should get additional scans to rule everything out.

There we were, the three of us, sitting in the front seat of the big brown Cadillac Sedan DeVille in an empty parking lot off I-10, blankly staring out the window. At least from the front seat, I had an unobstructed view. Speechless, a rarity for me, I had so many questions but couldn't ask any of them and didn't even know where to begin. I felt paralyzed.

My mom finally spoke. "Are you okay?" she asked.

Honestly, I didn't know if I was okay. Based on the initial X-ray results, things didn't appear promising.

"No," I said.

We were talking about my sister. My other half. My best friend. How could I be okay right now? We had one stop to make before heading home to Houston. We wanted to tell my grandfather the news of Celia in person. As much as I longed to hurry to the hospital to see her, I understood the magnitude of this conversation and why it needed to happen in person and not over the phone.

Celia and I had an extraordinary bond with our grandfather, Papa. We could do no wrong in his eyes and often went to him for advice, not to mention extra spending money, which he always gave us. "Don't tell your mother, but here's a little spending money for you to buy something nice," he'd always tell us.

Wharton sat a little more than halfway between San Marcos and Houston if you didn't count all the backroads. My parents knew this path very well as they had traveled it a lot when my dad was stationed at Bergstrom Air Force Base in Austin and my mother was attending college at UT.

We drove up to Papa's store, the small building with metal siding and the big red sign, "Joe's Package Store." Behind the counter sat Papa on my favorite wooden chair with the green vinyl cushion.

I could see the excitement on his face when he saw us drive up. But I could tell that he was puzzled, that he knew something was amiss as we walked into his store on a random Thursday afternoon with no notice.

A very sage and discerning man, he asked, "Where is Bubela, and why isn't she with you?"

He called Celia "Bubela," a Yiddish term of endearment for darling, sweetheart, or honey. By contrast, he called me "Bondit," Yiddish for mischievous or pain in the neck.

"Daddy, sit down," said my mother. "Celia is in the hospital having surgery tomorrow, and here's all we know." She proceeded to tell him everything she knew, and as she spoke, his eyes grew sadder and sadder. To watch him at that moment was heartbreaking. It's bad enough for a parent or sister to absorb this information, but being a grandparent takes sadness and helplessness to a whole new level.

"This shouldn't be happening to her. It should be me," he said. "I've already lived my life."

As much as I wanted to get to my sister, I didn't want to leave my grandfather. "Papa, please come home with us. I don't want to leave you here by yourself," I pleaded with him.

But he wanted to stay at home. I think he needed time by himself to process everything. It broke my heart to see him wave goodbye as we drove away.

Chapter 7

The hour drive to Houston seemed like it took three days. I had done this drive a million times, but today, it was as if I'd never seen these roads before. Nothing seemed normal.

We drove straight to the hospital. When we got to Celia's room, I wanted to run and jump into her bed, throw my arms around her, and tell her we'd get through this, whatever this turned out to be. After all, she helped me through one of the scariest days and times of my young life, and I would do the same for her. We were sisters, and nothing could break our bond.

Instead, I walked into her hospital room with a smile.

"Wow, you'll do anything for attention, won't you?" I said. My ultimate defense mechanism of sarcasm reared its ugly head again.

Feeling my tension, she laughed at my bad humor.

"Oh, Judy. How did you do on your finals?" she asked.

Seriously? She was lying in a hospital bed, awaiting a major surgery in less than twenty-four hours and she wanted to know how I did on my finals? My selfless, loving sister. Why couldn't I be more like her?

At that point, I don't even think I remembered taking any final exams, much less how I did on them. But we talked about my tests and other useless information to skirt the real elephant in the room. Then the doctor walked in.

Dr. Garcia, a renowned cardiothoracic surgeon, came to the United States from Cuba with a considerable presence, a thick but understandable accent, and confidence that made me feel like we got the best of the best. Aside from his physical aura, I noticed he wore a diamond pinky ring and a giant diamond-encrusted Rolex. He had a piece of paper in his hand with a drawing that looked like a heart.

"Because the tumor is sitting so close to the heart, we will perform the equivalent of open-heart surgery without opening her actual heart," he explained.

It didn't sound real, and I couldn't grasp that he was talking about Celia. Instead, my thoughts concentrated on his flashy bling as he spoke. In some ways, the simple act of staring at these gaudy status-wheeling pieces of jewelry calmed my nerves.

"Do you have any questions for me?" he asked.

I looked straight into his eyes. "Is my sister going to be okay?"

He smiled back. "I'll take good care of her," he said.

It wasn't lost on me that he didn't answer my question.

We said our goodbyes and went home to let Celia get some sleep. While she lived on her own in an apartment close to my parents' house, she still had a bedroom at home. I slept in her room that evening. I think I just wanted to feel close to her even though she hadn't slept in that bed in months.

When we arrived at the hospital the following day, we gathered in her room and tried to keep it light and chatty.

"I like your surgery hat and booties," I said.

"Maybe they'll give you some, and we can be twins," she said.

"We're already twins," I said with a smile.

As they wheeled her away, I gave her one last kiss.

"I love you so much, and we will get through this together no matter the outcome," I told her with tears.

"I love you," she said. I truly believed that we got through everything in our lives because we did it together. Why would this be different?

We settled into the waiting room and watched all morning as surgeons came in and out, calling families to a private room or to the hallway to give updates on their loved ones. Waiting for what felt like days, we all fell asleep at one point. Dr. Garcia finally summoned my parents and me to the hallway.

"The surgery went well. We removed a large mass about the size of a grapefruit. It sat too close to her heart, so we couldn't get it all. I also had to remove a small portion of her lung where the mass formed."

As he spoke, my ears started ringing, and I could hear my heart pounding in my chest. I felt faint. My mom started crying uncontrollably, and my dad had to grab her before she fell. Was he describing Celia? I almost asked him if he had the right patient. How could this be? I just knew this couldn't be real, and soon we'd wake up from this nightmare.

"She's got a long recovery road ahead," he said. "While I'm not a pathologist, I think this looks like thymoma, which would be cancer of the thymus gland."

Whatever that meant. Unfortunately, Google didn't exist in 1983, and the public library served as our search engine. I'd later learn that thymoma is a rare malignancy frequently associated with neuromuscular disorders with some patients reporting coughing and chest pains.

As Dr. Garcia continued talking, my mother cried, "This is my fault. I did this to her."

The doctor tried calming her down by telling her that wasn't possible. She didn't believe him, and to this day, I still don't think she considers any other theory than my sister got cancer because she had cancer first.

We had to wait a few more hours before we could see Celia in the ICU. When we were able to go in, I don't think I could have prepared myself for what I saw. Lying in bed, my vibrant five-foot-ten raven-haired sister was hooked to a ventilator with tubes coming out everywhere, surrounded by loud beeping machines. It felt like a scene straight out of *General Hospital.*

My mom and dad looked so small and fragile as they walked into the room. Here was their baby, their firstborn, their life. Despite all the noises coming from the machines, an eerily quiet calm surrounded us. Celia opened her eyes, and although she had a tube down her throat, she tried to talk. A small tear ran down her cheek as I looked into her eyes, willing her not to speak. I unconsciously wiped it away.

"You can't talk," I told her.

She just stared into my eyes. She looked so scared, and I had never felt more helpless. As I held her hand, I silently prayed to God that she would be okay and get through this. I knew she would have a long recovery, but I'd be right by her side. If I could switch places with her, I'd have done it in a minute although I knew she'd never let me do that.

My parents and I returned to the cold windowless waiting room to gather our thoughts. How had this tumor grown in such a short period?

"You need to consult with an oncologist," Dr. Garcia said. "If you don't have one, I can give you names." Fortunately, from my father's and mother's recent experiences, we believed we had one of the best, Dr. Blossom Zanger, to help my sister.

Chapter 8

A few days later, Celia moved from the ICU to her room. Once she started to recover from surgery, Dr. Zanger came to discuss the next steps. She explained that from her estimation, the mass appeared to be Hodgkin's disease, not thymoma, the cancer Dr. Garcia thought it to be.

"If she had to get cancer, this is the one to get as Hodgkin's disease is 99.9% percent curable through chemotherapy and radiation," Dr. Zanger said.

Finally, welcome news.

"Celia will have ten chemotherapy treatments—one every other week—and then she'll have radiation, and we will go from there," Blossom said.

'Okay, this is doable,' I thought. 'She's got this.'

The first treatment came while she was still in the hospital.

"You'll need to eat a light lunch before you get the chemotherapy, so just fill out the menu, and someone will bring you your selection," the nurse told her.

Celia did not think about the outcome and decided on a plain hamburger and orange sherbet. My mom and dad had to leave the hospital, so I stayed with her during and after the treatment. I sat on her bed, and we read celebrity magazines and gossiped, two of our favorite pastimes, while the IV dripped into her arm. We had no idea how she would feel during or after, so every few minutes, I'd ask how she was feeling and if she thought she was going to be sick. About forty-five minutes after the IV bag emptied, she yelled, "Get me the bowl. I'm going to throw up."

Usually, when I'm around people vomiting, I vomit, too. But this time, I felt a sense of protection and just did what I had to do: take care of her. She spilled everything into the tray and lifted her head to look as I held her hair back. We both started laughing hysterically. The color orange was on her bedsheets, her nightgown, everywhere.

"Your bed looks like a big orange Cheeto," I laughed. Being able to find a little humor in this horrible moment, I knew we'd be just fine. It's safe to say she no longer ate anything with color ahead of future treatments.

The next day, my mom brought a cake to the hospital decorated with icing that read: "1 down, 9 to go."

If it had only been that simple. Over the following months, after Celia left the hospital and returned to work, she had several setbacks. While her chemotherapy regimen initially seemed to be working, she kept developing fevers, which meant she had infections somewhere in her body.

"The chemotherapy isn't working as I had hoped, so I'm changing course and starting different therapies to treat the Hodgkin's," Dr. Zanger explained. Like the initial protocol, the new treatment first showed promise and even shrunk the remaining tumor in her chest cavity. But that glimmer of light soon dimmed when Dr. Zanger informed us that the medicine had stopped working.

*   *   *

There's never a convenient time for someone to get sick. And it's tough for the ill person to deal with it because they feel like a burden to everyone around them. They don't choose to be sick. Celia had to endure cancer and all the crappy things about the disease, like puking your guts out after chemo treatments, losing your hair, and constantly being tired. Also, the see-saw ride of gaining and losing weight.

Yet she felt guilty about what our family was going through. "I'm so sorry I'm putting you through all of this," she constantly said.

The truth is, I felt guilty that she had cancer and I didn't. Just like how she felt guilty when I got attacked. When you are close to someone, their pain becomes your pain, and if you could change places with them so they wouldn't suffer, you'd do it in a heartbeat. This represented us. We'd come a long way from our sibling rivalry days where her jealousy of me ran deep, and I wanted everything she had. But our love for each other stood firm.

Back at school, with my head not in it and my heart even further away, I had the worst semester, walking around campus lost and in a constant state of worry. The unknown is always more complicated to grasp and being back at school put me in the unknown category.

Even if I had been right by my sister's side, no one, not even her doctors, understood why she wasn't getting better or why the cancer wasn't going into remission. With today's advancements in cancer treatment, it's hard to imagine how little was known about many types of the disease in 1983. Even though Dr. Zanger felt confident she could treat Celia's Hodgkin's disease and put it into remission, no two cancers are the same, no matter what statistics show.

Celia would experience these patterns of the chemo working, and then they'd begin radiation. Once completed, more scans, but nothing changed, or the tumors reappeared. And she kept getting high fevers. Each time her temperature spiked, she'd go to the emergency room. This was exhausting for her and my parents. I swear my mom and dad aged so much during this period, even though they were both only forty-eight years old.

One weekend while I was home from school, we moved my sister out of her apartment and back to my parents' house.

"How did you accumulate so many shoes, clothes, magazines, and junk?" I asked her. "You have so much stuff."

"People who live in glass houses don't throw stones," my mother said to me. Celia had the same hoarding and packrat tendencies as her little sister.

Around this time, Celia started losing her hair. "Shave it all off. I'm over it," she said.

Her hair meant everything to her. Long, dark, and thick, it shed everywhere. While difficult for everyone, it devastated my mother the most since she had personally gone through the same experience of losing her hair two years earlier. But her hair grew back, and so would Celia's. We went shopping for wigs and bought her several different styles to see what looked best.

"I love the shorter style. It looks super cute and sassy," I told her.

"It's not my hair," she said.

"No, it's not. But the good news is if you get tired of it, you can become a blonde." I tried making her laugh, but even my sarcasm couldn't help at this point.

During this time, Celia went back to work as the HR Director at AMF Tuboscope, the oilfield division of AMF, the sporting equipment company. She even belonged to the office bowling team and had a bowling ball with her name printed on it. This job helped keep her mind off having cancer, and she loved it so much.

"As soon as I start making thirty thousand a year, I will buy you a Louis Vuitton handbag," she told my mom after she first got the job. I worked at Saks Fifth Avenue at the time and received a thirty percent employee discount off anything in the store. The day my sister got a pay raise to $30,000, a lot of money in 1981, she kept her promise and, along with my discount, bought my mother a Louis Vuitton handbag. She loved making others happy, especially our mother.

Back at school, I received a letter from Celia shortly after my last final exam:

> I don't know when you will get this card, but if you get it after you return from your last final—just a note to say, 'You made it!' You survived one year of college, even

through all the ups and downs. No matter what, hang in there. You will do just fine in the long run. I can't wait for you to come home.

And I couldn't wait to get home to her either. I could always count on Celia to be there to cheer me on with everything in my life.

Sadly, Celia had to stop working around the end of June 1983. Too tired and finding it increasingly hard for her to keep up with all the demands of her job, she gave her notice. This devastated her and her co-workers. And unfortunately, her hospital stays became more frequent, too, with Dr. Zanger constantly changing her treatments to help get her cancer into remission.

I spent the month of June being with Celia as much as I could. My mother was off for the summer from teaching elementary school, which allowed us to spend time together. And then July came, the real turning point of the story.

Chapter 9

In July 1983, Dr. Zanger ran some scans and tests to determine if Celia's Hodgkin's disease was in remission. The new therapies, which initially showed progress, no longer did, and at this point, all treatment protocols had become experimental. But Dr. Zanger never gave up hope, and neither did we.

"We do have one more option to explore," she said. "A bone marrow transplant where we take healthy, non-cancerous bone marrow of a perfectly matched donor and transfer it to Celia." It sounded simple enough until we understood how to find the match.

Today, the National Bone Marrow Registry helps find perfect donor matches in other states, but it did not exist in 1983. Immediate family members were the only way to find an ideal fit. That meant either my parents or me.

Dr. Zanger discouraged my parents because of their prior illnesses.

But I wasn't deterred. "I'll do it," I quickly said. I just knew I'd be a match and be the reason my sister would survive this horrible nightmare. A simple blood test stood between life and death, and I couldn't take that test fast enough.

"If you're a match, we'll perform a procedure where they suck your healthy bone marrow out and infuse it into Celia," Dr. Zanger explained. "It's pretty painful, and you'll need several days to recover."

"I don't care. I'm ready," I said.

At this point, I would have given my right arm and leg if it meant my sister would survive, so no amount of pain could scare me away.

"What happens after my procedure?" I asked Dr. Zanger.

"We zap Celia full of radiation to kill off her bone marrow and then place her in a plastic bubble," she explained.

"You'll be like John Travolta in that movie, *The Boy in the Plastic Bubble*," I said.

We both got a good laugh out of the thought of her being in a bubble, like in the movie. My parents didn't think it was funny.

"Enough," they scolded us. We could still find humor and be silly together, even in scary times.

Dr. Zanger continued, "She'd have to be in this bubble because her immune system will be too fragile, and she could contract anything near her. With the unhealthy bone marrow gone, she would then receive Judy's bone marrow through an IV infusion, and we'd wait to see if it worked. Of course, there's no guarantee it will work even if we do this."

The discussion would be moot because the day after I took the blood test to determine if I matched Celia, Dr. Zanger walked into my sister's hospital room to tell us the bad news: I wasn't a match. We were running out of options.

I felt as if I totally failed my sister and let her and my parents down. How could I not be a perfect match? This became another dark day for me, and I wasn't sure how I'd ever overcome it. That was because I had no idea what the next six weeks would bring.

Dr. Zanger, always the optimist, said, "There are some other experimental treatments we're working with, and we should consider them for Celia." She continued with a gut punch, "But I have to warn you that right now, we're only showing a twenty-five percent survival rate among people taking these drugs."

As if we weren't already living our lives under a dark cloud, the words "twenty-five percent survival rate" hung heavy in the air. I sat next to Celia on the bed, holding her hand. When Dr. Zanger explained how the treatments worked and all the possible side effects, my sister squeezed my hand, looked directly at me and then at my parents, and said to the doctor, "Does this mean I'd only have a twenty-five percent chance to live?"

For some reason, the unflappable Dr. Zanger could barely answer her. And while it would have been easy for my parents to tell her what to do, they didn't. The decision had to be hers.

"Can I take some time to think about this and discuss it with my family?" she asked.

Throughout Celia's entire cancer journey, we discussed every detail with her. My parents held nothing back because it was important to them that she understood every aspect of her illness—the good and the bad. It wasn't always easy, especially for my parents.

While contemplating her decision, my mother and I made an appointment to speak to our family internist, Dr. Holmsten, the doctor who had taken the initial scan that revealed the tumor the year before.

"We need your advice on what to do or what else we should be doing," we told him.

This conversation will haunt me forever.

"It's hard to say what else can be done for Celia since her cancer is terminal," he said.

My mother and I looked at him. "Terminal?"

We never considered her cancer terminal. No doctor had ever used the word, especially Dr. Zanger, until that day. Even though we knew the drugs used to treat Celia's cancer were experimental, no one ever told us it was terminal cancer. Yes, we understood Celia's prognosis was not good, but terminal? Maybe we were naïve, but we never lost hope by not calling it terminal cancer. My mother and I felt as if we were hit by a truck when Dr.

Holmsten used that word. We just sat across from him at his desk and cried.

The next day, Dr. Zanger came back to Celia's hospital room. Again, I took my place next to her on the bed, holding her hand.

"What have you decided?" Dr. Zanger asked.

"I want to try the new treatment," Celia said.

Dr. Zanger immediately went into action and started her on the new chemotherapy and radiation protocols. One of the side effects of the experimental drugs was shingles. Celia developed a horrible, painful case that wrapped around her waist. And even in as much pain as she was, she took it in stride—like she did everything through her miserable cancer journey.

A few weeks later, Dr. Zanger informed us that the new treatment didn't work, and we were out of options. Even though she felt we had no more choices, my parents gathered all of Celia's medical records and went to one of the top cancer hospitals in the country: M.D. Anderson.

When my parents returned home from their meeting at M.D. Anderson, they told me the doctors said there was nothing else they could or would try without making her a total experiment. Celia wouldn't want that, and neither would we.

"Who will tell her what we found out?" my father asked.

"I'll tell her," my mom replied.

As my mother sat on the bed telling Celia the doctors said there was nothing else they could do, my sister looked into my mother's eyes and cried, "Dammit. I won't be able to give you grandchildren." This again demonstrated my sister's selfless concern for my parents' well-being over her fear and anger of dying.

With our birthday around the corner, even being in the hospital wouldn't prevent my mother from throwing a big birthday bash. She pulled out all the stops: balloons, streamers, posters, presents, party hats, cakes and other desserts, and a constant stream of family and friends coming in and out of her room.

The nurses and doctors looked the other way, allowing us to celebrate, with some stopping by to join the festivities. The smile on Celia's face told the whole story. Life seemed ordinary for just those few hours, and we nearly forgot about reality and cancer. It's amazing what a good party can do for the soul.

After the birthday party wound down and everyone went home, I climbed into her bed.

"Mama knows how to throw a party, even in a hospital," Celia said.

"Did you count all the people in your room?" I asked.

Even though she was tired, we kept talking about all our observations from the day. And then it got heavy. "I'm scared, but not about dying," Celia said. "I'm scared for Mommy and Daddy. I'm worried they aren't going to be able to deal with me no longer being here."

"I promise I will take care of them as best as I can," I said. "I'm sure I'll continue giving them fits and frustration, so they'll never be bored."

And then we both laughed. Honestly, I had no idea what to do or say. A child is not supposed to die before a parent. I mean, it wasn't written anywhere, but it was logical. Parents are older, so naturally, they should pass before their children. This notion of her dying before our parents became hard to grasp and heartbreaking for Celia. I know she carried a lot of guilt about leaving them. We then turned the conversation to me.

I thought I'd had tough conversations in my life before. Wrong.

"I'm so proud of you, and I'm so sorry I won't be here to see you grow up and help keep you out of trouble," she said.

I'm not going to lie; she always protected me from my parents and even myself.

"If I had to choose a sister, I couldn't have picked anyone better than you," Celia said. "You have to promise me that you'll never stop living, never give up on what you want, and always follow your dreams. You are the most important person to me, and I'll love you forever."

I sat there and cried. I wasn't sure I could stop.

Then she joked, "I only hope you won't be as reckless as me since I was such a hell-raiser."

That tongue-in-cheek comparison made me laugh out loud. Celia, the angel, versus Judy, the limit-tester.

After I finished crying, which felt like hours, I finally spoke.

"You are the best friend I'll ever have and being your sister has been the most important thing in my life. I'm so proud of everything you've done and have always wanted to be just like you. I'm not sure why this happened to you and not to me. I don't know how I'll ever get by without you. But I do know I will never forget you, and I'll love you forever. And I promise to do the best I can to make you proud."

And then, after who knows how long, a nurse came to wake me up. I had fallen asleep lying next to Celia.

The days following our birthday celebration were agonizing. While Dr. Zanger couldn't tell us how much longer Celia had to live, we were close to the end. About a week after our birthday, Celia decided to come home.

Several rabbis visited Celia in those final days and helped explain every funeral detail. We discussed everything with no topic off-limits, including the funeral service, the casket, what she'd wear, etc. Whatever she wanted to know, we'd find an answer. We somehow believed being transparent with Celia about the process of dying would help us deal with her imminent death more quickly. Who knows if it worked or not?

"I know our family plot is in Wharton, but can you find a cemetery in Houston closer to you, so you'll always come and visit me?" she asked.

My parents would have done anything she wanted, but the more Celia thought about it, the more she wanted to be at rest in Wharton, so she'd be with our family.

"After I die, what will you do?" she asked us.

None of us could even venture a response.

"I think you should go away and relax," she said.

At that moment, we all decided that after her funeral and sitting shiva, the Jewish mourning period, the three of us would go to Cancun, one of Celia's favorite destinations.

"It will be a great place for you to chill out and remember me," she told us. "And get a yummy margarita to toast me, too."

Before I left for school, I tried to convince my parents to let me stay home. "I don't want to leave," I cried.

"We know you don't, but it's best if you go back and take your mind off things here at home," my parents told me.

I drove my sister's car back to San Marcos and followed my ex-boyfriend, Randy, who went to school at UT in Austin. Randy and I had a complicated relationship. My first boyfriend, but not the first boy I'd kissed.

That title belonged to a boy named Greg. They say you never forget your first kiss and for me, that was very true. I think I swallowed more of his saliva than my own, and he licked my face. Talk about swapping spit.

I also vividly remember my first kiss with Randy. It happened in the front seat of his blue Camaro. He took me by surprise as he leaned over the gear shift. "Can I kiss you?" he asked. "Uh-huh," I squeaked out. I'd never felt anything like it and thought, "Now, this is what a first kiss should feel like."

But Randy and I had a lot of other firsts—at least for me—and several ups and downs during high school, college, after college, and beyond. He hurt me, I hurt him, and we went several years without speaking. Many believed us destined for one another, but I didn't see it that way, and in his heart, I don't think Randy did either.

"Haveson, if we had ever gotten married, we'd probably have killed each other," he once said to me. "We're too much alike." He wasn't wrong. I loved Randy and probably always will.

Celia liked Randy, too, except when he made me cry. Randy ultimately married a wonderful woman named Heather, and they had a beautiful family together. And thankfully, we are still friends today. Life always works out in the end.

I finally said my goodbyes to my parents and Celia.

"I love you, and I'll see you real soon," I told her.

"Behave yourself, Judy. I love you," she replied through tears.

I had no idea if that would be the last time I saw my sister alive.

The Rosh Hashanah holiday fell during the week I went back to school. While my parents didn't attend high holiday services, my mother made a nice dinner with Celia's favorites, including matzah ball soup, brisket, and potato kugel. By the time my parents helped my sister downstairs to sit at the table for the meal, she was too weak and wiped out to eat.

Fred stopped by to see her but decided against coming into the house. Like Fred's and my relationship, he and Celia had a special bond. Only eleven years old when Celia arrived, he used to, according to my mother, call her "my baby." Watching her die brought unimaginable pain to him. To honor Celia's memory as is Jewish custom, when Fred and Kay welcomed their daughter Nancy three years later, they gave her Celia's Hebrew name, Tzviah Hannah.

On Thursday night, after I'd arrived back at school, I called my mom.

"How are things going tonight?" I asked.

"Not great, but she's hanging in there," she said.

"After my test tomorrow, I'm driving to Austin to spend the weekend with Abbe," I told her. Abbe was my close friend from junior high school. "If anything happens, you call her apartment right away."

After I hung up the phone, I tried to sleep. I had the room to myself that night because my roommate was staying with her boyfriend. Around midnight, something woke me, and I sat straight up in my bed. I felt a tight feeling in my chest. I also felt a cold draft that made me shiver. As I sat in bed trying to catch my breath, I smelled a familiar sweet scent I recognized right away: White Shoulders perfume.

I quickly turned on the lights to see if my roommate had a perfume bottle on the dresser but found nothing. Celia wore White Shoulders. She practically bathed in the bottle, and you could smell her before you saw her in the morning.

I frantically called my mother and asked, "Did Celia die?"

"No," she said. "She's in bed between your father and me. She is having a difficult time breathing and sleeping. The hospice nurse will come in the morning, but we want to keep her close for tonight."

I couldn't understand the gravity of pain my parents felt watching their first-born baby girl passing away before their eyes. They were so brave for me.

"Mama, I swear Celia was in my room with me. I know it. And I could smell White Shoulders, what else could that have been?" I couldn't shake the feeling.

The following day, I took my test and left for Austin. When I drove up to Abbe's apartment, she met me in the driveway and told me my mom had called.

"Did she die?" I cried.

"No, but she's in the hospital, and you're to wait by the phone for your mom to call you back in a few hours," Abbe said.

Abbe and I had been close since we were fourteen, after meeting when her family moved to Houston from Denver. She lived around the corner from me, and when the two of us weren't talking on the phone, we were together in person. We were part of each other's families, so knowing that Celia didn't have much time left upset Abbe considerably.

We went upstairs and waited for the phone to ring. "Did she die?" I asked when I heard my mom on the phone.

"No, but you need to come home. It's time," she said through tears. "Your father will fly to Austin, and you'll pick him up at the airport, so he can drive home with you."

I'm not sure I said anything after that other than, "Please tell her to wait for me."

I met my father at his gate, and when I saw him, I ran and jumped into his arms and held on tight. I couldn't stop crying. To lighten the mood, he stepped back, looked me over from head to toe, and asked, "What is that schmatta you're wearing?"

Flashdance fashion ruled in 1983. Jennifer Beals' character wore sweatshirts with the neck ripped out, hanging off one shoulder. Adding to my ensemble, I wore another fad from the early 80s: jelly shoes. These plastic shoes came in different colors, and mine were fuchsia.

Thankfully my smart-mouth father made me laugh even if only for a moment.

"Is she still alive?" I finally asked him.

"Yes, but it won't be much longer."

We stopped at a payphone before leaving the airport, and my father called my mom. "I'm here, and you should see your daughter's get-up," he said.

He'd never move past my outfit. I thought I looked stylish, and I knew Celia would agree.

"Someone wants to talk to you," he said to me.

At first, I shook my head no. Then I started to cry but took a deep breath and composed myself. "Hi, Celia, I'll be home real soon," I squeaked.

"How was your test, and why are you crying?" she asked.

I could barely understand her through her labored breathing. It sounded like her lungs were filled with fluid.

"It was fine, and I'm not crying. I have a cold," I said.

She laughed. "You're a bad liar." And then she said, "What are you wearing?"

I was glad my 1980s *Flashdance* outfit gave us all a diversion for a while.

My dad next called his sister in New Jersey. "Barbara, we're near the end. I'm driving back to Houston right now with Judy, but I'll call you in the morning. You'll need to book your flight for tomorrow."

I couldn't handle my father's tears.

We pulled up to our house around 11:00 p.m., and, like the night before her first surgery, I slept in my sister's bed that evening. I could smell her on the sheets and pillow, and oddly, it comforted me.

The following day we got to the hospital around 8:00 a.m.

"You need to prepare yourself because Celia doesn't look like she did last week," my mother said as she held my hand.

I immediately crawled into her bed to lie next to her. As she looked into my eyes, I held her hand.

"Thank you for waiting for me," I said.

"I'd never leave you without saying goodbye," she replied.

For the next few hours, we kept her comfortable. She struggled to breathe and became very agitated.

"Can you please step out of the room," my father asked my mother and me. "I need a few minutes alone with her."

As we stood in the hallway, we held on to one another because all we heard were loud cries and moans coming out of my sister's room.

"Is that Daddy?" I asked.

"Yes," my mom cried.

While we waited, I went to the payphone and called Uncle Joe to update him.

"Uncle Joe, it's almost over," I cried.

"I don't believe you," he screamed.

I couldn't understand why he sounded so angry at me.

"Let me talk to your mother," he demanded.

Even though his harsh words hurt me, I understood this was his grief talking.

Back in my sister's room, my mom fidgeted with Celia's pillow, and my dad paced the floor. I parked myself next to her bed and didn't leave.

"I just saw Papa George," my sister whispered.

"Who did you see?" my father asked.

"Papa George," she said. "He wants me to go to Dunhill's of London and pick up cigars." No one said a word.

Papa George, my father's dad, died in 1959 when my sister wasn't yet two years old. According to my dad, he smoked Dunhill's of London cigars, but there's no way Celia could have known that because until she mentioned it, my dad didn't even remember those were the cigars he smoked.

My mother sat on one side of her head and my father on the other side of her head. I sat at the foot of the bed.

"What time is it?" she asked.

"It's 10:30," all three of us responded simultaneously.

"It's time for me to go," she said.

"Go where?" we screamed.

"Home."

And then she closed her eyes.

There is no way to adequately describe watching someone take their final breath. It was like an out-of-body experience with everything moving in slow motion. I screamed, but I couldn't hear a sound.

"Take this pill, it will help sedate you," a nurse said to me.

It had no effect. I just kept stroking Celia's face to try and get her to wake up.

"Please wake up, Celia. Please wake up, please wake up," I cried. "I'm not ready for you to go." I turned to the nurse and said, "She's still warm, and her legs are twitching. She's not gone yet.

I couldn't believe it or accept it. In some ways, I still don't.

Chapter 10

September 10, 1983, fell on a Saturday. On the Jewish calendar that year, it fell between the high holidays of Rosh Hashanah and Yom Kippur, known as Shabbat Shuvah, or the Sabbath of the Return. It's one of the holier Sabbaths on the calendar.

With my cousin Fred's earlier help, my parents had already made funeral arrangements to have Celia's service the next day, customary in Judaism since Jews do not embalm the body, believing it should return to the earth naturally.

The morning of the funeral, my Aunt Barbara, who had arrived from New Jersey the night before, said to me, "This will be one of the hardest days of your life, but lean on loved ones who will try to bring you peace."

While I've had tough days in my life, nothing will ever match the difficulty and sadness of this one day.

My parents were still members of Shearith Israel, the synagogue in Wharton, but our family wasn't fond of its rabbi. "I'd like Rabbi Laibson to give my eulogy," Celia had told us when discussing her funeral. Rabbi Howard Laibson, a new rabbi in Houston at the time, often visited Celia in the hospital and agreed to be part of her service.

"I'm so honored she asked me to conduct her service," he said. For someone who didn't know my sister very well, his words captured her soul and brought so much comfort to my parents and me:

> Unlike many of you, I didn't know Celia very long. Our relationship began last July. But in that short period, I came to know her as a good, honest, sincere human being, one I would have been proud to call a friend.
>
> There is often a unique intensity in a relationship when both parties know that one of them faces death. The gaps in my perspective on Celia have been filled in considerable measure by her family. So with their help and from my own experience with her, this is what I will remember about Celia.
>
> First and foremost was her capacity to give. Celia was often concerned about others and what they needed. Whenever she could, she tried to provide it for them, a quality of hers from the beginning. When she was only three, a playmate admired one of her dolls. Celia gave it to her. Just like that. That's the way she was.
>
> And no one knew this better than her immediate family. She loved to give herself to each of you. Whether it was buying Judy new clothes, supposedly on loan, never asking to be repaid or engineering a free vacation for you, Bob, and Barbara, to San Francisco, knowing you could use a sense of uplift. Celia always found a reason to give away the love she felt for you. That's just the way she was. And, of course, you will all miss her for that.
>
> Celia was also very trusting. Somewhere along the line, she decided to look for the good in people. Somewhere along the line, she decided to accept people at face value. Occasionally, this trusting attitude bordered on the naive

and gullible. I know this was frustrating for many of you who cared about her.

She was the kind of person described as trusting others too much. But then, Bob, as you pointed out, the fault wasn't hers. Instead, it was with those who weren't worthy of her trust. For her part, Celia refused to become cynical. She would go on being open to people, trusting them, and seeing their good. She preferred to live that way, even to the last moment, and it was one of the most refreshing things about her.

Still, the one thing that stands out the most when I think of Celia is the uncommon closeness she felt for her family. It was as if all she cared about was their happiness. Judy, I know you'll miss how she kept tabs on how you were doing, both at school and socially. She always wanted the best for you, as you know. And even though she's not here to encourage you, you'll still reach for the heights Celia hoped for you.

And Bob and Barbara, Celia loved you so much. All she wanted toward the end was to spend her final days at home with you. And you were terrific. You didn't pamper her; you didn't try to protect her from the truth about her condition. She knew what was happening, and she needed to talk about it openly and honestly. You encouraged her to do so even though it was often hard for you. And that was the greatest mitzvah you could have done.

There was so much love there, among all of you. You were all fortunate. As we discussed before Celia died, even though she was to live for too-short a time, she knew more love from her family than many people who lived twice her years.

I must return to one subject. In Celia's last weeks, when her terrible illness became apparent, she approached the eventuality of her death with incredible maturity—having a supportive family, willing to talk about anything and everything: the funeral details, the Jewish burial rites, death itself. I believe she came to terms with her death in an admirable way. But she asked a troubling question: "Why me?"

Indeed, why should one be afflicted by such a horrible disease, one who is so young? The question is meaningful and of utmost significance. Because Celia deserved better, she was a good, kind, caring person who didn't have a mean bone in her body. She earned better than to be struck down in such a terrible way.

When she asked, "Why me?" as we all ask on her behalf, the question reflects our sadness and anger over the fact that the world lost such a fine and gentle person. It isn't fair. It isn't just. Ultimately, Celia understood that this wasn't punishment for some misdeed. We live in an imperfect world. Her sadness and anger, like ours, are appropriate to the situation.

That is why we reach out to one another now for support. That is how we are able, somehow, to reach down and find the strength to withstand the pain of this tragedy. That is how we go on living. And this we must do now. Celia wouldn't have it any other way.

In my sister's conversation with Rabbi Laibson, I found it ironic that she talked about her illness being a punishment for something she had done wrong. I had felt the same after being raped six years earlier. But the difference was I survived, and she didn't. And now I'd have to live with that for the rest of my life. Why did God spare me and not Celia? I don't think I'll ever understand it.

The days following the funeral were gut-wrenching. Family and friends surrounded us, and food deliveries were non-stop. Jews and food: a mystery.

"How will we ever eat all of this food?" I asked my mom.

"Trust me, if we don't eat it, others will," she said.

A parade of people came in and out of our home for days to pay their respects, and it felt as if each person brought more food with them. But what we didn't eat, they did.

As is customary in Judaism, the mourning period, called shiva, occurs over seven days. For the truly religious, all mirrors are covered, and hard benches replace sofas. Vanity and comfort are secondary. For my family, we did a hybrid version of shiva. We covered some mirrors (but not in my room; I knew Celia would want me to look good), sat on our furniture, and only held three days of mourning. On what would have been the last day of shiva, my parents and I flew to Cancun, fulfilling my sister's request.

We spent our time lying on the beach and reminiscing about Celia through laughter, tears, and silence. "To Celia," we toasted through tears with the promised margaritas. None of us could fully grasp the magnitude of this loss or how our lives could go on without her. But for her sake and memory, we couldn't stop living.

A few days after her funeral, we received a hand-written letter from Dr. Zanger:

Dear Barbara, Bob & Judy,

When Dr. Conlon called me on Saturday night to tell me Celia had died, I was shocked. For the past six months, I kept feeling this shouldn't happen. So, when he called me, I was somewhat taken aback and suddenly realized that there was no reprieve.

I could not attend the funeral due to a minor health problem, but I thought about her all day. Her case was the most frustrating, disappointing, and saddest I have ever encountered.

But the most unusual thing of all was not any of the medical aspects but Celia herself. I have never encountered a person, old or young, with so much courage. Every step of the way, she behaved like true royalty. She tolerated pain and discomfort with scarcely a murmur of complaint. She continued to give of herself during every possible moment that she was able, right up until the end when she wrote us such a beautiful thank-you note.

She never became angry or hostile to those of us who could not give her life. When death stared her in the face, she remained steadfast in her bravery.

In her 25 years, she gave more to the world than most of us in our 70-80. Such a person is not easily forgotten.

It gives me a little comfort to realize that in terms of universal time, each of us has such a small moment here anyway that what matters is what we do with that moment more than if our moment is 25, 50, or 75 years.

I humbly submit my condolences and pray that you will accept them.

I have no idea if it is customary for a doctor to send a letter to a family apologizing for not giving life to a loved one. Dr. Zanger's words summed up everything we'd been feeling over the past nine-month nightmare. Utter sadness and frustration that this happened in the first place to someone like my sister, whom she described as courageous and like royalty.

Her letter comforted my parents and me, but I hated reading it. I recently found it in a stack of cards and letters I'd packed away. And even though I'd read this letter hundreds of times, one particular sentence struck me and gave me such clarity after re-reading it: "It gives me a little comfort to realize that in terms of universal time, each of us has such a small moment here anyway, that what matters is what we do with that moment more than if our moment is 25, 50, or 75 years."

It's so true. We're only here for a moment. No one knows their destiny in life, but no matter how many years we're supposed to be here, what we do with our time—our moment—matters most. A life cut too short, but Celia left us, especially me, genuine gifts of kindness, strength, courage, acceptance, and love—most notably the love of family.

Shortly after my sister passed away, several people gave my family copies of Harold Kushner's book, *When Bad Things Happen to Good People*. I swear we amassed at least a dozen copies. I realize this was a kind gesture meant only to help us in the healing process, but I couldn't read it. I didn't need a book to tell me that bad things happen to good people.

My sister's been gone for many years, but in some respects, it's as fresh and raw as if it happened yesterday. I once had a friend ask me, right before her father died, if I ever got over losing my sister. I gave her a simple response: "I'll get back to you."

You never get "over it," but you do keep going—because life goes on.

At only nineteen years old, I wondered what my life would look like now without my confidante and best friend by my side? Only time would tell. While technically now an "only child," I couldn't imagine ever declaring that status to anyone who asked. One thing I knew for sure, Celia would always remain in my heart, and she's been with me in everything I've done in my life, every step of the way.

Part Two

Chapter 11

Shortly after Celia passed away, with the support of my parents, I decided to come home from Southwest Texas State University and enroll at the University of Houston (UH).

"Your father and I have been talking, and we think it's best if you come home this semester and enroll at UH," my mom said.

I could tell she had struggled with this discussion. On one hand, I'd become fiercely independent, living on my own at college. But on the other hand, I found it difficult to get out of bed most mornings.

"I'm so glad you said something first because I wasn't sure how to tell you I'm ready to come home," I said to my mother as we were sitting at the kitchen table when I was home for winter break.

I missed my sister even more than I thought possible. Honestly, if I'd stayed in San Marcos any longer, I'm pretty sure I would have flunked out of school. Unfortunately, I couldn't enroll directly into UH to finish my communications degree because I needed to complete many core courses that I despised, like math, English, and science. I fell far behind after Celia died, so I enrolled in Houston Community College for those classes, and in the following fall semester, I transferred to the University of Houston.

*   *   *

Music has been a big part of my life since I was a child. My father always played music on the radio or a record player in our house. Yes, a record player. That foreign object with a rotating turntable and needle arm, which, when hit just right, would scratch across the vinyl, giving the music that familiar crackling sound. My father had an eclectic record collection, including everyone from Benny Goodman, Frank Sinatra, and Ella Fitzgerald to Sergio Mendes & Brasil '66, Neil Diamond, and The Fifth Dimension.

Celia also had a great record collection that I took ownership of after she died. This included many 45s like her prized possession of "She Loves You" by The Beatles. She had bought it with allowance money at the five-and-dime store in Wharton when The Beatles first came to America in 1964.

To play 45s on a record player, you used a round yellow plastic thingamajig to fit the small disc on the turntable. We'd have endless dance parties listening to our records and often convinced our mother to buy us the latest 45 the minute the song played on the radio.

My mother played music on the car radio, and I quickly learned the words to almost every song. Celia and I loved that we each had theme songs for our names; hers was "Cecilia" by Simon & Garfunkel and mine was "Hey Jude" by The Beatles.

"We'd get in the car, and 'Hey Jude' would come on the radio, and you would sit in your car seat singing along," my mom told me.

This is probably why I love Paul McCartney. Today, I still remember song lyrics to music from forty or fifty years ago.

"If you would learn your schoolwork as quickly as you learned lyrics to songs, you'd be a genius," my mom would always tell me.

My love of music turned into a fascination with musical artists and bands. I would imitate performers like Diana Ross and

The Supremes, Sonny & Cher, and The Jackson 5, always mesmerized by their flashy costumes and wild dance moves. I wanted to be a backup singer/dancer one day, even though I couldn't sing a note or dance a step.

My mother convinced me to try out for the musical *South Pacific* in high school. I won a part in the chorus singing, "I'm Gonna Wash That Man Right Out of My Hair." Of course, anyone who tried out got the same part. It was my first and last stage performance, and while I never followed my passion for musical performance, I did pursue a career in the music industry.

* * *

Before starting courses at UH, I wanted to get a job. Community college was boring, and with my parents going back to work, being alone with my thoughts all day sounded dreadful. My life changed when I started an internship at a Houston radio station and met a new friend—my soul sister—who helped me get to the other side of my pain.

My mother's first cousin, Andy, worked in Los Angeles as an entertainment attorney for ABC. One of his friends was a big honcho at ABC Radio, and he facilitated getting me an internship at KSRR-FM, the ABC-owned-and-operated radio station in town.

On my first day as the new programming department intern at 97 Rock, one of the most popular radio stations in Houston at the time, a girl came bouncing through the office and plopped down in the chair next to me.

Rachel, the programming director's secretary, said, "Hannah, have you met our new intern, Judy?"

"No, I'm so glad to meet you!" Hannah said.

Hannah, a beautiful super tall girl, worked as the morning and afternoon sportscaster.

"What a fun job! I love sports," I told her.

I did love sports and enjoyed going to sporting events. My father used to take us to Houston Astros baseball games, and I even became an Astros Buddy one summer, an opportunity for kids to meet players before home games.

But it wasn't sports that drew me to Hannah. Something about her made me think we could be friends. Barely a year since I had lost my sister, I left school and the friends I made there, and most of my other friends were away at college doing their own thing. Since being home, I had mainly been hanging out with my parents when not in class. Meeting Hannah was unexpected, exciting, and comforting.

Not that I couldn't make new friends, but at that time in my life, I didn't feel very worthy of anything and carried so much survivor's guilt, I could barely function, much less put myself out there. In some ways, Hannah represented a sister-like figure for me. Also, her height, personality, and klutziness reminded me of Celia.

There's a great quote I love: "The universe doesn't give you the people you want; it gives you the people you need." At this point in my life, I needed Hannah, whether she knew it or not. She helped me get over some very dark times and encouraged me to live my life, exactly what Celia wanted for me, too.

Hannah was just two years older than me, and we instantly connected over fashion, boys, clubbing, pop culture, impaired judgment, and everything in between. We even became part of each other's families. On Christmas, I'd go to her house, and she'd come to my house for Passover. And boy, did I have a crush on her younger brother, Mark. She and I made a hilarious duo with her standing five foot ten and me five foot three (just like Celia and me). Many of her friends affectionately referred to me as Hannah's "short" friend with major league ta-tas (by comparison, she was as flat as a board, like Celia, too). I would have gladly traded big boobs for height.

Our stature and chest size and the fact that Hannah was Catholic were our only differences. Our fashion style, hairstyles, music preferences, and horrible taste in boyfriends were very similar. Hannah and I indeed were partners in crime and always there for one another, giving sage advice to get through any problem, like when I bounced my first check and called her crying.

"I can't believe I bounced a check," I said. "What am I going to do? I'm going to have the worst credit ever."

She laughed out loud. "Please, I bounce checks all the time," she said. "And I seriously doubt this will be the last time you do this."

Talk about the blind leading the blind in personal finances.

We would regularly shut down clubs and bars with our antics. I felt so carefree whenever we'd go dancing at the hottest clubs in Houston: The Metropol, NRG, or our favorite, Fast 'N Cool, a fine establishment that showcased dancers in cages like canaries.

"I want to dance in one of the cages," I screamed to Hannah one night.

"You're crazy," she said.

Instead, I opted for one of the large platforms at the front of the room.

"Hey, Hannah, I'm over here," I yelled to her while dancing as if I belonged up there.

"Havey, what are you doing up there?"

Honestly, I had no idea what I was doing, but I knew I'd never felt more alive.

We also had some of the most epic birthday celebrations for each other, at least the ones we can remember. *Judy's turning 22, she graduated, and she has a new gold card*, she wrote on a flier that she posted all over the radio station, inviting everyone to a party she planned for me.

At a Tex-Mex restaurant we both loved, the tequila flowed steadily. Someone tapped my shoulder while I was about to take God knows what number of tequila shots (honestly, I lost count). I turned around to find my father staring at me. I froze.

"If you're going to keep doing tequila shots, let me show you how to do them the right way," he said.

He proceeded to show me and everyone else how to properly take a tequila shot, including throwing salt over your right shoulder. To this day, I don't think throwing salt is significant, but we threw salt over our right shoulders all night long.

I guess the evening ended, but I have no memory of it. I remember waking up in a bed at my parents' house with the biggest hangover. Yes, another epic celebration courtesy of Hannah and Judy.

* * *

Being the sportscaster at the radio station, Hannah often got tickets to sporting events around the city. Together we attended countless Houston Astros baseball games, Houston Rockets basketball games, and Houston Oilers football games. We also scammed our way into other marquee sporting events that had nothing to do with Houston but everything to do with having a good time and getting into trouble.

One of those events was the 1987 Super Bowl in Los Angeles at the famous Rose Bowl stadium. The New York Giants played the Denver Broncos that year. Hannah and I decided to take a road trip to Los Angeles with two of our other friends, Jenny and Andrea, who worked in sales at the radio station.

"I only have two tickets to the game," Hannah said. "But we can scalp two tickets when we get there. People are always out front trying to get rid of tickets."

When we got to the stadium, we searched high and low for tickets. With no one selling any, we decided Jenny and Andrea would hand us their ticket stubs through the fence for us to get back in. While many called me a scam artist, I preferred to think of myself as a problem-solver. I always found ways to make things happen, especially when it involved Hannah and our escapades.

Jenny and Andrea went inside, but we lost them. While aimlessly walking around the stadium grounds, Hannah and I saw two cute guys waiting to get in.

I turned to Hannah. "I've got a plan; follow me."

We walked up to them and flirted.

"Hey, our friends just went in, and they were supposed to find us at the fence to hand us their ticket stubs so we could get in, too, but we lost them," we said in our best Texas accents. "Do you think y'all could pass your ticket stubs through the fence so we could get in, and then we'd give them back to you?"

"Sure, no problem," they replied. "Just make sure you give them back to us because we go to a lot of big games together, and these tickets are part of our collection."

We agreed. Once Hannah and I made it inside the gate, we looked all around for the guys who generously helped us, but they were nowhere in sight. We figured they would come to their seats at some point and find us, so we gave up.

It turns out their seats were way better than Hannah's original tickets. Because the New York Giants were playing, many fans from the New York area were at the game, and we were in their section. Not only were we surrounded by a bunch of raucous New Yorkers, but a few rows ahead were some members of the 1986 New York Mets team.

I looked at Hannah and said, "I hate the Mets!"

It wasn't so much that I hated the Mets, but I despised this 1986 Mets team. They had beat the Houston Astros the year before in the National League Championship Series and went on to the World Series. Okay, they won the World Series that year, but I, along with many of my fellow Houstonians, felt they were just a bunch of pompous babies.

"They're a bunch of thugs," I said.

"Okay but keep it to yourself before we get arrested or kicked out," Hannah replied.

Fair comment, and I behaved, for the most part. Not even their presence could take away the fun we had at this game. We didn't have a team to root for since neither of us had ties to New York or Denver, but since we were sitting amongst so many New Yorkers, we started rooting for the Giants, or at least I did.

John Elway was making his Super Bowl debut as Denver's star quarterback, and many people were rooting for him to win. The Giants won the game, and I officially became a Giants fan. We never found the guys who gave us their ticket stubs. I'm sure they never forgave us either.

Hannah's talent catapulted her into a storied broadcasting career. I cried when she eventually left Houston. "I'm so sad you're leaving, but I'm so excited for your future," I told her. "I'll always be your biggest fan."

In some ways, it felt like losing a sister all over again. But watching her success through the years made me so happy, and I knew, no matter what, we'd always have an unbreakable soul-sister bond.

* * *

I had some of the best and craziest times during my years at the radio station. I could never imagine all the experience I'd gain through this job. While technically an intern, I couldn't receive school credit because the internship didn't come through the Communications Department at UH. Essentially, I just hung out, mainly in the broadcast booth or production studio, learning the ropes.

Each studio had its function, but both smelled of cigarette smoke and bad cologne. You could always tell when one of the female DJs had a shift because of a sweet-smelling candle or floral perfume that filled the air. Production studios were used to record radio ad spots and promotional material, while the broadcast booth was strictly for live on-air broadcasts. I used to love watching the DJs do their shows from the booth.

I felt so grown up finally doing something other than selling clothes or being a camp counselor, my high school jobs.

Before starting my internship, Andy, the program director, offered me a paid position working in the research department. I would be responsible for making those annoying calls to random people, often interrupting their dinner hour to ask them survey questions about music.

"That sounds so boring, and while I know I'd get paid, I'd rather work for free and be your intern."

"Are you sure your parents would agree with you?" he asked.

"They probably wouldn't be too happy with my decision," I answered.

But I'm so glad I followed my gut. I learned something different every day, like the fine art of filing record albums in alphabetical order. My new desk sat in a long and narrow closet with floor-to-ceiling shelving to store all the record albums.

"The first thing I want you to do is re-file every album the DJ uses during their shift," said Michael, the station's Music Director, and my direct boss. "Oh, and in alphabetical order. The DJs get super cranky with misfiled albums," he added.

I spent hours upon hours re-filing the albums in alphabetical order. At one point, I became so intimate with the LPs that I could tell you the album and song order of almost every artist. For example, A1, Aerosmith's *Greatest Hits*, and A2, Aerosmith's *Toys in the Attic*, each had "Walk This Way." But if the DJ wanted to play the full version of the song, he needed A2, not A1, since the greatest hits albums always had the radio or edited version of songs, mainly because of curse words.

And for the overnight DJs, you always programmed the album versions of Lynyrd Skynyrd's "Freebird," Led Zeppelin's "Stairway to Heaven," and The Beatles' "Hey Jude" so they'd have enough time to use the bathroom and make it back on air before the songs ended.

These tasks didn't bother me at all. But I did have nightmares that all the albums fell and buried me alive. My record filing skills were supreme, and my hard work paid off quickly. I soon added more and more responsibilities and eventually programmed the music for the DJs to play.

"All you have to do is write the song title and artist in each box on this form, and don't forget to write the album number," Michael directed me. How could I ever forget the album number? I knew every single one by heart. I couldn't believe I got to program the music. I remember getting all giddy when I'd listen to the radio station and hear a song play that I'd selected. Or I'd be angry when I knew the DJ played the song from the wrong album, or worse, the wrong music—such a power trip.

My internship was only supposed to be for that summer. I don't know if my timing or hard work and dedication helped me, but it all paid off. Before my internship ended, I started making money. Michael sent a memo to the entire staff to make it official, too:

> Please join me in welcoming Judy Haveson to the ranks of ABC paid employees. Her parents are thrilled that she is now getting paid for what she does in the Music Department. When you see Judy[2] (short for Judy Judy), ask her for a loan.

I felt invincible that day. I may have only been making minimum wage, but I felt like a million dollars. I desperately wanted to share this news with Celia. This event represented one of many events to come that I'd never be able to communicate with her about. But fortunately, I had my parents and Hannah. And both were so proud of me. I knew Celia was proud of me, too.

Oh, and that paid research department job? Eventually, I got promoted to oversee the entire department and the people who made the calls. Yep, always go with your gut, I thought. Two short years later, before I graduated college, I became Research Director for 97 Rock. This job came with a raise, a business card, and an office in the computer room, a step up from the music library closet.

I officially did it. But as excited as I felt, I still had that pang of sadness that I couldn't share this news with the one person above all others who would be so proud and excited: Celia.

Chapter 12

Working at a radio station came with a lot of perks. You were the first to know when an artist or band released a new song or album, and when they went on tour, you often got tickets to see them in concert for free. Occasionally I also met the artists when they dropped by the radio station before a show for a bit of self-promotion.

I felt like a kid in a candy store working at 97 Rock but always had to act cool since it was customary to come face to face with some of my rock heroes. However, I quickly realized most "rock heroes" didn't belong on pedestals.

My concert-loving days started at age twelve during the Houston Livestock Show and Rodeo. My parents took Celia and me to see KC and the Sunshine Band. In addition to famous Country and Western artists, the rodeo planners would throw a Pop or Rock act into the mix to expand their country audience.

From that moment, live music became my jam, mainly concerts. And I loved seeing live shows with my parents and Celia, too. Together we saw legendary musical artists, including Frank Sinatra, Neil Diamond, Liza Minnelli with Joel Grey, and Barbra Streisand, to name a few.

My musical tastes have always been eclectic, and I attribute that to my father and sister. I thought I'd never see anything or anyone better than KC and the Sunshine Band, until my sister took my best friend Melinda and me to see Billy Joel in 1979.

"How would you and Melinda like to go see Billy Joel in concert?" my sister casually asked me one day.

"Yes, yes, yes," I replied.

I like to count Billy Joel as my first real concert since he played in an actual music venue, not one surrounded by cows and horses.

*   *   *

Over the years, I saw and met a variety of bands and artists, elevating my coolness factor, or so I thought. Among the greats included Paul McCartney, Gloria Estefan and Miami Sound Machine, Whitney Houston, Billy Joel, George Michael, Donny Osmond, Barry Manilow, Patrick Swayze, Michael Jackson, Paula Abdul, Olivia Newton-John, Styx, Genesis, Earth, Wind & Fire, The Cars, Bruce Springsteen, The Jacksons, Diana Ross, Queen, Rick Springfield, Rod Stewart, Tom Petty, The Eagles, Fleetwood Mac, Heart, Santana, Journey, ZZ Top, The Doobie Brothers, Madonna, Van Halen, The Who, The Rolling Stones, and many more.

Many of these memorable encounters and concerts included VIP treatment and access, like eating Mexican food and playing miniature golf with Donny Osmond or seeing The Jacksons with Abbe at the Astrodome when I was on crutches. But the most unforgettable person I ever met was Sir Elton John, though technically, I met him before his knighthood.

Elton John's music is a part of the soundtrack of my life. Celia got me hooked. We listened to the album *Goodbye Yellow Brick Road* until the needle on the record player could no longer find the groove in the vinyl.

I started my long obsession with attending Elton John concerts in high school and never stopped going to his shows. I even saw Elton John and Billy Joel's duet concert tour twice with Melinda. The first time was in San Antonio for my thirtieth birthday.

Melinda and I drove to San Antonio and stayed at a hotel along the Riverwalk.

"I wish we could get stoned before the concert," Melinda said.

"I'll take care of it," I said. I called Randy and told him Melinda and I had tickets to see Elton and Billy in concert for my birthday, and we needed a party favor.

"Consider it an early birthday present," he said.

He gave me a joint and Melinda and I smoked it in our hotel room before the concert. It had been years since either of us had gotten high; we almost forgot how.

"It's not working. I feel nothing," Melinda said.

"Give it time. It will kick in," I said.

And boy, did it ever kick in. Walking along the Riverwalk, I prayed we wouldn't fall into the water.

"I think I'm wasted," Melinda said.

"No, I know you are," I snorted.

"What the hell just happened?" Melinda screamed, looking up as she spoke.

"Oh my gosh, a bird just shit on you," I laughed.

I quickly walked her to the nearest bathroom to clean her up, praying neither of us would fall into the river. We couldn't stop laughing, but we eventually made our way to the concert, and it did not disappoint.

The tour headed to Houston the following year, in time for Melinda's thirtieth birthday, so I told her I'd buy the tickets. We didn't get a chance to repeat the wild fun in Houston with party favors because shortly before the concert, Melinda had news.

"I'm pregnant," she said.

"Way to spoil the fun," I joked.

Of course, the concert still rocked, and we probably enjoyed it more this time around.

Then came the time I met Elton John. Like many of my meetings with other musical artists and bands, this wasn't just a casual backstage posed-photo cattle call. The gathering included a small intimate session for radio programmers.

After serious throat surgery, Elton debuted *Reg Strikes Back*, when many thought he'd never fully recover or sing the same again. Around this time, Elton John also started to tone down his striking appearance and lifestyle and began auctioning off the flamboyant costumes he used to wear at his concerts. The new and improved Elton John had arrived.

My boss was invited to the party but declined, and Darien, one of the station's DJs, and I got the golden tickets.

"Wait, why is there a white baby grand piano in the middle of the room?" I asked Darien as we walked inside the hotel ballroom.

"We're obviously in the wrong place." We both laughed and made a beeline straight to the bar.

"Would you like some crab cakes?" asked the waiter passing the hors d'oeuvres.

I turned to Darien and said, "No way am I eating because I may throw up when I meet Elton John."

I politely passed on the crab cakes. I could imagine the scene, "Hello, Elton. So nice to meet you ... " and then I'd puke my guts on his shoes. I drank water instead.

After about twenty minutes, the local promotion guy for the record label took the microphone to welcome the fifteen people in the room to Dallas. "Without further ado, ladies and gentlemen, Mr. Elton John."

I was pretty sure I didn't breathe for about five minutes. He walked through the room wearing a subdued outfit: an understated suit, his signature eyewear, and a straw hat.

Darien and I waited our turn for a picture and then stepped up to pose with Elton standing between us, his arms draped across our shoulders. I wore a bright pink silk dress, and I prayed he couldn't see the sweat forming in my armpits. My hair matched the 1987 required style of tight perm curls, but I wouldn't have cared if it were bright pink and matched my dress.

When they filled out the paper name tags, instead of writing my name as Judy Haveson, they wrote June Haveson.

When we walked up to take our picture, Elton extended his hand and said, "Hello, June, nice to meet you."

I shyly replied, "Actually, my name is Judy."

He replied with a wink and said, "I like that name better."

If I hadn't been a fan before, this made me a fan for life. I felt faint, standing mere inches away from Elton John.

He sat at the white baby grand piano with people around him, humming, singing, and dancing as he played his most famous songs. This went on for more than an hour. He played hit song after hit song: "Rocket Man," "Bennie and The Jets," "Candle In The Wind," "Crocodile Rock," "Goodbye Yellow Brick Road," and "Your Song." He took breaks and talked about the music, what it meant, his life at the time when he'd written the songs, and other fascinating stories. I felt as if he sang directly to me the entire time, especially as he made eye contact more than once.

I don't think I ever really processed all the emotions I felt meeting Elton John. He was just another person who put his pants on one leg at a time, but he also wasn't. He was Sir Elton John. I couldn't stop thinking about Celia when I stood in his presence. After all, she introduced me to his music. She loved him so much, and I only wished she were with me. But the whole time, I felt as if she were, standing right next to me.

When I saw Elton John in concert after that meeting— and I attended several more shows—I felt a special connection. Not just anyone can say they stood next to Elton John's piano as he sang to them. Or maybe they could, but it didn't matter to me.

Chapter 13

During my tenure at the radio station, 97 Rock changed ownership and music formats multiple times: from album rock to adult contemporary to high-energy dance music. I became a mainstay in the programming department through all the music and company changes. I eventually worked as the Music Director and Music Manager.

Record promoters often visited program and music directors to persuade them to play their artists on the air. I instantly hit it off with Ken and Shanna, the promotion team from SBK Records, a new label. Ken, the executive from New York, had traveled to Texas to work with his local rep, Shanna. They took me to dinner one night, and while we talked about SBK's music, the conversation turned personal as Ken asked about everything from my non-existent dating life to living in Houston.

"You don't have a boyfriend?" he asked me.

"Not at the moment," I told him.

"Maybe you need to live in a bigger city," he said.

I stared at him. "Houston is a big city, or didn't you notice?"

"Sure, but do you want to move to Los Angeles?"

"What?" I asked, curious what he meant.

"We're looking for a National Promotions Manager for the small markets, and think you'd be perfect," he said.

Record promoters split markets up by city population; the top ten markets included New York, Los Angeles, Chicago, and Houston. Markets eleven through twenty-five had towns like Phoenix, Tampa, and Denver. Markets twenty-five and below represented the rest of the country.

"Are you serious?" I asked him again.

He said yes, and we discussed flying me to New York to meet with his boss.

The next thing I knew, I was on a plane to New York City, meeting with Ken and his boss, Daniel, and getting a life-changing job offer I never saw coming.

"What an incredible opportunity," I told them. "Can I have a few days to think about it and discuss it with my family?"

If only Celia were there to help me make the decision. She'd know what I should do.

Before I flew home to Houston, I met up with one of my closest, free-spirited, and confident childhood friends, Alysa, who lived in New York City. Alysa and I met when we were twelve years old. We became instant friends. While we didn't go to the same junior high, we did go to the same high school and eventually to UH together.

While still attending UH, Alysa's parents decided to move to Los Angeles.

"I can't believe you're leaving me," I cried while sitting in her front yard the day the moving vans showed up.

"We'll always stay in touch, and you know that," she assured me.

As the last moving van pulled away and their cars followed, I sat on the curb of her driveway and just cried and cried and cried. She eventually moved to New York City from LA.

Back at her apartment, Alysa and I analyzed and over-analyzed the pros and cons of moving to LA for this job.

"The pros heavily outweigh the cons, except for leaving my parents and the familiarity of living in Houston," I said.

My parents and I were extremely close, probably to a fault. And while we became even closer after Celia died, I never wanted them to smother me. I needed my space, and they granted it to me. I'd always been an independent creature—probably because of that incident on the first day of kindergarten—but moving across the country and not having them nearby scared me.

Having courageously moved from Texas to California to New York, Alysa helped me realize I could do this. "Listen, if you don't like it, move back," she said. "Don't live your life wondering what if. Life's too short for not taking advantage of great opportunities. I just wish the job was in New York."

So did I.

I went back to Texas and had a long conversation with my parents. While they were sad about the thought of me moving away, they supported me one hundred percent. So, along with their encouragement, I gave notice at the radio station and accepted the position at SBK Records.

Saying goodbye to my co-workers at the radio station proved more difficult than I had imagined. Even though it wasn't the same station as when I first started, I had been in the same building for almost six years. At the time, the longest relationship of its kind I had ever had. Before I left, I asked the general manager, Susan, to please write a letter of recommendation for me, in case I needed it in the future. I had no idea what she would write or say about me, but when I read her letter, her words overwhelmed me.

> As the Music Manager, Judy was an invaluable asset to the programming, promotion, and research departments. Her enthusiastic personality motivated the air and research staff. Judy is a tireless worker who possesses excellent people skills, and I strongly recommend her for any position.

I couldn't think of a better way to wrap up my radio career. Look out, Hollywood, here I come.

Chapter 14

The night before I moved to Los Angeles, we celebrated Passover at my parents' house. It wasn't a big gathering for our Seder that year, just my mom, dad, grandfather, and me. Our family holiday gatherings weren't the big celebrations they once were since Celia died. Even though it had been seven years since she'd passed away, we still didn't feel comfortable celebrating without her. And with my moving across the country the following day, no one was in the mood for a big event. Especially my father.

"Since I'm leaving for Vancouver on business the morning after the Seder, and Judy is flying to Los Angeles that day, too, I've booked us a room at the airport hotel, and we'll be leaving directly after dinner," he said. "This way, she won't have to rush to make her plane."

My mother, a brilliant and wise person, knew my father better than himself. She understood his motives, and they had nothing to do with making this convenient for me. He struggled to say goodbye and wanted to spend every minute with me before I got on that plane. While my mom also grappled with saying goodbye, she reluctantly allowed these theatrics because she realized this event was more overwhelming for him than it was for her.

Leaving my parents' house that night ranked high among the most challenging things I've ever done. There were a lot of tears all around. No one said goodbye. Instead, we said "see you soon." My grandfather slipped me money, something he'd done my entire life.

"You've got this, and I'm so proud of you," my mother said through tears as she held me longer than usual.

Then my father and I drove away. I'm sure I didn't stop crying until we drove up to the hotel. The minute we checked in; I called my mom. "You miss me already," she said.

"More than you know," I replied.

"Melinda called right after you pulled out of the driveway," she said. "She was crying so hard I could barely understand her. I think she's more upset that you're leaving than I am, and she kept apologizing, saying she should be comforting me, not the other way around."

Melinda being so upset helped my mom forget her sadness in some respects.

My dad and I checked into our room on the concierge level and decided to indulge in the hospitality suite. Since we were both stuffed from the Seder meal, watching people fill their faces with pizza and other appetizers made me nauseous. I'm sure that wasn't the only reason I had nervous butterflies in my stomach.

My entire life, my father always told me, "If that's what you want to do—you can do it." No matter what I searched for in my life, he'd always say this to me. Not as a way of granting permission, but rather to help me make my own decisions. While his words always sounded like the name of a Dale Carnegie self-esteem workshop, they held such meaning to me.

A man of few words (something I did not inherit) and even fewer emotions, when he spoke, I listened. It's not as if I have an enormous sense of self-doubt or poor self-confidence, but for some reason, my father always had a way of helping me gain clarity in my decisions—good or bad.

Morning came quickly, and I remember hearing my dad getting dressed. I always knew he was ready to go to work when I smelled his cologne. The lights were off in the bedroom, but he walked to the bed and sat on the edge.

"I'm so proud of you, and you're going to do great things," he said through his tears. "But no matter what, remember I'm always here."

Whenever he displayed any emotion, it shook me to my core. But no matter how sad I became leaving my parents, friends, and all things familiar, I knew I had to do this. I didn't know what lay ahead for me, but one thing I knew for sure, I was ready, and I couldn't turn back.

* * *

I landed at LAX and took a deep breath. "I'm here; I can do this," I thought. After picking up the few suitcases I had brought with me and getting my rental car, I drove straight to my new apartment to get my keys. Driving along the 405, I exited Santa Monica Boulevard into snarling traffic.

My apartment was in West Hollywood, or "Beverly Hills adjacent," near big celebrity hot spots like Le Dome and Spago. I wanted to live at the beach, but everyone warned me that LA is a great big freeway with nothing but traffic. Instead, I opted for a place near my new office where I could be in my parking garage in one song on the radio if I hit the stoplights just right.

"What is with all this traffic? Is this normal?" I asked my landlord.

"Tonight is the Oscars. Welcome to Hollywood!" he said.

I loved my new tiny apartment. When Hannah and I visited Los Angeles for fun, we stayed at Le Parc, a small hotel in West Hollywood. The cute room had a sunken living room and a big bedroom and dressing area. It was also convenient for everything. My new apartment was located directly down the street from Le Parc. So perfect although it had an oven the size of an Easy-Bake and a compact refrigerator. And as I learned when looking for a place to live, the fact that the apartment even had a fridge came as a big bonus.

"Many of the apartments I'm going to show you today don't come with refrigerators," said the apartment locator working with me.

"Excuse me? Do you mean I have to buy a refrigerator for an apartment I'm renting?"

"Oh no, you have to rent one," she replied. "Everyone does that in LA."

I did hear that you shouldn't be overly impressed by all the wealth and materialism in LA because most people rented and leased everything. Apparently, this included refrigerators.

As I was leaving my apartment for the hotel I'd be staying in for the next few days, my neighbor came out his door and introduced himself to me. "Hi, I'm John, but my friends call me Stubbs."

I just stared at him. I didn't want to know why his friends called him that, but he continued.

"Welcome to West Hollywood, where men are men and women don't matter. Honey, we'll take great care of you."

I instantly loved Stubbs. And I would love him even more the night the earth shook, and I met him in the hallway.

"It's just a tremor," he told me.

"I'm only used to hurricanes, not earthquakes," I said.

After leaving my apartment, I headed to my hotel, the Hyatt on Sunset. Also known as the Riot Hyatt, thanks to stories of legendary rock bands like Led Zeppelin, The Who, The Doors, and others who stayed there. It's not hard to imagine where the nickname originated.

Fortunately, there were no riots that night, but plenty of glitz and glamour for all to see. Oscar-wannabes walked through the lobby, donning their long gowns and tuxedos. I guess they were looking for a party or their next role. I sat in the lobby and people-watched for hours with nothing else to do that evening. I didn't recognize anyone famous and figured the most special people would be at the awards ceremony and not trolling in the lobby of the Hyatt. Still, I couldn't believe my first night in Hollywood fell on the night of the Academy Awards.

I had a lot of courage and confidence to move across the country alone, not knowing anyone in town, or I'd lost my mind. I did have Joel, my friend from high school, and cousins who lived in LA. Andy, his wife, Randy, and their boys, Matt and Jonny, lived in the Hollywood Hills. Andy is the person who helped me get the internship at 97 Rock. They often invited me to their house, and I loved having them live so close. But other than that, I knew no one.

After Oscar left town and the Sunset Strip cleared of traffic, I made my way to my new office. Everyone welcomed me, and they were so friendly. I had a huge office with a big window looking directly at Sunset Boulevard. Across the street sat the famed Tower Records. I seriously couldn't believe my life.

SBK Records, a relatively new label, had recently been created by three men steeped in music industry lore. The leading man, Charles Koppelman, before founding SBK Records, headed EMI Publishing, one of the largest music publishing companies in the world.

Every time he would sign a new artist, they became instant stars. He worked with some of the era's great hitmakers, including Barbra Streisand, Cher, Dolly Parton, Billy Joel, and Donna Summer; he indeed had the Midas touch. And through EMI Publishing, he owned the rights to pretty much every song you have ever heard, including "Happy Birthday."

The origin story of SBK is that Charles' son, Brian, worked as an A&R (Artist and Repertoire) manager for another record label, Elektra. He scouted new talent. While attending Tufts University, he went to a bar in Boston and heard a woman singing with a voice like none other. He brought her to his dad, and they gave her a publishing deal and got her signed to Elektra Records. The artist—Tracy Chapman—sold millions and millions of albums.

Charles decided he wanted in on the record label side of the business, so he got together with two friends (Stephen Swid and Martin Bandier), forming SBK Records. One of his first successful acts was Wilson Phillips, the trio of daughters from The Mamas & the Papas and The Beach Boys. I had promoted Wilson

Phillips, and other artists, to radio stations in small markets around the country.

In my new role as National Promotions Manager, I'd now sit on the other side of the desk from my days as a music director at the radio station, using a different brain. I wondered, how will I do this? I didn't know, but there was no turning back now.

Chapter 15

Before starting my new job at SBK Records, I bought several maps. And not just maps of the USA that you could hang on a wall. I purchased the granddaddy of maps—a Road Atlas—and one for every country section. These maps became my bible for all the upcoming road trips I'd take to visit radio stations across the country.

Before every trip, I got a yellow highlighter and marked each route I'd take once I left the airport. It reminded me of our family road trips and the AAA TripTiks, but on steroids. In 1990-91, there were no portable cell phones or GPS, and using good old-fashioned maps and lots of quarters for the payphone was the only way to figure out where you were going. Oh, and stopping at a gas station to ask for directions, too.

"I think it's time for you to hit the road to start visiting radio stations, and the best place to begin is the Southeast region," Ken said. "You'll fly to Atlanta and meet up with Monte."
It reminded me of the *Mission Impossible* TV series, where the agent received his assignments, if he chose to accept them.

Monte, based in Atlanta, promoted SBK's music to the entire Southeast region of the country: Georgia, Florida, Alabama, Mississippi, and parts of Louisiana. I'd been talking with Monte over the phone for several weeks, and we had struck up a flirtatious friendship, but I assumed he treated all the girls this way. Regardless, I couldn't wait to meet him.

* * *

The morning after I arrived in Atlanta, Monte came to the hotel to pick me up. "I'm in the lobby, so come down when you're ready," he said.

When I got off the elevator and saw him waiting for me, I stared. He was more gorgeous than I imagined. My knees nearly gave out as I stared at his dark hair, beautiful eyes, and wicked smile.

I walked up to him and probably too enthusiastically said, "Monte, it's so nice to meet you in person finally. I'm Judy."

He looked at me curiously as if he didn't believe me and that I must be someone else.

"What are you staring at?" I nervously asked him.

"I'm staring at you," he said.

Okay, awkward. "Why?" I knew my cheeks were bright red.

With a broad smile and a slight laugh, he said, "Ken told me not to be shocked when I finally met you and not to make you feel self-conscious because of your weight problem."

What? Ken had pulled the ultimate prank and punked Monte.

"You got off the elevator, and I was shocked, but not for the reasons he said. I told him I'd been talking to you for weeks and couldn't believe he described the same person; you're so tiny and cute," he said.

He quickly added that it wouldn't have mattered if I had a weight problem or not. Good to know. We got in his car and called Ken from his car phone.

"Hey, Ken, I'm here with Judy," he said.

Ken laughed and said, "I told you she was a looker."

That evening after work, we met Hannah, who lived in Atlanta at the time, for dinner.

"Havey, he's so cute," she told me.

"I know," is all I could say.

After dinner, we went to a nightclub and danced and drank into the early morning hours. I knew I'd pay dearly for this fun the next day.

Bright and early the following day, nursing a slight hangover from the night before, Monte picked me up from the hotel, and we were off to Alabama. We started in Gadsden, home of the Holy Bible, and on to Huntsville. From there, we went to Birmingham and stopped for the night. In Birmingham, I learned the phrase, "Whatever it takes."

As a record promoter, you had to do whatever it took to get your song played on the radio. This didn't include illegal or illicit behavior, but if a program or music director wanted to go to a strip club, you went.

"I'm sorry, we're going where?" I asked Monte.

"Judy, if you go to this strip club, we'll get him to add our record to his playlist for this week. Besides, you're better looking than any of the girls in that club," Monte said, as he gave me the most panty-busting smile he knew.

I'd do just about anything for him, including a striptease dance at the club. We went to the strip club, and the program director added our song. And I didn't have to strip—all in all, a successful night.

The following day, we visited more radio stations in Birmingham before continuing to Montgomery. While there were no strip clubs for us at this stop, lots of drinks greeted us. One program director loved to drink. And she could drink like a fish.

"Come on, Monte, let's get drinkin'," she enthusiastically exclaimed in her Southern twang.

I decided not to indulge. Someone had to be responsible. Monte tried hard to keep up with her. I have never seen a woman drink so much.

"I can't drive," Monte slurred.

Duh.

"We need to keep going to get as close to Mobile tonight. Are you good to drive?" he asked.

I nodded. After an hour or so I felt tired and decided to stop. Ever familiar with roadside motels from years of family road trips, I pulled off the highway at the first sighting of a clean establishment.

"Stay here and don't move," I told him as I got out of the car to check us into the hotel.

With the late hour and Monte still drunk and almost passed out, I decided to get one hotel room since the likelihood Monte would make it to his room was slim to none.

"This should be an interesting story for Ken about why we got one room for us," Monte laughed.

"Let's just keep him guessing," I said.

Monte went on to have a successful career running a record label he created with his brother, representing some of the most famous musical acts of all time. But for a tiny moment, we were just two Jews road-trippin' through Alabama—laughing and drinking all the way.

* * *

"After your Southeast journey, I think you're ready to explore the country solo," Ken said. "For your next assignment, I want you to visit radio stations in Minnesota, Montana, and North Dakota."

I'd never been to these states, so I was excited about the adventure ahead.

"I'm coming to visit you, so get ready to add some music to your playlists," I told the program and music directors at all the stations in those states.

"We never get anyone from New York or LA to visit us," said the program director in Grand Forks, North Dakota. "This is going to be great fun."

If I'm being honest, I couldn't even pick out Grand Forks on a map, or North Dakota at all, for that matter. But I had my trusted road atlas, so I knew I'd be just fine.

I flew into Minneapolis and took one of those puddle jumpers to Duluth. The end of Interstate 35, or beginning, depending on how you viewed it, ran through Duluth. I knew I-35 very well because it ran directly through Texas, from Dallas to Mexico. Just outside of Duluth, in Hibbing, sat the home of Robert Zimmerman, a.k.a. Bob Dylan. Years later, while playing a trivia game, this fact came up, and I looked like a genius answering the question about the birthplace of Bob Dylan.

While not yet officially winter, snow blanketed the ground. After dark, I arrived at the rental car facility, and the friendly man behind the counter handed me a map and a plastic contraption.

"What is this?" I asked him.

"It's a snow scraper," he said energetically.

"What exactly is it I'm supposed to do with this?"

He looked at me like I had just asked him how to drive a car. "It's to scrape snow off your car window," he said.

Sure enough, the following morning, with snow all over my windshield, the plastic contraption came in handy. Luckily, I saw several people in the parking lot scraping snow off their car windshields and started doing what they did.

* * *

One of the best things about visiting small towns and cities is the people you encounter. Everyone was friendly and always trying to help, especially when I was lost. While I had no shortage of maps at my disposal, I still got lost. I've never been good at directions, and in fact, I can sometimes get lost in my own neighborhood.

When I first moved to Los Angeles, I spent more time turning around than going straight to my destination. "Go east towards the mountains and go west towards the ocean," everyone instructed me when I moved to LA. Of course, if you couldn't see said mountains or ocean, how would you know in which direction you were going? Hence the reason I was constantly turning around.

But in small-town USA, there were no such directional landmarks to follow except when visiting a radio station. "You need to drive about two blocks to the stop sign, hang a left for about a mile, and then hang a right and go about two more miles. When you get to the end of the road, look up. You're in the right spot if you see the radio tower."

And these directions worked ninety percent of the time.

One day, Ken announced he was joining me in Montana.

"It's supposed to be so beautiful, and I don't want you to get lost," he said.

Ken, a born and bred New Yorker, believed New York City to be the center of the universe and anything west of New Jersey uninhabited land.

"I'm driving," Ken said when I picked him up at the airport. "There's nothing but open roads in Montana, and I want to drive fast and bury the needle."

He floored it before I could stop him, driving so fast I couldn't feel my face.

"Are those sirens?" I asked as I white-knuckled the side of the door. "Oh my gosh, we're getting pulled over."

He just laughed and pulled the car over. "Where did he come from? We're the only car on the road."

The police officer slowly walked up to Ken's side of the car. I half expected him to ask us to get out of the car and lay face down on the highway.

"Hi, officer, how can we help you?" Ken said.

"Do you know how fast you were going, son?" he drawled.

"I think about seventy-five," Ken replied.

"More like ninety-five," the officer sniped.

"I'm from New York, and we don't have any roads like this, so I was just seeing how fast I could go," Ken explained like it was normal.

"Well, in Montana, we don't give tickets for excessive speed. We give tickets for excessive fuel usage. That will be five dollars," the officer told us.

What? A five-dollar excessive fuel ticket? Where were we? Ken gave the officer the money, and we were off. And once we were out of sight of the officer, he buried the needle again.

I'm just glad we didn't get arrested.

Chapter 16

One Saturday night in January 1991, I sat in a hotel room in Sacramento, California, having just left a Guys Next Door concert. They were one of the bands on SBK Records, our answer to the New Kids on the Block. In 1991, New Kids on the Block dominated the boy band craze, and every record label wanted a piece of the popularity. But while the Guys Next Door were cute, NKOTB came first and had talent. For some reason, that didn't seem to matter to teenage girls with raging hormones. They just needed cute boys and a reason to scream at them.

After the concert, while I was in my hotel room watching *Saturday Night Live*, Ken called me.

"Are you alone?" he asked seductively.

"I'm in Sacramento. Who would I be with?" I replied.

"With one of the Guys, of course."

"I'm older than fifteen. Why are you calling anyway? I need sleep," I whined.

"Well, you better sleep tonight because we need you in Louisville, Kentucky on Tuesday. You're going on the road for three months."

I couldn't understand what he was trying to tell me.

"One of our artists on tour needs promotional help coordinating backstage parties, radio station visits, and record store signings," he explained. "And since the opening band is also ours, we think it's best to have someone from the promotions department be with both acts at all times, and we decided that person would be you."

"How much underwear will I need for three months?" I asked.

Ken cleared his throat. I quickly recovered when I realized I had asked that question out loud.

"Well, I'll agree if you agree that I won't have to travel on the stinky, crowded tour bus."

I mean, I had to draw the line somewhere. I may not have been a total princess, but I did have my limits, and smelly tour buses were a hard limit.

"Sure, Judy, you can fly from city to city," he quickly agreed.

Later, I found out he only agreed because logistically, flying would prove to be impossible, and he knew I'd end up on the bus.

On January 16, 1991, I left sunny LA for Louisville, Kentucky, landing in blizzard-like conditions with temperatures hovering around twenty degrees. I now understood the meaning of California Dreamin'.

The musical artist I joined was the rapper Vanilla Ice. The label began promoting the Iceman the prior year when Monte heard his song, "Ice Ice Baby," on the radio while traveling through the South. He quickly called our boss and told him the phones at the radio station were "blowing up" (industry jargon for the song being a big hit), and we needed to get him on the label before another label got him first. SBK purchased the rights to his song and album, cleaned up his image (somewhat), and the rest is history. Okay, a long history that had several twists and turns, but history, nonetheless.

Because I lived in Los Angeles, I got to take him around town to different events, including the MTV Video Awards.

Vanilla Ice, whose real name is Robbie Van Winkle, wasn't a "big" star yet, so he didn't get the big star treatment of limos and red carpets. Instead, he got stuck with me, picking him up from his hotel in my Honda Prelude.

Shortly afterward, his single, "Ice Ice Baby," soared to number one on the Billboard charts, and you couldn't turn on a radio station anywhere in the country and not hear it playing. That's when he became a bona fide star. Now he rode in limos and walked red carpets.

"You'll miss riding in my Honda Prelude," I told him.

He laughed and rolled his eyes.

Once you have a successful album or hit song, the next step to solidifying stardom is a concert tour. While Vanilla Ice had been touring with MC Hammer, the record company quickly put together a headliner tour for just him, designed to promote sales for the album *To the Extreme* and the hit song "Ice, Ice Baby." He had other songs like "Play that Funky Music," but they all sounded the same.

That didn't stop the legions of Vanilla Ice fans, though. The album sold more than thirteen million copies worldwide. The Vanilla Ice craze officially hit full force, and the concert tour guaranteed to make him an even bigger star.

The label decided to put one of their lesser-known artists on tour as the opening act for Vanilla Ice. These acts, also referred to as "T-shirt Bands," helped sell merchandise before the star took the stage.

RIFF were five boys from Paterson, New Jersey, who sang acapella. They had wicked talent and appeared in the movie *Lean on Me*, starring Morgan Freeman as a high school principal who helped his students graduate and make something of their lives. The boys of RIFF attended the high school portrayed in the movie, with the script loosely based on their story.

Unfortunately for RIFF, in the early 1990s, another acapella boy band topped the charts: Boyz II Men. Like the Guys Next Door with New Kids on the Block, there wasn't enough room on the radio for both, but the label counted on the Vanilla Ice tour exposure to launch RIFF into the spotlight.

When I arrived in Louisville, I knew I had a lot of work coordinating promotional appearances and other activities for both bands. I was always up for a challenge, and at least I would be flying from city to city instead of riding the bus. That thought didn't last long.

On January 16, 1991, in addition to the Vanilla Ice concert in Louisville, Kentucky, the first Gulf War began, which was perhaps more historically significant than the Iceman on stage in Louisville. Being surrounded by so many patriotic people in Kentucky, I quickly realized I was no longer in Los Angeles.

I now sat smack dab in the middle of America's heartland, where the only things that mattered were God and Country, and everyone bled red, white, and blue. I hadn't seen so many American flags on display since I visited Washington, D.C. with my family. It felt like I was witnessing a significant time in history. So much so that at the end of every show, Vanilla Ice brought out a giant American flag and led the audience in singing the national anthem.

As I made my way backstage after his performance, I prepared myself for Vanilla Ice to question my appearance and try to persuade me to leave.

Instead, he greeted me with a massive grin on his face.

"Hey, everyone, it's Judy! Did you bring your Honda Prelude?"

And so it began.

*　*　*

The Vanilla Ice tour, also known as the *To the Extreme* concert tour, would take us throughout the Midwest, the Northeast, and Southern states. While I had traveled to many states during various road trips with my parents and as the national promotions manager for SBK Records, there were still several states to check off my list.

After this one concert tour, there were only two states I didn't visit: South Dakota and Alaska. And I still haven't seen them to date. Also why I went to North Dakota and not South Dakota remains a mystery.

"But Ken, you said I could fly from stop to stop and not sleep on the stinky tour bus," I whined to my boss over the phone after the Louisville concert when he informed me flying was not an option.

"Stop being such a princess," he responded.

Easy for him to say since he wouldn't dare step foot on a tour bus. Although much better than a Greyhound or school bus, the tour bus had close quarters for all.

The smell alone included a combination of gym socks and sour milk, enough to make you sick. And if that wasn't bad enough, all the guys—seven in total—loved White Castle hamburgers. If you've never smelled the stench of grease at a White Castle restaurant, you haven't lived. Paired with usual boy smells, I don't have to say more. It was not good. Luckily, I befriended the bus driver, Steve, and politely explained my dilemma.

"I typically don't allow people to sleep on the sofa in front of the bus because it's a little risky if I have to jam on the brakes," he explained.

I batted my eyelashes at him. "But Steve, you can't let me sleep back there. Just thinking of the smell, I want to retch."

Steve bent his "no sleeping on the sofa" rule, and I took my place for the next three months at the front of the bus. I had my pillow and used my winter coat and Vanilla Ice tour jacket as my blankets. Fortunately, the bus had heat, so Steve continuously blasted it. Mainly to keep us warm and kill any germs permeating the air. I hoped I would survive the long three months ahead on the road.

Each night after the concert ended, both bands would hang out backstage to meet with radio station staff and promotional winners. Known as the Meet & Greet, groupies would inevitably be in tow. Vanilla Ice was only twenty-three years old, but that didn't stop women of all ages from throwing themselves and their intimate items his way. Everyone wanted a piece of this guy. This must be how women treated Frank Sinatra and Elvis Presley back in the day.

Once the Meet & Greet ended—around midnight or 1:00 a.m. most nights—we'd drive away. Steve slept during the day to rest up for the drive to the next stop. It took a while for us to settle down after each show, and most of us fell asleep well after 2:00 a.m.

Some days we would have a rest day in between cities, but most of the time we went straight to another show. All the band equipment rode on a separate rig, and that crew left well ahead of us to set up early in the morning the next day. On those rare occasions when we had the day off, I always tried to explore the city or relax in my hotel room. While that is how it mainly worked out, there were always cities where things didn't go as planned.

February 4, 1991: New York City. We had two days off in New York, and they were jam-packed with promotional appearances and record company meetings. We had traveled all night after the Minneapolis concert and arrived late in the night in New York City.

"Goodbye, and I'll see you at the Beacon Theatre on Wednesday," I said to Ice after checking into the hotel.

Officially off-duty for these two days, I had finally settled into my room when the phone rang.

"Judy, there's no way I'm staying at this hotel. It's hot, and the windows don't open. I want a new hotel," Ice said loudly.

"No hotel room windows open in New York City. They worry people will jump," I told him, not knowing if that was true. "It's 2:00 a.m.," I said. "Can this wait until the morning, so I can call the travel agent at a decent hour to rebook us?"

"Call her at home. I want to get out of this hotel now," he barked.

I calmly told him I would while I chugged down the little bottles of bourbon from the minibar.

"Cheri, I'm so sorry to wake you, but Ice hates the hotel and wants to move to a new one. Anything you can do?"

Cheri quickly called another hotel, and within the hour, we moved. The following day, I called a local florist and sent Cheri a large bouquet thanking her for all her help. And I put it on Ice's bill.

*   *   *

February 11, 1991: Nashville, Tennessee. We left Columbia, South Carolina, after the show on February 10 and headed to Nashville. Fortunately, we would have a day off before the February 12 concert. I couldn't wait to get a day in Nashville to myself. After checking into the hotel and taking a long hot shower, I hear a frantic knock on my door.

"Judy, quick, Ice was riding someone's motorcycle, and he flipped it and fell down a hill!"

I thought, please, please tell me this is a nightmare or a bad practical joke. I threw on my clothes and ran into the lobby, where I saw a commotion in the parking lot. Sure enough, Ice sat on the ground surrounded by his staff and what appeared to be a doctor.

"Are you kidding me right now?" I asked him.

He just smiled up at me and said, "Oops."

Fortunately, he had no broken bones or scratches on his face.

On February 14, 1991, we were headed to Atlanta, Georgia. I had been looking forward to this because we were staying at a nice hotel, and I'd be able to see Hannah and her boyfriend, Dan. I hadn't seen Hannah in what felt like forever.

After traveling all night from Chattanooga, we arrived in Atlanta early in the morning. I had the worst sinus infection. I was notorious for getting upper respiratory and bronchial infections, and because of all the travel, lack of sleep, changing weather, and poor eating, I got it bad. After I checked into my hotel room, I called Hannah. "I'm sick," I said.

Not like I had to tell her since you could barely recognize my voice.

"I'm taking you to my doctor, so get ready, and I'll be right there," she said.

When she arrived at the hotel, she asked me how I let myself get this bad. How? Let's see. In the middle of winter, I was living on a bus, using my coat as a blanket, and getting on average, three hours of sleep a night. That pretty much summed it up.

The doctor was not as understanding as Hannah. "You will take these antibiotics for seven days and get plenty of rest."

I wasn't sure how much rest I'd get living on a bus, but I promised to try.

The concert fell on Valentine's Day, so Ice bought all the women working the venue and his tour single red roses as an added touch. He then bought several dozen more and threw them into the audience. Afterward, I brought Hannah and Dan backstage to meet Ice. I'm sure that will always be one of the highlights of their life. We stood next to a giant speaker with thunderous sounds blaring out of it; I thought we'd all suffer permanent hearing loss. I snuck out of the concert, and Hannah and Dan took me back to my hotel to sleep. I felt almost like my normal self by morning when we were off to the next stop.

The one show I couldn't wait for was on February 23 in Houston. I would finally make it home. The night before, we had been in Alexandria, Louisiana, and since we were less than four hours from Houston, instead of sleeping in Alexandria, we drove on to Houston. When we were outside of the city, off Interstate 10, we stopped for breakfast, and I called my mom.

We decided she would meet me since I would be busy that night with the concert. I'd never been happier to see my mother in my entire life. I practically jumped into her arms in the parking lot. I brought her into the restaurant and introduced her to everyone.

"You're Judy's mother? You look like her sister," one of the guys said.

"They're just trying to butter you up, Mama."

They told my mom about the tour and how much fun we had. And then one of the guys said, "Hey, Barbara, come check out where your daughter is sleeping on the road."

I practically tripped over myself to get in front of her so she wouldn't step foot on the tour bus. Too late. I'm not sure if shock or disgust filled her or both, but the look on her face resembled sheer panic. I quickly explained how I slept in the front on the sofa, not on the bunks. Thankfully, Steve corroborated my story.

On March 6, we had a concert in Johnstown, Pennsylvania, and the temperatures were in the teens. Thankfully, we just had a small Meet & Greet after the show and were able to start driving toward Buffalo, New York before midnight. Even though I had always heard how cold Buffalo winters were and about lake effect snow, nothing prepared me for the frigid temperatures. I needed more sweaters and warm socks.

We pulled into the hotel parking lot at about 4:00 a.m. and I headed to my room. The thought of jumping into bed and pulling the blankets up excited me. I couldn't wait to open the door, practically shoving the key card in the slot. Dragging my suitcase behind me, I opened the door, turned on the lights, and found two people sleeping in the bed.

"What the hell are you doing in our room?" one of the occupants screamed at me.

"Your room? They gave me a key to this room," I said.

Now fully awake, I hurried back to the check-in desk. The hotel couldn't stop apologizing to both of us. This episode scarred me for life, and to this day, I knock on the door loudly before entering a hotel room.

When we finally got the rooms sorted out, I jumped into bed and got a few hours of sleep. Fortunately, we didn't have much going on during the day, so I went shopping at the local mall.

"The mall is about a ten-minute walk from our hotel, but you better watch things because a huge snowstorm is coming our way," said the concierge.

With the sun shining and the skies crystal blue, I thought he was being overly dramatic with his weather forecast. I found the mall and got what I needed in record time. I left the mall to walk back to the hotel and entered a blizzard. Snow started falling at about an inch a minute, with the strong winds blowing it sideways, meaning the winds blew me sideways, too. I could barely stay on my feet. As I trudged across the parking lot, I couldn't see in front of my face. I thought I would be buried alive in the snow, and no one would find me.

To make matters worse, I'd lost my markers to get back to the hotel because snow covered everything. Over an hour later, I eventually found my way back to the hotel. It took me another hour to thaw out, but at least I had new fuzzy socks to keep my feet warm.

We were nearing the end of the tour on March 28 when we stopped in Hershey, Pennsylvania. I couldn't wait to get back to LA. The Passover holiday had begun, and this would be one of the first times I missed a Seder with my family. I called my mom and cried. "I can't believe I'm not with you," I sobbed. "I just want to come home. I'm sick of this bus."

I'm sure my tears were more about exhaustion than missing the Passover Seder, but it made no difference. I just wanted to get off the bus and into my bed.

By this point of the tour, everyone hated each other. Tempers were short, and attitudes were long. The countdown to the finish line officially began. We did get a lot of Hershey chocolate, so at least I could eat my way into a sugar coma through the next few days.

Chapter 17

The Vanilla Ice tour finally came to an end on March 31, 1991. I couldn't have been more thrilled. I needed to recharge my batteries and fast. Fifty-six cities in under three months traveling by bus would make anyone tired. But I got to see parts of the country I would never have seen if not for this experience.

I couldn't wait to get into a regular slower-paced routine and spend time exploring Los Angeles. I still traveled around to radio stations, but I stayed more local and mainly went to Arizona, Nevada, and California. I also had a new boss: Jeff, who had come on because he'd worked with Ken at another record company. I loved the work, but right from the beginning Jeff and I clashed, which made things miserable.

I decided I would surprise my parents and go home for the Fourth of July weekend to make myself feel better. It had been several months since I'd been home, and I couldn't wait to see them.

"I miss Papa," I told my mother while hanging out at home. "I want to drive to Wharton and see him. Can I please borrow your car?"

"Of course, he will be thrilled," my mom said.

I drove to Wharton the following day to surprise him.

"Well, I'll be," he said with the biggest smile as I walked into his house.

The setting felt so familiar, and it made me so happy.

"Why didn't you tell me you were coming? I would have had Mildred make a roast." Mildred, his housekeeper, made the best roast that Papa knew I loved.

"I wanted to surprise you."

We talked about LA and my job and everything in between.

"I'm having a hard time with my new boss," I told him. "He's not very nice, and I'm not sure what to do."

He looked at me and very wisely said, "Judy, you're not going to please everyone all the time. Just do the best you can, and whatever happens is meant to happen. But you will always know you did your best."

His simple advice always felt so powerful.

When I finally said I needed to get home, he walked me to my car and did what he'd always done my entire life. "Here's a little spending money to buy yourself something nice. But don't tell your mother."

He stood on the front porch step and waved goodbye as I drove off. I couldn't shake the strange feeling that this goodbye might be our last.

When I got back to LA, things at work became even more challenging to deal with than before I'd gone to Houston. It seemed I couldn't do anything right in Jeff's eyes. But I powered through and did the very best job I could.

To stay away from Jeff, I hit the road to visit radio stations in Central California. On my way, I picked up several dozen donuts and drove to Bakersfield to deliver the treats to program and music directors. Going back home to LA, my car phone rang, and I saw my father's number pop up.

"Where are you?" he asked.

"I'm driving back from Bakersfield," I said.

"Can you pull over for a minute?"

A strange request, but I said that I would. He waited for me to get off the highway and come to a safe stop.

"Papa had a stroke, and Mommy is with him now."

My heart started pounding in my chest, and I wasn't sure I could stop my tears. "Is he going to be okay?"

"We don't know, but it's not good," my father said. "His left side appears paralyzed, and he can't speak. The doctor says we need to move him to a nursing home."

"He'll never let you do that," I said. "He'd rather die than have that happen. You can't let them do that, Daddy. Promise me."

"I agree, but we just need to wait and see how he recovers," my father said.

"I'll call you when I get back to my apartment, but I will get on the next plane home," I said.

"Judy, we don't think that's a good idea," he said. "He's in pretty bad shape, and we want you to remember how he was when you were with him last month."

And then I remembered that feeling I had when I drove away from his house as he waved goodbye. I knew it didn't feel right.

My grandfather rarely got sick and had always taken good care of himself. Even though he was one of the most stubborn people I knew, he was my rock.

His community in Wharton loved him, too. Of course, like in any town or city, seedy characters occasionally lurked in the shadows, and his liquor store was robbed on several occasions. In this case, his stubbornness was an asset. Instead of just giving the thugs his money, he would sometimes resist and chase them down the street. A couple of times, he suffered injuries when the would-be robbers pistol-whipped him with the barrel of their guns.

The police always told him, "Mr. Roth, you need to stop chasing these punks and leave that up to us. You're going to get yourself killed." And he'd reply, "I know, but they just can't take what's not theirs." He may have been right, but his life meant more to so many people than any amount of money stolen. Like I said, strong and stubborn.

Besides his liquor store, he loved working in his yard. One time we visited him when he was eighty-three years old. We drove up to the house but couldn't find him anywhere. What we saw in the yard stopped us in our tracks. My grandfather was standing on his roof with a chainsaw.

"Daddy, what are you doing on the roof? Get down from there this instant," screamed my mother.

"I just needed to cut this tree branch before it fell on the house," he replied.

I'd also add fearless when describing him.

The thought of this courageous man lying in a hospital bed from a stroke broke my heart. It's not that I believed my grandfather would live forever, it's that I couldn't imagine a life without him in it. That's the circle of life. And he led such a rich life, not necessarily monetarily, but in other aspects.

My grandfather always taught me to appreciate money but to know there's more to life. "Work hard for your family, but take the time to enjoy your life; otherwise, it will pass you by before you know it."

My mother wouldn't agree to put my grandfather in a nursing home, knowing he didn't want that. But the decision never became hers to make. On August 11, 1991, my grandfather peacefully passed away at eight-six while still in the hospital. I flew home for the funeral the same day.

Two weeks later, after returning from my grandfather's funeral, I went to work one morning, and my boss, Jeff, called me into his office. "I have Ken and Daniel on the phone," he said.

"Hi, there, how are you?" I said into the speaker.

Daniel started the conversation. "Judy, we think you're a great person, but sometimes jobs don't match personalities. While we like you, we don't think this job is working out, so we think it's best if we part ways," he said.

I just sat there, staring at the speaker. With my heart pounding in my chest, I said, "Wait, are you firing me?"

Jeff spoke first. "Well, it's more like we're eliminating your position," he said.

I glared at him. I didn't know what to say. I knew this guy didn't like me, but why did he get me fired or get my position eliminated?

Daniel finally spoke after a very long, awkward silence. "Is she still there?" he asked.

Jeff confirmed my presence and then tried to console me.

"Please don't speak to me," I snapped. I got up and walked out of the room.

Ken eventually called me. "I'm so sorry, Judy. I hope you won't have any ill feelings towards me, but sometimes these things happen."

I got that, but did it have to happen to me? I felt like such a failure. I couldn't believe I'd moved my entire life to California and for the past two years I had worked so hard, only to be informed that they had eliminated my position and fired me over the phone.

And to add insult to injury, I'd just lost my grandfather and would be flying home to Houston later in the week to be a bridesmaid in Melinda's wedding. I couldn't let her know what had happened. She'd be so upset, and I didn't want to take anything away from her happiness.

After I packed everything up in my office and said my goodbyes, I stopped at the pharmacy to pick up my prescriptions. Walking out of the store, located in Beverly Hills, a panhandler was harassing people while begging for money.

"Do you have any spare change, so I can get something to eat?" he asked.

I politely said no, but he didn't like my answer.

"Oh, you're just a rich little girl in Beverly Hills, probably living off Daddy's money or a trust fund, but you can't spare a dollar for someone in need," he screamed at me.

I was in no mood for his judgment. It probably wasn't the most brilliant reaction, but I yelled back at him. "Excuse me, but you have no idea who I am. I lost my job a few hours ago, so I'm no better off than you are now. But the difference between you and me is that I'll find a job to take care of myself and not harass people walking out of drugstores."

He stared at me as I shakily got in my car and drove away.

When I got home, I called my friend Alysa because I knew she could cheer me up.

"I got fired," I cried.

She started laughing.

"I'm glad you think this is funny. Did you not understand what I just said? I got fired."

She finally contained her laughter long enough to speak. "So did I!" she said.

Then I started laughing. What were the chances that two friends on two different coasts would lose their jobs on the same day? It's as if the universe spoke to us and said, "This sucks, but you're not alone, and it's all going to be okay."

Getting fired comes with different stages of grief, like death: denial, anger, bargaining, depression, and acceptance. Most times, you never see it coming. I always believed getting fired was conditional. When hired to do a job, and you don't meet the expectations of that job, you lose your job. Or, if you do something idiotic, you'll probably be fired, too. But to be told, "We just feel it's best if we part ways," didn't help me understand why I got fired. Whatever the reason, I had to accept the reality that I no longer had a job. Now what would I do?

Later that week, I flew home to Houston for Melinda's wedding. I knew I had to put on an Academy-award-winning performance and not let anyone know about my unemployment. That proved to be more difficult than I'd imagined. With Melinda being so proud of me and all I'd accomplished, she had bragged a lot about me to her friends. So not only did I let myself down, but now I'd let Melinda down—and I couldn't even tell her yet.

I already expected to endure the endless annoying questions about my dating life that inevitably come with being single at a friend's wedding. "How's the dating life in LA? Have you met anyone special? You know you're going to be next. How can such a pretty girl still be single?" But now, I had the added pleasure of dodging questions from people asking me about my fantastic job and enviable life in Hollywood.

"How's Los Angeles, Judy, and are you enjoying your new life there?" asked many members of Melinda's bridal party.

I just smiled. "Everything is great," I said. I didn't think it would be appropriate for me to blurt out, "Well, it sucks. I just lost my job."

I felt like I wore a sign that said, "Ask me about the job I got fired from but can't tell you about." Too much to handle, so I kept the drinks coming my way.

After spending a week in Houston following Melinda's wedding, I flew back to LA and tried to figure out what to do with my life. As I saw it, I had two choices: stay in Los Angeles and find another job in the music industry or go home to Houston, defeated, and start over.

Ultimately, I came home but decided to keep my belongings in storage in LA. Honestly, I didn't know what to do. While I wanted to return to Texas for the familiarity, family, and friends, part of me didn't want to give up on LA.

"What if I find another job after returning home?" I asked my mom.

"Then you'll go back," she said.

She made it sound so simple. At this point, my only job experience included working at a radio station and in the music industry, and I wasn't sure there would be anything for me in Houston. In my mind, this move back home wouldn't be permanent.

"The movers are coming tomorrow to put all my things in storage, and then I'll get on the road to come home," I told my parents.

"Are you sure you don't want one of us to fly to LA and drive back to Texas with you?" my mom asked.

I wanted to make the drive alone for soul-searching about what I wanted to do next in my life. My parents worried about my solo trek home, and my mom later told me she held her breath until she saw my car pull into her driveway.

In your twenties, appearances matter. You constantly worry about wearing cute clothes, driving the right car, dating the best-looking boy or girl, and how others judge your life choices. Right or wrong, my biggest fear of coming back to Texas centered on people saying, "Oh, look at Judy, she moved to LA and got fired and had to come home."

How would it look, and what would I say for my sudden return to Houston? Also, when you're in your twenties, you don't understand that none of it matters. Instead of worrying about how others would perceive me, I should have just concentrated on my survival and what would make me happy moving forward.

I also couldn't move past the feeling of letting Celia down. I promised her I would make her proud, but losing my job was one of my least proud moments.

I made it halfway between Phoenix and Tucson and decided to stop for the night. Of course, I forgot to check the fuel gauge before leaving LA and only noticed the low fuel indicator as I got outside of Phoenix. "Please, please, God, let me make it to the next gas station. I promise I'll be better at checking to see if I have enough gas if you just let me make it to the next stop," I prayed aloud while frantically searching for a gas station.

My prayers were answered. I found not only a well-lit gas station but a clean hotel right next door, just off the interstate. I checked in for the night, making sure I had a parking space for my car right outside my room to keep an eye on it. The next day I got an early start and kept driving until I reached the New Mexico Texas border. I stopped at another gas station. While I needed to fill the tank, I also needed to get my car inspected.

"If I had a dime for every person who crossed over this border to get their Texas State inspection, I wouldn't need to work here anymore," said the attendant when I pulled up.

"While living in California, I never switched my Texas plates and let the inspection expire," I told him.

He nodded and said, "That's what they all tell me."

That little station made more money on state inspections than fuel. This stretch of Interstate 10 was familiar to me as I'd traveled on it with my parents and Celia driving home from our vacation out west. But driving solo is a whole different experience since there's no one to talk to in the car. Fortunately, I had the trusty portable CD player that I had hooked up through the cigarette lighter to listen to music instead of the radio. There weren't many stations with a strong signal in the middle of nowhere. Luckily, I never felt too alone on the highway since every eighteen-wheeler I passed acknowledged me. I thought if I ever did run into trouble, I could flag one of them down, and they'd help. Still, I was anxious to get home.

I finally made it to San Antonio and decided to stop again.

"I just can't drive anymore," I said to my parents when I got to the hotel. "I'll see you tomorrow afternoon."

I half expected one or both to fly to San Antonio in the morning and drive home with me. I couldn't wait to get home, but even with just five hours left to go, my body felt exhausted.

The following day I made it home in record time. When I drove up to my parents' driveway, I started crying. I'm pretty sure my tears were full of mixed emotions. While I was so happy to see my parents and not be driving anymore, sadness overwhelmed me for what I had left behind. And I couldn't shake the worry about what lay ahead.

Once home, I didn't realize how much I truly missed everything and everyone in the two years since I had left. I had moved to Los Angeles because I needed to escape. Houston represented everything about Celia and her not being there anymore. I carried so much loneliness, sadness, and guilt, making it the right time to get away from those emotions.

I eventually had to let Melinda know I no longer worked at the record label. Still, I didn't tell her until well after she had returned from her honeymoon. I also didn't tell her about my "eliminated position" or the exact timing of my departure because, at that point, it didn't matter. She just cared about my being home.

But several months later, when we were out for a walk and talking about my former job and life, I finally came clean.

"What made you leave your job at the record label?" she asked.

I paused. "I've been keeping something from you that I need to share," I fessed up. "A few days before your wedding, I was fired from SBK Records. I didn't want to tell you at the time because I didn't want you to be upset or worried. It was your wedding, and there was no need for me to be a downer or take away any happiness from your weekend."

She just stared at me. For a moment, I thought, oh my gosh, is she mad at me? I couldn't bear it if she were mad at me. And then I thought, why would she be mad at me?

It turns out she felt the opposite of angry. She started to cry.

"That's the most selfless thing anyone has ever done for me," she said.

I always felt Melinda and I were more like sisters, but now I truly believed it.

While my time in Los Angeles didn't end the way I'd hoped or envisioned, in a way, it probably played out how it should have. I left Houston a naïve twenty-five-year-old girl who had barely been away from home or her parents and came back an independent twenty-seven-year-old woman who'd traveled the country and made adult decisions about her life and career.

Yes, getting fired made me feel like a big fat failure, but my short time away from home would end up having been the best decision. I learned so much about myself and finally started grasping the concept that things happen for a reason, even if they don't make sense to you at the time.

Chapter 18

In 1991, Google didn't exist because neither did the internet. If you wanted to search for any information, like finding a job, you had to read the want ads in the newspaper or go to a public library.

"Anything new in the job section this morning?" my mom would ask as we sat at the kitchen table, and I pored over the classifieds.

"Not yet," I'd reply and sigh.

Returning home from California with no job or prospects meant I had to move home. While I loved having my meals cooked and laundry cleaned, I had lived on my own for five years. But now, here I sat, unemployed, twenty-seven years old, and living in my parents' house, with their rules. Something had to change, and fast.

I started camping out at the local library, reading books about everything from finding the perfect job to writing a foolproof resume. I even hung out in the job reference section of bookstores and bought a copy of the book *Congratulations, You've Been Fired,* an advice guide for helping women recently fired and seeking employment. If ever a book spoke directly to me, this one did. I read that book cover to cover. Finding work turned into a full-time job, minus the paycheck.

But even with everything I did, I still had no idea what I wanted to do with my life. I loved working in the music industry but didn't think I'd be able to find a job in the field in Houston.

"Maybe you need to sign on with a temporary staffing agency to gain experience in other areas and earn some money, too," my father advised.

I hesitantly agreed and got my first assignment as a secretary for an insurance company whose office happened to be in my father's building.

This job ranked right at the top as the most boring experience of my life. During my lunch break, I'd hide in my dad's office.

"How's your day going?" he asked me every day.

"I hate office work, and I'm bored," I complained. "All they want me to do is make copies, file, and type. Glad I went to college for this."

As much as my father loved seeing me every day at lunchtime, he got tired of my constant kvetching and needed me to move on. Then he gave me an idea.

"You need to network," he said.

"Huh?" I said.

"Make a list of everyone you worked with in the past and start calling them to find out if they know of any jobs or can connect you with anyone who may know of jobs."

That turned out to be very sage advice. Joe, a former co-worker, introduced me to his college friend, Dave, who recently began a company for large-scale events such as outdoor concerts and conventions. The company sold all the concession stands where people bought food, drinks, T-shirts, and other tchotchkes. He hired me as his admin assistant to help manage all the vendors.

The 1992 Republican National Convention—George H. W. Bush's re-election campaign—became our first big contract. Our role included selling all concession booths to people who wanted to sell their products. Being a political junkie, I loved watching the conventions on television, especially the state roll call. But I never knew what happened behind the scenes and all the outlandish stuff you could buy.

"How many booths does one convention need that will sell red, white, and blue hats and T-shirts?" I asked Dave.

In every corner of the convention center, you saw the contagious patriotic spirit of the delegates. I attended the convention and brought my mother with me as a bonus. I'd seen a lot of music concerts in my life, but this proved to be so much more.

The stars of the show also weren't necessarily the president and vice president. The actual celebrities were decked out in their "I Love USA" apparel, proudly waving American flags.

Even though the convention and everyone in attendance supported Republican candidates, party affiliation made no difference during this four-day lovefest. Everyone patriotically displayed their American pride, regardless of which political party they kept.

After recovering from the convention, we started our next contract for Lollapalooza, a massive outdoor concert in Houston. In 1992, grunge rock ruled the music scene, and the big acts performing at this concert included the Red Hot Chili Peppers, Pearl Jam, Ice Cube, and The Jesus and Mary Chain. This project brought back memories of my time working at the radio station and being on the road with Vanilla Ice. I felt in my element.

While the bands appeared on stage, the real show occurred upfront in the mosh pit. Raucous "fans" bumped, jumped, and slammed so hard that people flew. And as an added treat, it had rained earlier in the day, making the grounds wet and muddy. It made no difference to anyone until the unthinkable happened. At around 3:00 p.m., at the height of the all-day concert, Dave frantically came up to me.

"We've run out of beer," he said.

"That's impossible; we're in Texas," I replied.

Instead of panicking, we rallied and turned into problem solvers. I guess my time with Vanilla Ice prepared me for this very moment. Nothing rattled me after that experience.

Fortunately, Dave had a connection with the Anheuser-Busch distributor, and he promised to have multiple kegs delivered within a half hour.

And thank God. I certainly didn't want to be the person announcing to this teeming crowd we'd run out of beer.

We won the contract for another big outdoor music festival in San Antonio a few months later. Like Lollapalooza, we were responsible for all the concession booths, including food and beverages. However, unlike the last time, we made sure not to run out of beer.

After the concert, I started looking for a new job. While I enjoyed working with Dave and coordinating fun events, I needed to find something more challenging and fulfilling.

* * *

Melinda's parents owned Al's Formal Wear, the biggest tuxedo and bridal apparel company in the Southwest. The company and her family were very well-known and very well-respected in Houston. Melinda and her siblings and their spouses all worked there, too. Her dad, Al, ran the company, and of all my friends' fathers, I found him to be one of the most admirable ones I had the pleasure of knowing.

Melinda mentioned my job search to her dad. He had recently created a high school prom Ambassador program and wanted to know if I would be interested in helping get it up and running.

"Do you think this is something you would like to do?" Melinda asked.

She didn't need to ask me twice. Every morning, I sat at my kitchen table and smiled and dialed my way through a giant list of Texas high schools. I began working ahead of prom season and registered high schools from all over the state. And with more than 3,200 high schools throughout Texas, that was a lot of phone calls.

The program turned out to be a huge success, and apparently, my enthusiasm impressed Melinda's dad. He offered me the position of Public Relations Director. While the job opportunity excited me, especially the chance to work with Melinda, I hesitated at first to accept it.

"I'm worried about working for my best friend's family because what if I do a poor job and make Melinda look bad, and then we won't be friends anymore," I told my dad when we discussed the pros and cons of the job. "Also, since I'm not part of the family, will there ever be an opportunity for more?"

No one could answer the last question until I started doing the job.

"All you can do is approach this job as you would any other and go into it with your eyes wide open. It sounds like an amazing opportunity for you to use your skill sets and gain experience for the future," my dad said.

I accepted the job and became the new Public Relations Director for Al's Formal Wear.

A few days before I started my job, my new boss and Marketing Director, Cindy—Melinda's older sister—called me.

"Judy, I'm so sorry to do this, but we just instituted a new drug policy at Al's requiring all new hires to be drug tested before they begin working with us."

I remained silent.

"Before you can start, we'll need you to take a drug test."

Usually, this would not be an issue. But the situation I found myself in at this moment couldn't have come at a worse time. Michael, a good friend from high school, and I had decided to party with friends and get high to celebrate my new job a few days earlier. It had been many years since I participated in this activity, and clearly, the universe got the last laugh.

"Michael," I yelped when I called him, "I'm freaking out right now. A drug test? I'm going to get fired before I even begin working. Help me," I cried to him over the phone.

"Here's what you're going to do," he said. He had experience in this area. "There's an herbal tea to flush out toxins, including traces of marijuana. Just follow the directions on the box, and in a day, you should be good to go. But I need to warn you. You'll be going to the bathroom all night."

If this worked, I didn't care if I had to go to the bathroom all week. I lived at home, and fortunately, I slept in the downstairs bedroom, away from my parents' bedroom upstairs. I followed the instructions on the box and called Michael while waiting.

"Nothing is happening," I told him.

"Give it time. I promise you; it will work."

About an hour later, I couldn't stop peeing. How is it possible for one person to pee so much? Nervous and fidgety, I finally fell asleep with no liquid left in my body.

The following day I went to the clinic to pee in a cup. I knew everyone in that office could see my deceit just by looking at me.

"How long before you get the results, and will you let me know before my employer?" I asked.

"We'll have the results in a few hours, and we'll let your employer know before you."

Yep, it's over, I thought. I went home and waited, and waited, and waited. Finally, I got a call from Cindy.

"Okay, Judy, you're good to go. We'll see you in the morning."

Of course, I shared this story with Melinda. "Can you imagine if it had been positive? Talk about making a great first impression with your family."

She just slapped her forehead and laughed. "Only you, Haveson; only you."

With my new job, I was finally able to move out of my parents' house and get an apartment. That meant getting all my stuff from Los Angeles to Houston. After the movers dropped off my belongings, I sat on the sofa, willing everything into place, and noticed movement coming from one of the boxes. I slowly opened the box and out jumped a mouse. I'm pretty sure my screams were heard throughout the apartment complex.

I called my mom. "I have no idea what's in that box, but I'm just going to throw it away," I told her.

I spent that night at Melinda's house fearful of meeting more stowaways from California.

As PR Director, I established working relationships with media contacts in the retail, fashion, and bridal industries. I wanted to be their first phone call when they wrote stories or produced television segments about weddings, proms, or other reasons to wear a tuxedo or formal wear.

The next four years had fun and challenging times. Still, I gained invaluable experience, learned to tolerate and accept all different types of personalities, and realized a lot about myself. I tackled every assignment like a boss, whether I knew how to do it or not. "Write a press release for this new bridal collection." I'd never written a press release, but that didn't stop me. "Call the fashion editor at the *Houston Chronicle* and get our tuxedos featured for prom." No problem, and I eventually became their first call. "Work with the display department to coordinate the fifteen bridal shows for the season." You got it.

I loved everything about this job, but the one thing that I couldn't move past, no matter how hard I worked or how well I did my job was this: there would never be any opportunities for advancement.

"Just as I thought before I accepted the job, there's just nowhere for me to go," I said to my father.

"Maybe you need to start looking around to see what else is out there," he replied.

I did and began applying for other jobs. I hated doing this behind the backs of Cindy and Melinda, but I just kept thinking I could do more in my career—and my life.

In addition to loving the work I did, I made some great friendships at Al's, particularly with the Advertising Director, Brad. He became my sounding board and confidante, concert and sporting event partner, and biggest cheerleader. He always said, "Judy, you'll do great things one day if you could just let the little things go." I always seemed to sweat the small stuff, which felt significant.

I also made another great friend at work, Strat. One day his sister-in-law, Renee, told him that her company, one of the top public relations firms in Houston, had job openings and asked if he knew of anyone.

He immediately thought of me. "You have to apply for a job there; you'd be perfect."

I met with Helen Vollmer, the president of Vollmer Public Relations. My first impression of her was that she had a bubbly, happy personality, but I could tell she didn't take crap from anyone. I instantly liked her.

"I'm very impressed with your portfolio for Al's Formal Wear," she told me. "And I want to hear more about your job at SBK Records, specifically touring with Vanilla Ice. What was that like?"

Yep, I knew that job would be a crowd favorite.

"I have two openings," she continued. "One is for an Account Executive, and the other is for a Senior Account Executive. Given your limited PR agency experience, I can't offer you the senior position, even though that's where you probably should be at your age." She was blunt but honest, and I liked this woman.

At thirty-two years old, I wasn't fazed by her declaration.

"That's fine; everyone's got to start somewhere," I said.

I guess that impressed her because I got the job. Honestly, I didn't care about the title. I just wanted to be challenged and do a brand-new job, and something told me I'd met my match with Helen. Also, I truly believed I wouldn't be an Account Executive forever because there were so many more opportunities for me at the firm.

Now came the hard part: telling Melinda I accepted a new job. I dreaded the thought. She and her family had given me such a fantastic opportunity and helped me reinvent myself after returning from California. But on the other hand, there wasn't anywhere else for me to go at the company.

"I'm going to be leaving Al's at the end of the year. I accepted a new job, and I'm starting in January."

She just stared at me and then asked why.

"I feel like I've done all I can at Al's, and I'm ready for more. I appreciate everything you and your entire family have done for me, and I hope you understand and aren't upset with me. I would die if this affected our friendship," I said.

I seriously would have been gutted if she were angry about this.

"Judy, I understand. You need to do what's best for you, and if you're happy, that's all that matters."

And that is why Melinda and I were friends. We always knew our friendship and happiness mattered most. Business is business, but the sister-like bond we shared was forever.

Chapter 19

Starting a new job is both exciting and terrifying. Exciting for the challenge of all the new things you'll experience and learn, and terrifying because of all those new things. And you always want to make a good impression on others, especially your bosses.

Imagine just two months into my new job at Vollmer PR when I had the owner of the company, Helen Vollmer, come into my office one morning, close the door behind her, and scream at me. "You better pull your head out of your ass, or I'll fire you."

Yes, I knew how to make a lasting impression.

It all began when Helen asked each employee for a photo for the company website. "We're updating our website and need you to submit a fun picture of yourself alongside your bio," she explained.

One early Friday morning, when just a few of us were in the office, my co-worker, Barry, said, "Hey, I thought it would be cool if I took my picture standing on the window ledge with the backdrop of skyscrapers. Will you take it?"

I also needed a picture for the website. "Sure," I replied. "Will you take my picture, too?"

The ledge measured about a foot wide, and I'm probably being generous. But that didn't stop us from the daredevil antics of stepping out our office windows to stand on the tiny ledge, hovering eight floors above the street to pose for photos.

Unbeknownst to us, Sandy, the office manager, also came into the office early that morning and saw us crawl out the window. After our impromptu photo shoot, she came into my office as we crawled back inside.

"Your lives are vital to us, and if you were to fall off that ledge, it would be a terrible thing. Please promise you'll never do that again."

We promised her and thought that ended the conversation, but it wasn't over. Not only did Helen threaten to fire both of us on the spot, and frankly, I'm surprised she didn't, but the building installed window guards, forever barring anyone from opening a window again.

I stayed in my office with the door closed for the rest of the day. I called my friend Jeff for support. "I just did the dumbest thing of my life, and I think I'm about to be fired."

He laughed. "What did you do?"

When I told him, I expected him to reply with something like, "Oh, that's not so bad" or "You'll be fine."

Instead, he sighed and said, "Yep, that was a pretty stupid thing to do, and you'll probably be fired."

Nothing like supportive friends to cheer you up.

Around lunchtime, Barry knocked and slid an envelope underneath the door. I opened the envelope to find pictures of me, standing on the ledge with blue skies and tall buildings behind me. At least the photos were good.

After my near miss of being fired what felt like moments after starting my new job, I vowed to do everything I could to gain back any respect I had lost from Helen and my other co-workers I freaked out that day. I had to make sure they remembered why they hired me instead of why they should fire me. And why did I always seem to sabotage my new jobs?

In 1997, most newspapers and magazines had limited internet access in their newsrooms, making pitching my new internet client, Travelocity, challenging. Travel and consumer products editors wouldn't be able to see the Travelocity site, much less write about it for their readers.

"I can fax over pages circling the steps you need to follow to book an airline ticket," I would say to different media contacts when pitching Travelocity. A big contrast to today, when you can email or text people or even slide into their DMs. We lived in a less instant-gratification world back then, and I found it easier in some respects.

While I missed the fast-paced world of the music industry, working in public relations and influencing public opinion was just as exciting. Like promoting new artists to radio stations, I found pitching clients to the media rewarding. My passion for media relations officially began by working on the Travelocity account.

With no online media databases like today, I had to be Nancy Drew—and sleuth different magazine and newspaper articles and then search the media guidebooks to find the contact's information. It wasn't always that easy, but when it was, I looked golden.

My primary responsibility was print publications like consumer magazines and daily newspapers. And while I had no shortage of media outlets to pitch Travelocity to, the holy grail for me was *People* magazine.

"Hi, I represent Travelocity, a new online travel site, and I wanted to talk to you about including it in your travel section," I said to the consumer editor over the phone.

Ever so confident this would lead to an article about the trend of e-commerce sites, specifically in the travel space, I could picture the Travelocity logo on the pages of *People* magazine.

But my bubble burst when the writer clapped back. "A travel website? The magazine is called *People*, which means we cover people. No, thanks."

Well, okay then. Of course, I had the last laugh when Travelocity appeared in their travel section a few years later when another writer decided to feature the most popular travel websites.

One day while meeting with Helen and Denisha, my direct supervisor, they said, "We want you to visit the Travelocity offices in Dallas and get to know Terry, the company's president, and make him your friend," Helen told me.

Besides being president of Travelocity, Terry was a well-known travel industry guru. He came up through the AMR Corporation, American Airlines, and The Sabre Group, all travel powerhouses. And while I hadn't met him, his reputation preceded him, and I won't lie, he intimidated me. I researched his background, and from what I could surmise, he didn't sound like a warm and fuzzy guy who wanted to be friends with a PR flack. All business, or so I thought.

"Me?" I asked them. "Will one of you be coming with me?"

When they said they believed I could handle this independently, I knew I needed a strategy. I called his executive assistant, Sharon, and befriended her first. Terry may have been the head of Travelocity, but Sharon ran the ship.

"Hey, Sharon, I'd like to meet with Terry to introduce myself. Any pointers you can give me?" I asked.

"Be a good listener," she replied, golden advice for sure.

With Sharon's help, I gained more access to Terry than even some of his direct reports. I also learned many life tips from Terry, like, "If you screw up, fail fast and don't make the same mistakes twice." That proved to be sage advice while working on this account.

I had some of the most challenging, rewarding, and memorable career moments working with Terry. I loved being part of a team that changed the travel industry and consumer behavior.

Working at Vollmer PR also had its challenges and rewards, and I loved every minute. Even though I was hired in at an entry-level position, I quickly rose through the ranks to a Senior Account Executive, Account Supervisor, and Management Supervisor. And just when I felt like everything in my life was in place as it should be, my parents surprised me with an announcement.

"We've decided to move to Florida."

Hearing this news, I pictured that scene from *A Torch Song Trilogy* when Harvey Fierstein's character asks his mother, played by Ann Bancroft, "Ma, why are you moving to Florida?" She replied, "It's what we do." I felt like I was living in a *Seinfeld* episode with my parents moving to Boca Del Vista. How cliché: my Jewish parents retiring to Florida to play golf!

But this became their plan, and now I cried as they drove away. Suddenly, despite how well my life appeared, I started questioning living in Houston. Yes, I had great friends and many relatives still living close by, but without my parents, did it matter? By then, all my friends were married with children and spending time with their single friends fell low on their priority list.

The year 1999 was the height of the internet age. In addition to Travelocity, Vollmer worked with several other internet and e-commerce companies, including jewelry designers, online banks, event companies, and more. San Francisco had become one of the hottest cities in the country for internet companies and start-ups, and I thought it would be awesome to live there.

I decided to float a wild idea to Helen since I no longer had ties to Houston. "I'm ready for a change and challenge. Can we open an office in San Francisco?"

She thought I'd lost my mind. And I might have. While the city by the bay wasn't an option, the idea of opening a new office wasn't as absurd as I thought.

"What about an office in Austin?" I countered.

"That could be an interesting idea," she said, "but we're getting ready to open an office in Dallas, and nothing can happen until then."

I could live with that.

When it rains, it pours, as the saying goes. And the best time to find a dream job is when you're not looking. I think they say that about a husband, too, although that never happened to me.

Hannah's sports broadcasting career had taken off as she blazed a trail for women in sports television. One day, she called me with an exciting proposal. "My new management company is looking for a PR person, and I want them to speak to you."

Her new Boulder-based management company represented several Olympians competing in the 2000 Summer Olympics in Australia. I flew to Boulder to meet with the owner and staff. This job would allow me to create a PR department within the management agency and promote all their clients, including Hannah.

"We love all your experience and what you've done promoting clients throughout your career. We think you'd be a perfect match for our company," the owner told me. I couldn't believe it.

I loved my job at Vollmer PR so much, and while this opportunity would be a real career changer, could I leave Helen? They'd given me so much, and I had much more to do at the agency.

"You have to follow your gut," my parents told me. "But things are going so well for you at Vollmer. Do you want to leave now?"

If only Celia were here to help me decide what to do. My parents were right, things were going well, but would I ever get an opportunity like this at Vollmer? I ultimately decided to accept the job in Boulder. Now I had to tell Helen and everyone else. I soon learned that they would not give me up without a fight.

"Before you decide, we want to take you to lunch," she told me.

I had already accepted the position in Boulder, but that didn't concern them because they just knew they'd be able to persuade me to stay. They selected Brennan's for lunch, a famous New Orleans restaurant and one of my absolute favorite places in Houston.

"You're already not playing fair," I told them.

It felt like an interrogation at the lunch table. Around the table sat Helen, her husband Allen, who was also co-owner of the firm, Denisha, and Carolyn, Helen's second in command.

"We don't want you to leave and are prepared to make you an offer you can't refuse," they said. "We would like to move you to Austin to be the General Manager/VP of our new office."

I couldn't believe it. And the new job title came with a big fat raise, too.

"Oh, and if you want to go to the Olympics in Australia, we can talk about that, too," added Allen.

I kept silent as I sat in utter disbelief. On the one hand, they didn't want to lose me and presented me with a fantastic opportunity. But on the other hand, did they only do this because I said I wanted to leave? I genuinely didn't know what to do. After some deep soul searching, I finally decided to stay at Vollmer. It became the most complex career decision I'd have to make. But talk about an ego-booster.

In October of 1999, as promised, we opened our Austin office, and I became the new General Manager/VP. In less than three years, I had gone from being the oldest Account Executive Helen had probably ever hired to running a new office in a new city. I loved my job.

As Vollmer expanded, Travelocity grew, too. In less than five years, it had become one of the largest and most recognized travel websites and one of the top consumer websites behind such behemoths as Amazon and eBay. My working relationship with Terry had strengthened as well.

While he still intimidated me at times, he respected me, too. The company's national and international expansion meant Terry wanted more.

"I think I want to explore other national PR agencies in New York to represent us moving forward. You guys have done an amazing job up to this point, but I'm worried you've taken us as far as you can."

These are not the words any PR agency wants to hear, especially from their top client.

"If you need someone to move to New York to service the Travelocity account, I'll do it," I told Denisha when we were discussing it.

"You would?" she asked.

"Yes, I would, in a heartbeat."

Honestly, I'd wanted to live in New York City since the first time I visited in high school. I loved the city's energy and activities and how close I'd be to my friends Alysa and Hannah. I also loved how I could be unmarried in my thirties and not be considered a spinster. I had spent so much time in New York on business over the years and was already familiar with the subways and different neighborhoods. I loved living in Austin, but I knew this opportunity to live in New York City was one I couldn't let pass me by.

But would Helen and the crew share Denisha's and my enthusiasm for the concept, and could we convince Terry this is what he needed to do?

Indeed, a far-fetched idea but one that proved to be brilliant. All parties agreed, and by October 2001, I would officially be working and living in New York City. I couldn't wait to get there.

"You belong in New York City, and frankly, I'm surprised you've never lived there," Terry said to me when we finalized our move.

Our new office space wouldn't be ready until early October, and I still needed to find a place to live. I flew to New York City on Thursday, September 6, 2001, with plans to scour the city for a place to live. On Monday, September 10, 2001, I signed a lease for my new apartment and flew home to Texas to prepare for my next chapter.

And then life happened again when the country suffered one of its darkest days.

Part Three

Chapter 20

Everyone has their own story from September 11, 2001, whether they were in New York City, Washington, D.C., or simply at work. Like previous generations knowing exactly where they were for the assassination of President Kennedy or when the Japanese bombed Pearl Harbor, we all remember the moment those planes hit the twin towers. Many of us were watching it live on TV. The world seems to stop when tragedy strikes, and for whatever reason, we always remember the moment—even when it occurred many years ago.

September 11 is a parallel moment in my personal history. September 11, 2001, which forever changed our nation, and September 11, 1983, which forever changed my life when I buried my sister, Celia. While she died on September 10, 1983, as is customary in Judaism, you conduct the burial within 24 hours, making her funeral the next day.

My whole world stopped the day Celia died, and I couldn't understand how people went about their business as if this horrible tragedy had never happened. Of course, it had only happened to my family and me, and this was our sorrow, not the world's. But indeed, life did go on that day.

The weekend before the nation's 9/11 attack, I was in New York attempting to find a place to live. Apartment hunting in New York City is unlike anywhere else in the United States. You can't put a deposit down until one month before your move-in date, so you can't start looking for a place to live until one month before your move-in date. Since we wouldn't be in our new PR offices until October 2001, I flew to New York to start the hunt in early September.

"What part of the city do you want to live in?" Alysa asked me. She had lived in New York City for more than fifteen years at this point and volunteered to help me find a place to live.

"Somewhere close to a subway to have an easy commute to my office," I told her.

I couldn't believe I wouldn't have a car anymore. I had leased my dream sports car a year earlier, a silver Lexus IS. I loved that car, but it made no sense to keep it. My lease didn't end for a few years, and I still owed money. At first, Fred said he'd take over the lease and let his youngest son, Jay, drive the car since he needed a vehicle at college. A great option if not for Jay being extraordinarily reckless and getting several speeding tickets while driving the sportscar. Of course, I found the tickets stuffed in the glove compartment when I took the car back. I wasn't surprised.

"Steven will sell it," Melinda told me.

Steven, Melinda's resourceful husband, especially when buying and selling cars, helped me. "I'll put it on eBay, and we'll see what we get."

A brilliant idea, and it worked. Now that I had sold my car, I needed to find an apartment.

And that's what Alysa, her one-year-old daughter, Alexandra, and I set out to do on Saturday, September 8, 2001. I had already seen several apartment buildings on the Upper West Side and Chelsea areas of the city the day before. Today, we'd be looking in Hoboken, New Jersey, and at an old building near the Financial District that had been converted to condos.

"I think we can take the Path train over to Hoboken from the World Trade Center," Alysa said.

As we walked through the lobby of the World Trade Center, I kept looking at the different stores and restaurants. "This reminds me of downtown Houston," I told her. "If you work here, you never need to leave because every conceivable thing is available to you."

It felt like a city inside a city. Being a Saturday, it wasn't nearly as crowded as I imagined it would have been during a weekday.

"I think it would be so cool to work down here," I said.

When we got back to her apartment, I felt defeated. "I didn't like anything, and everything is so freaking expensive," I said. "I found a building on West 50th Street that looks interesting, so I think I'll go check it out and then head to Grand Central to catch my train to Hannah's house."

I was spending the weekend in Connecticut with Hannah and her daughters before going back to Texas. While I wasn't excited about living essentially in the middle of Times Square, the brand-new modern building changed my mind.

"We have a great one bedroom on the ninth floor," said Carol, the leasing agent at The Gershwin building. "And you're next to every major subway stop, too. It's the perfect location."

Even more perfect was how close I'd be to my office. Steps away from West 53rd Street and 7th Avenue, the office building made for an easy commute from the apartment building at West 50th Street between Broadway and 8th Avenue. A no-brainer, even though I'd be living in the middle of tourist central. But I couldn't beat the commute.

"I'll think about it and let you know on Monday," I told Carol.

I got to Hannah's house later that afternoon, and she agreed that it would be an excellent place for my first apartment in New York City. "The beauty of Manhattan apartment living is moving if you hate it after a year," Hannah said. "That's what I did when I first got here."

I had all the paperwork with me, so I signed the lease, transferred my money (and I mean all my money), and faxed it to Carol on September 10, 2001.

"The next time you'll see me, I'll be living in New York City," I told Hannah as I hugged her goodbye.

We couldn't believe we'd both be living in the same part of the country again.

"It's been forever since we've been so close to each other," she said—a bonus to this move for sure.

When I got to LaGuardia to board my flight back to Dallas that night, the pilot made an unwelcome announcement.

"Ladies and gentlemen, there seems to be a big storm heading our way, so we're just going to board everyone and then push off the gate and wait for instructions. Our best guess is that we'll probably have a 10:00 p.m. or later departure because this storm is nasty, but we want to try and get everyone out tonight," the pilot informed us. "The good news is that we're heading south. All those traveling west tonight aren't as lucky because that's the storm's direction."

As I read a magazine, my cell rang with Terry on the other line. "Are you still in New York?" he asked.

"I'm on the plane at LaGuardia, but we're not going anywhere. Are you back from London?" He had been in London for the week and made a stop in New York on his way back to Dallas.

"No, I'm on the plane at Kennedy and in the same situation. Tomorrow morning, please come to the office, so we can talk about a new launch."

And then we hung up. My plane finally departed LaGuardia around 10:30 p.m. and landed at DFW Airport around 1:00 a.m. Beyond exhausted, I couldn't wait to get to my apartment and sleep.

The following day I woke up, took a shower, and turned on *The Today Show*. With a worried look on her face, Katie Couric said, "We've noticed a small aircraft has crashed into the World Trade Center." I thought, oh wow, I was just there. I couldn't walk away from the television and kept watching to see what else she said. I then heard Katie say, "Another plane just hit the other tower." Obviously, not a coincidence. What was happening? Both towers were now on fire.

I didn't have much time to process anything because my cell rang. "It's Terry. Are you back in Dallas?"

I replied yes.

"Please get to our offices right away and find Helen."

I quickly got dressed and got in my car. On my way, I tried to reach my parents. They weren't home, and neither answered their cell phones. I'd have to call them later, I thought to myself.

Travelocity's offices, still part of The Sabre Group, which used to be part of American Airlines, sat on the outskirts of DFW Airport. Whenever running late for a meeting, I'd drive directly through the airport. And while I'd done this drive a million times, today looked different.

Because of what had just happened at the World Trade Center, all flights across the country were instantly grounded. I'll be haunted forever by the scene of driving through DFW and seeing hundreds of planes lined up on every runway. Some were at gates, but most were in the middle of the tarmac. It was surreal.

Before I got to the office, I finally reached my father.

"Daddy, where are you?" I could barely squeak out.

"I'm at the golf club. What's wrong?" he innocently asked.

"Daddy, we're under attack. Two planes just hit the World Trade Center, and another one hit the Pentagon, and they don't know where the fourth one is, but they think it's headed to the Capitol."

He was silent for a moment.

"Are you still in New York?" he nervously asked.

"No, I got home late last night but just barely. My flight had a four-hour delay from a big storm, but I got home. I have to go to Travelocity's offices right now, but it's so eerie with these planes everywhere. It looks like a shopping mall parking lot at Christmas but with planes."

He told me to be careful and call him when I got back to my office.

"And Judy, we'll need to talk about your moving to New York right away."

I knew what he meant, seeing as the city was under attack as we spoke, but even so, I wanted to move there. Why wouldn't I?

I hung up with my father, and my cell rang again with Melinda on the line. "Are you in New York?" she asked.

"No, I got home last night," I told her.

"Okay, just checking," she replied, sounding relieved. "We're in Vegas and just rented a car to drive back to Houston."

Nothing felt normal that day.

I made it to Terry's office.

"We've got a situation," he said.

Shortly after the attacks, the F.B.I discovered one of the hijackers of American Airlines Flight 77 had purchased his ticket on a Travelocity-powered website. The Feds were on their way to the office to speak to management.

We worked tirelessly to help minimize the story's narrative and concentrate on assisting customers stranded worldwide. A few days later, an article in *The New York Times* highlighted this finding:

> There is less information on American Airlines Flight 77 than the others. But the F.B.I. document provided to the German police showed that Nawaf al-Hamzi of San Diego booked a ticket with Travelocity, the Internet travel agency, on Aug. 25, using an address on Linwood Plaza in Fort Lee, N.J., and paid for it with a Visa card. Apparently, as a backup, he bought a second reservation through Travelocity using a Wayne, N.J., address. […] Salem al-Hamzi, who apparently lived in San Antonio at one time, booked his ticket through Travelocity using the same Fort Lee address.

This was not the publicity we wanted for Travelocity. I remember thinking, "How is it that the F.B.I figured out where some terrorists purchased airline tickets but didn't have information that this horrific attack would happen?" I was angry and scared but knew I had to pull it together to help my client. I had other thoughts about how much money I'd just spent to secure an apartment in a city I didn't know I'd ever make it to.

None of us slept much in the days and weeks following the attacks, but in some ways, helping others proved the perfect solution for coping with the unthinkable act that had just happened to our country. We had no idea if Travelocity, much less the travel industry, would survive this catastrophe since, for most people, boarding an airplane ranked at the bottom of their priorities, much less traveling anywhere for fun or business.

Travelocity's VP of Public Relations, and a good friend of mine, Al, went into crisis mode. "We have a lot of work to do, and I will need everyone to focus and work together," he said.

When I'd notice Al getting panicky, I'd say, "Al, you need to breathe." He didn't always appreciate my comforting words and a few times barked, "No, you breathe." Years later, we still recall those moments with laughter. There's no way to adequately put into perspective the amount of stress and total fear we all felt during this event. But in some ways, this tragedy bonded us forever.

It's still hard to fathom the events of 9/11 and how our country forever changed. And just as the families and friends of the victims struggled to understand why or how something like this could happen to their loved ones, I spent many days—and years—after my sister's passing asking why Celia and why not me? I'm sure she had similar thoughts after my rape.

I never figured it out and decided the question could never be answered. Full disclosure: it took me a long time and a lot of therapy to realize this. Unlike the 9/11 victims' families and friends, I said goodbye to my sister because I knew her ultimate fate.

While many people fled the city in droves for fear of a repeat attack, I never wanted to get someplace faster, even with the future uncertain. I count moving to New York City—a month after 9/11—among my most extraordinary life experiences. Texas will always be my home, but I had never been happier to be a part of such a vibrant city that, after one horrific day in history, I would soon call home.

Chapter 21

They say moving is a good idea until you start packing. My moving adventure to New York City marked the sixth time I'd relocated in ten years, making me practically a professional mover at this point. But far from a professional packer.

"Before you officially move to the Big Apple, we want you to spend a few months in the Dallas office getting all your client work in order," Helen told me.

Now I'd have to pack up my stuff in Austin, put it in storage, and then hire movers to haul it to New York City. I got exhausted just thinking about all this coordination.

Since I'd moved from Los Angeles to Houston, I'd somehow amassed more stuff, making my parents refer to me as a borderline hoarder. I should have taken the time to purge my belongings, especially since my New York City apartment would have nearly fifty percent less space than my sprawling two-bedroom, two-bathroom Austin abode with a living/dining room, washer/dryer and a balcony. But why be practical?

"Do you want me to come to Austin and help you pack and throw things away?" my mother asked.

"No, I just threw everything in boxes, and once the movers deliver everything, I'll get rid of what I don't need," I said to my mother.

I'd live to regret this.

After spending about two months in our Dallas office, the time came for me to leave for New York City. While I wanted to make this move, it hit me that I was leaving Texas once again. I secretly wondered if this would be for good.

Flying into New York City is always a rush of excitement when you first see the famous city skyline, especially the Empire State Building. But this flyover brought a real punch to the gut. Gone were the twin towers that helped define Manhattan's character.

Instead of the buildings, smoke billowed up from the rubble. I'd seen the pictures on TV over the past month, but nothing could have prepared me for the utter destruction of what would forever be called Ground Zero. And not only did I get a bird's-eye view from the plane, but I also got a closeup while driving in from Newark, heading towards the Lincoln Tunnel.

I arrived in New York on a Wednesday, but I couldn't move into my apartment until Monday.

"I have to work on Monday when my apartment will be ready, and the movers are bringing my life to New York. Do you think you and Daddy can come to help me unpack and move in?" I asked my mother.

Before my parents came to town, and while I had time off from work, I decided to explore my new neighborhood and scope out where to buy essentials like area rugs and lamps. I had become used to wall-to-wall carpeting and overhead light fixtures that didn't exist in a tiny New York City apartment.

ABC Carpet & Home was the only place to shop for rugs and lighting, according to multiple people. The large store couldn't fit all its merchandise in one building, so two buildings sat directly across the street from each other. One building housed items like lamps and other must-have trinkets for a stylish Manhattan high-rise. The other building had rugs.

Walking around the showroom, I noticed huge rugs hanging from the ceiling with huge price tags to accompany them. I'm pretty sure the least expensive carpet I saw was $15,000.

"How can I help you today? Looking for anything specific?" the sales lady asked me.

"Um, I'm just browsing, but your rugs are so beautiful and expensive," I quipped, lightening the mood.

"My dear, these aren't simply rugs; they're an investment," she replied.

"Oh, I'm not looking for an investment. I'm just looking for something to walk on," I said straight.

She wasn't amused. So I left. Who paid $25,000 for a rug to put in an 800-square-foot apartment? What was I missing? Or was this just the price of living in Manhattan?

When my parents arrived, and I told my mom about my experience, she persuaded me to go back to the store. We returned to the scene of the expensive rugs, and my mother went to work.

"Excuse me, but where are your less expensive rugs?" she asked the first salesman she saw.

"Just follow that staircase down to our basement," he replied.

What? Where did that staircase come from, and why didn't Miss Snooty Pants tell me about it? How did my mother do that, and how would I ever make it by myself in this city?

After we reached the bottom of the stairs, we entered rug nirvana. Stacks and stacks of rugs from the floor to ceiling lay before us. It would take me days to go through them all, but fortunately, I wasn't a picky person and found three beautiful rugs for my living room, dining nook, and bedroom.

"Will you deliver and set the rugs?" my father asked the man.

"Yes, sir, but it's an extra hundred-dollar charge for setting each rug," he said.

Now I knew I had officially arrived in New York City.

The following Monday, I left my parents at my apartment to wait for the movers, and I walked the three short blocks to work.

"I'm here," I told my mom ten minutes later, sitting at my desk. And I thought the commute I had when I lived in LA was short.

About an hour after I got to the office, my mother called me. "The movers are here, and we don't have room for all your stuff. Did you throw away anything before you left Austin?"

I hadn't.

"I didn't have much time to pack before I left for Dallas, so I just stuffed everything into boxes. I knew you'd be able to help me throw things away."

I'm not sure my mother loved anything more than throwing away clutter. I knew she'd be up for the challenge. About an hour later, she called me back.

"We are stacking boxes in the hallway because there is no more room inside your apartment."

I was sure I would be a favorite neighbor after this. After about the fifteenth box, they finally got in a groove.

"I unpack the box, and your father takes the box apart," she explained. "But when you get home, be careful where you walk because there's not a single space without your crap."

By the time I got home from work, my parents were exhausted. And my mother hadn't exaggerated. My stuff sat all over the floor, and you could barely walk through the room. I laughed at the sight of my father sitting in the chair, breaking down box after box as my mother unpacked. I loved these two so much.

"I asked your mother if you'd notice if we just threw away a few boxes with your stuff still in them," he said sarcastically.

Truth: I probably wouldn't have noticed at all. I couldn't think how I could ever repay them for all their help getting me settled. This was symbolic of my relationship with my parents and theirs with me. We would do anything to make the other's life easier. Even though we no longer lived in the same city, we were still a very tight unit. And we shared a lot of laughs as well as tears.

If Celia could have been there with us, everything would have been perfect.

My father's unpacking and box skills were nothing compared to his supreme knowledge of the New York City subway system.

"How do you know which subway line to take?" I asked him multiple times that weekend.

"Because I skipped school a lot to come into Manhattan. Besides, the subway lines are still the same," he said.

Born in Bayonne, New Jersey, across the Hudson River, my father spent many afternoons traveling to Manhattan. He and his hoodlum friends would often skip school or Hebrew school and come into the city and go to Times Square or wherever else they could find trouble. Who knew one day I'd be the recipient of his subway knowledge?

Living in the heart of the Theatre District and Times Square meant busy streets, loud noises, and excitement at every corner. When you weren't dodging the constant flow of tourists jamming the streets, you had to deal with significant events like the Macy's Thanksgiving Day Parade marching down your block.

But the granddaddy of them all and what persuaded me to start looking for a new apartment when my lease came up was Dick Clark's Rockin' in New Year's Eve Party.

When I left my apartment, the friendly NYPD officer standing at West 50th Street and Broadway said, "To get back in, you'll need to prove you live there."

"You're kidding me, right?" I asked.

He wasn't joking. I had never heard of frozen zones, but apparently, I lived right in the middle of one. The first New Year's Eve after 9/11, the NYPD had a significant presence, making my neighborhood probably one of the safest in the city. But I had to get out of there for the evening. I joined my friend Karen and some of her friends for dinner on the Upper East Side.

Around 1:00 a.m., I decided to brave the crowds and make my way home. "Do you think we'll be able to enter the frozen zone for me to get home?" I asked my cab driver.

"Oh, it's probably all cleaned up by now, and you won't even be able to tell anyone was there," he replied.

I couldn't believe it. Less than an hour after the ball dropped in Times Square, with millions of people jamming the streets, it looked as if no celebration had occurred. I guess this is where all our tax dollars went.

Despite the congestion of my neighborhood, I did love the convenient access to every subway line and my office. I could get anywhere in the city within steps of my apartment.

"Maybe I'll just renew my lease and deal with it," I told my mother. "I can't imagine moving again."

And then the NFL kickoff came to town. This event wasn't a marching parade with a few streets closed. It consisted of an entire frozen zone of multiple roads and avenues, all outside my doorstep.

To kick off the season in big, bold fashion, the NFL solicited the help of New Jersey's favorite son, Jon Bon Jovi. He performed on a stage in the middle of Times Square. It sounds simple enough until you add the extra flare of dropping him on stage via a helicopter hovering overhead. Streets were closed, and now we also had closed air space. New Year's Eve no longer represented my nightmare on Broadway.

Naturally, since he arrived via copter, he would leave the same way and then be shuttled over to MetLife Stadium for the football game. Even though the kickoff show lasted only about half an hour, the whole ordeal lasted the entire night. Yep, time to move. Fortunately, my mother and father had helped me purge all my crap, guaranteeing my next move would be easier.

*   *   *

With my job and apartment in order, I found myself with a lot of time to concentrate on the one thing I'd been neglecting the most: me.

To steal a quote from a *Sex and the City* episode, "In New York, they say, you're always looking for a job, a boyfriend, or an apartment. So let's say you have two out of three, and they're fabulous. Why do we let the thing we don't have affect how we feel about all the things we do have?"

Was this me? I had a great job and a lovely apartment, albeit in the middle of Times Square, but I didn't have a boyfriend—and hadn't had one in several years. I did have a vast collection of first dates. Was this the thing that would eventually taint my view of all the goodness in my life? And would I let it?

Chapter 22

Growing up in Houston, if you weren't married with children by your ten-year high school reunion, you might as well enter the convent. By this standard, I was well on my way to becoming the first Jewish nun.

Most of my graduating high school class was almost married, married, married with children, or for one poor soul, on her second divorce by the time this milestone celebration rolled around. Me? I wasn't even close to any category. But I wasn't worried about it. I had plenty of time. At only twenty-eight, I could hardly be called a spinster.

There's an old Joan Rivers joke: "My mother was so desperate for me to get married. Outside our house, she put a sign: 'Last girl before the freeway.'" My mother adopted this sentiment. While I like to think she wasn't desperate, I knew she suffered from anxiety about whether I'd ever get married.

Desperate times called for desperate measures when she set me up with a boy she met on an airplane. On the way home from visiting her brother, my Uncle Joe, in St. Louis, she spoke with a young man waiting to board the flight. Their conversation continued on the plane, and by the time they landed in Houston, she'd planned my wedding.

"Who is that guy Mama is walking off the plane with?" I asked my father while we waited at the gate.

"It's probably one of your uncle's friends," he replied.

"Judy, this is Michael," my mother said with a big grin.

"Hi," was about all I could manage to say.

When he didn't leave our side as we made our way to baggage claim, I became suspicious. I caught up with my father and grabbed his hand. "Do you think Mama is trying to set me up with this guy?"

My father just looked at me and replied, "What do you think? You know your mother."

Yes, I knew her very well, but I couldn't believe she would pick up a strange guy on an airplane and try to pawn him off on me.

We collected her luggage, and as we walked away, she said to Michael, "You have my number, so give me a call, and we can set up a time for you to come for dinner."

I had my answer. This "last girl before freeway" had a whole new meaning.

"I can't believe you invited him to our house for dinner," I screamed as we walked to the car.

"What do you have to lose, Judy? He's a nice guy in law school, and you may find you like him."

Was she kidding me right now? Had I gotten to the point where I needed my mommy fixing me up on dates?

"Who are you, the yenta from *Fiddler on the Roof*?" I asked.

My dad, knowing better, didn't say a word and kept walking—and laughing.

I decided that if my mom could invite Michael to our home for dinner, I could invite some friends. Strength in numbers, of course. My girlfriend, Annette, had recently married, and I thought she and her husband, Kenny, would be the perfect people to join me.

"Please come and save me," I begged her. "You can bring Kenny, and y'all will serve as a great diversion for me."

Annette went to law school, so I figured she could start talking legalese and get things going if the conversation got dull.

The evening started okay, and everyone enjoyed the meal my mother spent all day preparing. What I didn't plan on, however, was Michael to be so charmed by Annette that if it weren't for the fact that she had recently married, he might have asked her out.

My mother's matchmaking services officially ended that night. A few months later, I ran into Michael at a bar. An awkward moment made me even more uncomfortable when he walked up and asked, "How's your friend, Annette?"

"Still married," I said.

* * *

Before I moved to New York City, Fred, my favorite cousin, sagely told me, "There are two million single Jewish guys in the city and two million married Jewish guys who hate their wives. You have four million opportunities to find yourself a man." Ah, yes, I was moving to mecca. But was I?

Ironically, when I first got to the Big Apple, Fred invited me to a board of directors dinner. He served as chairman for the company. The event took place at the famed French restaurant, Le Bernardin. Since Kay wouldn't come to New York with him for the dinner event, he wanted me to be his date for the evening. I guess he figured I needed practice before I launched what would become my side career of dating in New York City.

"I have appointments all day, so plan on meeting me at the restaurant," he told me.

I arrived on time, but he was late. Texas oil company executives filled the room, and their wives played the part well with their gaudy jewels and big Texas hair.

"I'm Judy Haveson, Fred Zeidman's cousin, and I'll be joining him for dinner tonight. He told me to meet him at the restaurant," I explained to one of the friendly gentlemen who greeted me.

He gave me the once over, which creeped me out. "Well, nice to meet you, Judy. Come on in and let's get you a drink," he said in his Texas drawl.

One of the wives who stood dripping in diamonds, condescendingly said to me, "How nice of Fred to invite you to dinner tonight."

I confidently replied, "Yes, he always calls on me when Kay isn't available."

She snarked back, "Of course he does."

I thought her response felt a bit odd. Still, I also felt her outfit looked like it belonged at a Cattle Baron's Ball and not at a French restaurant in New York City. The only thing missing was spurs on her boots. The man who initially greeted me walked up to my side and started in with even more odd questions.

"How long have you known Fred? And where did y'all meet?"

"I'm his cousin," I said.

How long did he think I knew him, and where did he think we met?

Finally, he said, "Well, we used to call you nieces back in our day."

And then he winked at me. Oh my Gawd! He thought I was a prostitute and Fred hired me to be his date. I didn't know what to say, so I channeled my inner Julia Roberts from *Pretty Woman*. "I can't be his niece since Fred's an only child."

Right about that moment, Fred walked in. "Hello, cousin!" he said.

They all turned to him with a knowing look. "Fred, they think I'm your niece," I said. "Shall I call Kay and tell her, or will you?"

The entire room erupted in laughter. While I wasn't the "hired" entertainment for the evening, it's safe to say I got the party started.

I decided to join the thousands of singles experimenting with internet dating. After all, I was a busy professional who had little time for a social life, so what better way to meet someone than in the privacy of my own home, using the internet? Innocent enough, or so I thought.

The whole concept of internet dating felt so bizarre: writing a description of who you are, whom you're looking for, what you believe makes the perfect partner, and what you learned from your last relationship. As if we ever really learn from our past relationships? Honestly, if we did, why would we be on these sites? Some brave souls posted their pictures, too. And what were the odds that the whole truth would be revealed, even with photos?

New York City's internet dating prospects included a plethora of men. My first encounter happened just after New Year's Eve 2001. While visiting my parents in Florida, I received an email from Jerry. He said, "I think I sent you an email a while back but never heard from you, so I tried again. Email back if you'd like."

When I first signed up for the service, I got many emails, and I mean *a lot*. But only because of the sheer volume of single people, mostly men, in New York City. If I didn't receive many emails, I would have been concerned. I honestly didn't remember this guy through my sea of notes, but I read through his profile, and he seemed to be someone I wouldn't mind meeting.

Jerry said he was thirty-nine years old, five foot nine, an investment banker, had an MBA, liked the theater, and enjoyed sushi. What the heck? I answered him back with, "Hi, Jerry, I don't remember seeing an email from you, but thanks for getting in touch with me. I enjoyed your profile. Let's chat some more, and when I get back to New York, maybe we can get together."

After New Year's, we had our first phone conversation, and it went pretty well. We decided to meet the next night for a drink at La Montparnasse, a bar at 2nd Avenue and East 51st Street. I got there first—a trait I picked up from my father—always be early, never be late. A few minutes later, in walked Jerry.

I know you can't judge a book by its cover or a guy by his picture on the internet, but there were some severe discrepancies in front of me. First, if he was five-nine, I was, too. I think he was about five-four. Throughout the conversation, I learned about other falsehoods in his profile. For starters, he was forty-three, not thirty-nine. I asked him why he lied about his age.

"If I reveal my real age, I will get emails from forty-year-old women, and I don't want to go out with women that old," he lamely explained.

"But you think it's okay to lie to women in their thirties about how old you are because they'll understand?"

He didn't have an answer for that either. Oh, it didn't end there. The investment banker portion of his profile was also a little fabricated. He wasn't precisely in investment banking; he wasn't precisely in anything. He was out of work. He did, however, have his own consulting company and was in the process of looking for a new project. So before me sat a forty-three-year-old, out-of-work guy who was truth-challenged. I ran home to call my mother and tell her to print the wedding invitations.

We drank one glass of wine and called it a night. He said he would call me, which I did not doubt. He called the next day, the next, and the next. I decided to give him another chance. We went to the movies and had sushi, so at least he didn't lie about that part.

A few days after our date, I came down with the worst stomach flu. Jerry wanted to come to my apartment to take care of me.

"That's very sweet, but I don't think it's a good idea seeing how contagious I am," I explained.

While I recognized he was just being sweet and caring, the last thing I was ready for was him coming to my apartment to hold my hair back while I puked in the toilet. The next day, I received a considerable flower arrangement of three dozen white, long-stem roses. I appreciated the sentiment, but it was a bit overwhelming, as were his twice-daily phone calls. I wondered if he put as much effort into finding a job.

Once the sickness fog lifted from my body, I started thinking about whether Jerry was a good match for me. All signs pointed to no. I called him and said, "Jerry, you're a super nice guy, but I don't think we're a match." Always good to be blunt and rip off the Band-Aid. I'm not sure if he understood because I continued to get hang-ups on my phone for the next several days. I felt sad for him because of all the lies he told in his profile. After almost a year, he was still online with the same descriptions of himself. And I thought only women were that vain.

One evening I decided to browse the internet, and I came across a very handsome man named Adam. According to his profile, he was between thirty-six and forty years old, was between five-eleven and six feet tall, and seemed fun from his responses. The profile survey asked: "Someone may want to contact you but not know what to say. Ask a question to help them." Adam's response was: "I enjoyed your profile; check out mine and let me know what you think." It was not the most original, but I thought this would be a great opportunity since it was so simple.

Also, the last part of the profile survey asked if you want to add anything that perhaps wasn't requested. Well, Adam boldly included that he was an unbelievable kisser. Was he kidding me? Who says that about themselves? I sent him an email that night that said: "Hi, Adam, I enjoyed your profile; check out mine, and let me know what you think. To steal a line from you. By the way, what makes you such an unbelievable kisser?"

Now the waiting game began. Would I get a response, or would my email get trashed? Another feature of this dating website was seeing if someone read your email and deleted it. Pretty awful, but hey, it happened. The next day, Adam responded to my email. "I'm going out of town this week but would love to get together with you when I return. Also, women have told me I'm an unbelievable kisser in the past. Maybe you can let me know your thoughts, too." At least he wasn't shy.

I emailed back. "I hope you have a nice time, wherever you're going. I look forward to meeting you when you return. And by the way, I've also been told I'm an incredible kisser, so maybe we need to put our skills to the test." Moments later, another response came in, "I look forward to that challenge."

I'd often been told my kissing talents were superb, and I had my dear high school friend, Cynthia, to thank for teaching me. No, I didn't kiss her, but she did teach me what to do. We would sit in her bedroom talking about the mechanics of the perfect kiss for hours. Unlike me, she had a boyfriend, so she got lots of practice. I only had my teddy bear, but that stuffed animal helped me master my skills, and I never had anyone complain.

The Monday after Adam returned from vacation and I returned from a business trip, we finally connected. My phone rang at work, and the guy on the other end, with a slight New York accent, said, "Hi, Judy, this is Adam from Matchmaker."

I was thrilled to hear from him, but then came his next statement. "By the way, my name is not Adam. It's Daniel."

My first thought was, here we go again, another truth-challenged loser. "What do you mean? Why did you say your name was Adam?"

"I gave a false name because I didn't want anyone I know to see I was on the site."

"Why, are you married, or in a fight with your wife?"

He laughed, but I was serious.

"Don't you think others will know who you are because your picture is there?" I asked.

He didn't seem to think so or understand my point. What was this? Should I even go any further with this one? A fake name? What other lies was he telling?

Instead of wondering, I asked. "What else are you lying about?"

He promised there was nothing he was hiding, and we continued talking. "Do you want to meet for a drink this evening?" he asked.

"Unfortunately, I have a party to go to, but if it turns out to be a bust, I'll take your number and give you a call."

He liked that idea.

About an hour into the party, I walked out into the hall, pulled out Daniel's (or Adam's) phone number, and called him.

"How's the party?" he asked.

"Don't ask. Are you still up for that drink?"

The next thing I knew, I was in a cab headed back uptown to meet him at a bar named Mica on East 51st Street and 2nd Avenue, two doors down from my first date with Jerry the "flower boy." Hopefully, this wasn't an omen.

As I would later learn, Daniel was everything his profile said, except his name. He was tall, handsome, and yes, I can confirm he was an incredible kisser. We had instant chemistry, and the conversation came so easily as we talked about our jobs, recent vacations, families, everything.

Even though our impromptu date went well, something about him didn't sit right. But then again, the thing I probably couldn't put my finger on was he appeared to be an ordinary guy. Daniel and I consistently saw each other for the next several months, but I would never call it a relationship. For starters, we never really spoke to each other during the week, and secondly, we mainly got together on Sunday nights for dinner and a movie. I guess I wasn't weekend-worthy for a Friday or Saturday night date.

Of course, this led me to believe he must be married or had so many other dates that he could never seem to fit me into a regular schedule. Around the beginning of summer, Daniel called me with some news. "As much as I hate to say this, I think it's best if we stop seeing each other."

Insert awkward silence.

"Summer is here, and I'm going to be spending a lot of time in The Hamptons or going to parties in the city, and I would hate it if I ran into you and I was with another girl," he said.

Was this guy for real?

"All along, I have told you that I have a problem with commitment," he continued.

Honey, commitment is not your biggest problem.

While Daniel spoke, I couldn't get the song lyric out of my head about players only loving you when they're playing you. It was summertime, so he couldn't see me anymore. Did that mean when the first leaf fell, he'd call me?

I responded very casually, "That's fine. I hope you have a great summer."

"Wow, you don't even sound upset. You're a pretty cool girl."

"Yep, I'm a pretty cool chick."

Not that he'd ever find out. In my estimation, if you reacted to guys like Daniel in the manner I did, they would call you back, and that was when you could have fun with them. While I wasn't a big player, this one was too easy.

Turns out I overestimated Daniel. He didn't even wait for the first leaf to fall. He called around the Fourth of July. He must have missed his ride out to The Hamptons. Regardless of his unbelievable kissing talents, I decided he could kiss my ass instead.

While surfing J-date, a dating site for Jewish singles, one night, I came across Jeff's profile and thought he looked interesting. He said he was a photographer and had traveled far and wide to get the perfect shot. He also mentioned he'd visited Marfa, Texas, and if anyone reading his profile knew what was special about Marfa, reach out and let him know. Being a Texas gal, and because one of my clients was the State of Texas Tourism Office, I instantly knew what Marfa was known for: the location of the James Dean/Elizabeth Taylor/Rock Hudson movie *Giant*. That was way too easy.

Jeff was impressed with my cinematic knowledge and Texas history, so we agreed to meet for a drink. He picked the bar at The Hudson Hotel in Midtown, near my office. The morning of my blind date with Jeff the photographer, I woke up with what felt like dust in my eye. As a contact lens wearer since the eighth grade, I was used to foreign particles flying in my eyes; and living in New York City, I had my fair share of dirt and God knows what clinging to my lenses. I quickly put in some eye drops and prayed the irritation would subside before my date later that evening. I also took several pairs of contact lenses with me in case I needed to change them throughout the day.

Before meeting Jeff, I decided to stop at the nail salon and get a quick manicure since the Hudson Hotel was close to my office. In theory, it was a good idea, but it being the dead of winter meant I couldn't put my gloves on after my manicure and had to walk to the hotel as my fingers dried.

By the time I arrived, I had frostbite. Not really, but my fingers were frozen and purple, and I was in excruciating pain. At this point, I'm not sure what hurt worse, my fingers or my scratchy eyes. Yes, my eyes were still irritated and now tearing up, making my nose run. Thankfully, I arrived at the hotel first and had time to go into the bathroom to put my fingers under hot water to try and warm them up and change lenses for the third time that day.

This was a good plan until I walked into the darkest bathroom I'd ever visited. I could barely see when I tried to freshen up my eye makeup. My mascara had now run down my face. I did the best I could. Jeff finally arrived, and we went to the bar to order drinks. He was a fascinating guy with great stories about photography and traveling the world.

I tried to concentrate on everything he said, but I was overwhelmed by the pain from my throbbing fingers and scratchy eyes. I excused myself to fix my eyes once again. I came back to the table, blotting my eyes with a tissue. They were full-on tearing now. I also tried to dry my runny nose. I must have looked like a massive cocaine addict.

About ten minutes later, I excused myself again because I wanted to scratch my eyes. This time, I came back to the table wearing my glasses. I apologized for all the disruptions and finally explained what was going on with my irritated eyes. He smiled. But not a sympathetic smile like he understood and wanted to take care of me. No. This smile was more like, "Oh, you are a total drug addict, and I'm sure you've been doing lines every time you go to the bathroom." I knew I should have rescheduled this date. I guess I didn't need my contacts or glasses because I never saw him again after that night.

I decided to go on hiatus from online dating. Frankly, it was exhausting, and I'd had enough. My friend Alysa said she and her husband Greg wanted to set me up with a good friend of theirs. He had just gotten out of a long-term relationship and wanted to meet new people. His name was Mitchell, he was Jewish, had a great job, and she and Greg liked him. That all sounded perfect to me.

The week before our date, I met my parents in Seaside, Florida, to spend time with the Zeidman cousins for the Fourth of July weekend. While in Seaside, a yellow fly stung my ankle. I had never heard of yellow flies, but apparently, they're related to horse flies. Only worse. Seaside was inundated with them that summer, and the doctor said being stung by one was equivalent to being stung by a wasp. My foot was now swollen, and I could barely walk. By the time I left to go home, I was still hobbling, and when I changed planes in Detroit, the flight attendant got me a wheelchair and upgraded me to first class to keep my foot elevated. Bottom line: I was in a whole lot of pain.

I called Mitchell when I got home. "A funny thing happened to me in Florida," I told him. "I was stung by a yellow fly, and I have a swollen foot."

"If you're still up for going out, we can keep it casual and local, so we don't have to walk too far," he said.

He was such a gentleman. When I arrived at the cafe, he greeted me by shaking my hand. This little gesture would turn out to be key to the story.

Our first stop was the bar at the new Ritz Carlton on Central Park South for drinks. Mitchell was everything Alysa and her husband said he'd be, and I enjoyed our conversation.

"I'm not ready to go home yet. Are you okay to go somewhere else?" he asked while paying our bill.

I said yes.

"How about the bar at the Rainbow Room?" he asked.

"Absolutely," I enthusiastically replied.

There we had another drink and kept talking. It was a great evening, and I couldn't wait to let Alysa know how much we hit it off.

When we left the Rainbow Room, we decided to call it quits since it was a school night, Sunday. I lived a few blocks from the Rainbow Room, and Mitchell walked me home. The doorman on duty was Rudy, a wonderful man who looked out for his residents. He gave me a curious eye when I walked up with a strange man since he hadn't seen me leave with him earlier. I gave him a knowing look, letting him know all was good.

Mitchell and I awkwardly stood on the sidewalk when we got to the building, not knowing what to do next. I extended my hand to close the silence.

"It was great to meet you and thank you so much for a fun evening."

Instead of shaking my hand back, he practically ripped it away. What was that about, I thought? Did I do something wrong by extending my hand? I assumed he'd do the same and reply with how he liked meeting me too and would like to call me again for another date. Wrong.

"Oh, did Alysa not tell you?" he asked.

Huh? Tell me what?

"I'm an Orthodox Jew, and I don't touch women."

Again huh?

"Ever?" I asked.

"No," he said.

"Are you gay?" I asked, not that there was anything wrong with that.

"No, I want to get married one day."

"You may want to start touching women," I said.

And he walked away.

Of course, I immediately wanted to call Alysa to ask her to explain how she could have left out this small detail. But it was too late, and she had a sleeping baby at home. I sent her an email with the subject line: CALL ME FIRST THING IN THE MORNING! I decided to call my parents to see if they could help me explain what the hell had just happened.

After going over every detail of the evening, including shaking his hand when I met him, my father, in all his wisdom, said, "He just didn't want to touch you!" But then he and my mother called bullshit on the whole thing since there was no way this guy was a total Orthodox Jew, seeing he used glassware and utensils at the places we had drinks and food, and he shook my hand when we first met. None of this made me feel any better, but the mileage I've gotten out of this one dating horror story is still going strong today.

I'd received two emails from two different men through J-date asking to connect. The first was from Mike, a forty-something guy who lived on the Upper West Side, and the other was from Adam, whom I gathered liked to cook since he wore a chef coat in his profile picture. I decided to respond in order of receipt.

Mike and I agreed to meet for dinner at a place near my apartment. I learned he was a born and bred New Yorker and had lived his entire life on the Upper West Side of Manhattan. His parents lived around the corner from him, too. He was currently unemployed but was close to landing a new job.

"It must be stressful looking for work," I said to fill the awkward gap of silence during our meal.

"Nah, it's okay. At least I have my parents to support me."

And that was pretty much how the entire conversation went. Mike had absolutely nothing to say. To make matters even more uncomfortable, he had a glass eye, and I couldn't tell where to look when he was talking, which he barely did the whole evening. We said our goodbyes, and he asked to see me again.

"I'm busy at work and will be traveling a lot over the next several months, but I'll touch base with you when I have time," I said.

I couldn't believe he wanted to see me again since we exchanged maybe twenty words the whole evening. I called my mother when I got home.

"Am I a bad person?"

"No, but what did you do?" she replied.

"I just went out with Mike, and we had nothing to say to each other, and he had a glass eye. I mean, I guess it's good we didn't talk that much because I didn't know where to look anyway when we did. I'm a horrible person, aren't I?"

Again, she said no. She was always so comforting and reassuring.

"Well, I know for sure I'm done with dating for a while," I said.

And then my loving, comforting, and reassuring mother barked, "Oh no, you're not. You have another guy who wants to talk to you, and you will go out with him."

Seriously?

"Okay, okay. I'll speak to him tomorrow."

The last girl before the freeway reared its ugly head again.

The next night Adam and I spoke over the phone, and we talked for hours. We agreed to meet the next night after work for a glass of wine at Ruth's Chris Steakhouse in Midtown, close to where both our offices were.

"So you're a tax accountant. That's exciting," I sarcastically said to him.

"Yes, but I don't think like one," he replied. I wasn't sure what that meant.

"Why are you wearing a chef's coat in your profile picture?"

"I like to cook," he said. "Last year, I took the twenty-two-week amateur culinary course at the French Culinary Institute, and I'm currently taking the twenty-week amateur pastry course."

He could have stopped at "I like to cook." Did I just win the lottery? A gainfully employed, handsome guy with a great smile who reminded me of my father in the hair department (bald) and, from all accounts, had lied about nothing on his profile, and liked to cook. Check, please.

We spent several hours talking about everything, including politics, which you should never discuss, especially on a first date. Somehow Bill Clinton's name came up, and I blurted out, "Oh, you mean Slick Willie?"

With wide eyes, I caught myself, slapped my hand over my mouth, and quickly said, "I'm so sorry; I didn't mean to say that out loud."

He replied, "Are you kidding me? I may marry you."

To be clear, I had no real issues against Bill Clinton. I even voted for him in his second term, much to my conservative father's chagrin. I didn't like his slickness and everything that happened with Monica Lewinsky. But apparently, my sarcastic wit endeared me to Adam, and he wanted to learn more.

Chapter 23

After our drink date, Adam called the next day to ask me out for an actual date for Saturday night.

"Unfortunately, I have plans for a friend's birthday," I told him.

I never cancelled plans with friends for a guy, and I wasn't going to start that terrible practice now, no matter how much I wanted to see Adam again.

"She lives in Connecticut, and I'm spending the night at her house."

Adam also lived in Connecticut, not too far from Hannah.

"If you'd like, I can pick you up at her house and drive you back to the city on Sunday and then we can have dinner," he said.

I called Hannah and asked if that would be okay, and she said way too eagerly, "Uh, yeah, it will be okay. That way, I can meet him."

"Hannah, I barely remember what he looks like, and now that I think about it, I don't know if I want you to meet him so soon."

"Havey, you will have him pick you up at my house, no arguments."

Never one to argue with Hannah, I agreed.

Adam drove to Hannah's house to pick me up and drive me back to the city that Sunday afternoon. Hannah's daughters at the time were six, four, and two. The four-year-old opened the door and quickly ran away, leaving Adam standing by himself. I wondered if she had some secret sense and was trying to tell me something. As I let him in the house, I noticed a tray of desserts in his hand.

"These are just some samples of pastries I made in class yesterday that I thought I'd share with you and Hannah."

Hannah and I looked at each other in amazement. Homemade macaroons, Linzer torte cookies, and other French delicacies I didn't even recognize filled the tray.

I also noticed the car he drove, a Mercedes convertible. I quickly assessed the situation in my head as we were walking up to his vehicle: friendly, well-mannered, handsome, gainfully employed—albeit a tax accountant—a man who drove a ridiculously fancy car and brought my friend a pastry platter for her and her daughters all while he volunteered to take me back to the city, so I didn't have to take the train.

Walking up to Adam's car, I saw Hannah mouthing, "Don't screw this up."

"I'm going out of town for a week, but we can get together when I'm back if that works," I said when he asked to see me again. The following week while in Dallas for work, we spoke on the phone every night. The conversation felt so natural and very comfortable. We made plans for dinner when I got back.

"What is all this?" I asked when I opened the door to let Adam into my apartment.

"Just a few things for me to make dinner for us," he said.

I stood in the doorway with my mouth open, shocked.

"You're going to make dinner in my kitchen?" I asked him. And then it dawned on me. "I don't think I've plugged in my stove."

And I was serious. I'd never used it and sometimes stored things in it. Fortunately, the stove worked, and I had removed my sweaters. Adam made the best dinner.

"I could seriously get used to this," I told him.

From that moment on, Adam and I were inseparable. Over the summer, we explored New York City or took drives through Connecticut. For the Fourth of July weekend, Adam invited me to his apartment.

"I have a grill and would like to make you dinner," he said.

Chicken Americana and grilled vegetables were on the menu, and for dessert, little mini tarts decorated with flags made from blueberries and strawberries. Oh, and he made the tart dough and pastry cream from scratch. I felt super inferior because it would all have been store-bought if I ever tried to make anything close.

We were in the kitchen, and as I watched him prepare the chicken, my stomach got queasy. The main ingredient of Chicken Americana is mustard, one of the many condiments I detest. It's probably in my top two. The other was mayonnaise, and I certainly didn't want this scene to turn out like the time in California when I refused to eat the hamburger and my father practically force-fed me. Many thoughts ran through my mind. How could I politely get out of this situation without eating the chicken? I came up with none.

How rude would it have been for me to say to him, "Uh, thanks for going to the trouble to make this awesome dinner, but the sight of mustard makes me ill?" I would hate me, too. Or worse, to have him make the meal and then not eat it. No, I had to suck it up.

Adam went to so much trouble to make this lovely dinner, and I won't lie, Hannah's words were circling in my head.

I started thinking of that *Seinfeld* episode when Jerry had dinner with a girl who served him mutton, and he kept spitting it out in his napkin but forgot to take the napkin out of his jacket and the girl's dog found it. Adam didn't have a dog, but I couldn't do that to him. No, I had to be mature about it and just eat the chicken.

"The chicken and everything are so good," I told him.

And while it wasn't that bad, the fact that I saw him slather mustard all over it before putting it on the grill, the chicken could have been dipped in chocolate, and I'd still have an issue with it. Of course, he never knew about the conversation in my warped mind during this meal until years later when he overheard me speaking to a friend.

"I can't stand mustard, and in fact, I get physically ill if I see it near my food," I said to my friend when we saw a man with mustard dripping down his chin while eating a hot dog.

Adam walked up and said, "Wait, you don't like mustard?"

Dammit!

"But what about that chicken I made you for the Fourth all those years ago?"

I had to fess up.

"Yes, well, I didn't want to be a total bitch and tell you I wouldn't eat the meal you made me just because I saw you douse the chicken in mustard."

Everyone got a good laugh—at my expense—and to this day, he never uses mustard when cooking. Or at least he never lets me see it.

However, the actual test of our new relationship came after we'd been dating for about two months.

August in New York City is probably the most miserable month and why many people flee the city en masse. It's hot, humid, and stinky from garbage and other unrecognizable city smells.

One hot August afternoon in 2003, while sitting at work on a conference call, all the lights started flickering. And then everything shut off. The phones didn't work, the lights wouldn't turn on, and the air conditioner compressors quit. Following the 9/11 terrorist attacks, New Yorkers were still on edge, especially when something unusual happened. Your mind automatically thought, "We're under attack."

Not knowing anything, everyone ran for the stairwell to get out of the building. Chaos met us on the street. Cars and buses were at a standstill, and people dodged cars and taxis in the middle of traffic. "What is going on? Are we under attack?" you could hear people asking anyone who appeared to be aware of the situation.

I immediately called Adam but couldn't get through because of spotty cell service. With my office at Broadway and West 53rd Street, I wasn't far from Adam's building on 6th Avenue and West 47th Street. I decided to walk to his office to find him. I stood outside his building, repeatedly calling both his office and cell. After several attempts, he finally picked up the phone.

"Why haven't you answered your phone?" I asked.

"I've been in a meeting. What is going on?"

Working in a more modernized building than mine, when the electricity shut off, his building's generator kicked on, and no one knew of the chaos happening below.

New York City is a walking town, and on most days, I loved walking here and there. But in August, with the temperature ninety plus degrees and the humidity over 1,000 percent, I cried. The scorching conditions made me hot, sticky, and miserable. Unfortunately, with the subways not running and buses and taxis jamming the streets, Adam and I had no choice but to walk to my apartment across town.

My building had a courtyard in front. It quickly became a gathering place for residents and neighbors passing through. It also became the stage for a play I called *Judy, This Is Your Life*.

Living in New York City, you inevitably see former guys you've dated around town, especially when they live in your neighborhood. But it's extra special when they descend upon your building while you're standing outside with the guy you're currently dating.

"Hey, Judy, I thought I'd walk over and see if you were hanging outside," said Josh, the guy who decided we weren't compatible to be in a relationship after one week, but still wanted to sleep with me. "Do you want to come over to my place?" he asked, totally ignoring Adam standing next to me.

"I'm okay, thanks though," I said. "Oh, and this is Adam; we're dating now."

Should I have said that? I thought we were dating, but I certainly wasn't ready to call him my boyfriend. And after this, would he even let me?

"Nice to meet you, Adam," he said and then turned to me, as if Adam weren't standing there. "Just let me know if you want to come over later, Judy. I'm making a big salad with everything I have to take out of my fridge."

Did he not get the part where I said Adam and I were dating? I just smiled awkwardly and said thanks.

The former date parade didn't end there. "Hey, Judy, I wanted to walk over to make sure you were okay," said Matt, the guy who returned bottled water at Starbucks in exchange for a paper cup and didn't understand why I ran my air conditioner when I wasn't home.

"Thank you," I awkwardly replied. "This is Adam; we're dating now."

I prayed this would be the last time I'd have to say this phrase that day. I quickly ran through the other guys I went out with to remember where they lived. Fortunately, the others were on the Upper East Side, so I didn't expect any other surprise pop-ins. Suddenly, I saw my neighbor, whose name I didn't know, and noticed he had a flashlight.

"Oh, hey, neighbor," I enthusiastically said. "Are you going up?"

"Yes, want to follow me?"

He had no idea that at that very moment, he saved me.

"Absolutely," I said. "Sorry, Matt, but we're going up now. Thanks for checking on me." And we were off.

The walk up thirty-one flights of stairs in the hot, pitch-black stairwell wasn't as miserable as the *Sex and the City* moment I'd just experienced in the courtyard. What were the chances of two guys I dated over a year before both showing up to check on me while the guy I'd hoped to be with longer than either of them stood next to me? Only me, and only in New York City.

Adam and I got to my apartment and stripped off the clothes sticking to our bodies. I put on shorts and a dry T-shirt, but poor Adam had to sit around in his boxers. I quickly searched for a flashlight and my Trimline telephone. This relic had been with me since I moved into my first apartment in Houston after college. The minute I plugged the phone in and got a dial tone, I called my mother.

"I'm okay, and I'm with Adam at my apartment," I told her when she sounded panicked hearing my voice.

"Do you even know what's going on?" she asked.

I had no idea the entire city had lost power. User error at an energy plant in Akron, Ohio led to a power overload. Eight states in the Midwest and Northeast were affected, and the outage ended up lasting up to twenty-nine hours in some states. While that all sounded bad, the nightmare of my past dating worlds colliding in the courtyard proved more disastrous. I didn't know whether I should bring it up to Adam or let it go? And what would I even say?

"That was entertaining," I finally said to him. "I hadn't seen either of those guys in over a year, and they both showed up simultaneously. Funny how these things work."

He replied, "Well, I would have checked on you, too."

I thought to myself, "I dodged a big bullet." My stifling apartment didn't provide much relief, but fortunately, I had a balcony, and we were able to open the sliding door and front door to let in a cross breeze. I faced west towards the Hudson River and could see New Jersey.

"Wait, I think the lights are on in New Jersey," I said.

"No, those are cars stuck on the West Side Highway," Adam explained.

My phone rang with my mother giving us updates. The ringing telephone sound brought people on the floor to my front door like ants to a picnic.

"Can I use your phone?" one after another said. I could have made serious money. And then, sometime during the night, the power came on because we woke up to the air conditioning blasting cold.

After about two months of going out, I started thinking Adam wasn't like the other guys I'd dated, mainly because he lasted more than a few dates, especially after surviving the blackout and parade of former dates.

My parents first met Adam when they came to New York City for a Hadassah convention. Before the conference started, we all went to brunch at Sarabeth's on the Upper West Side. On the way to the restaurant, my mother walked with Adam and didn't stop talking to him the entire way to the restaurant.

"I hope she lets him get a few words in, and she doesn't say anything to embarrass me," I said to my father.

"Don't count on it," he replied.

They instantly fell in love with him, and I knew they'd probably have a challenging time letting go if we ever broke up. They loved him, and not just because he cooked, which was a big bonus knowing they often wondered how I kept myself fed with my limited knowledge around the kitchen. I think they grew fond of him because they saw him treat me with respect and kindness. As the months went on, Adam and I grew closer and closer, and we spent all our spare time together.

In June 2004, Adam and I decided to take a vacation to Grand Cayman. We spent five days there, and afterward, we flew home through Florida to see my parents. They were both turning seventy that year and had decided to throw a party. My uncle Joe would be there for the party, and I couldn't wait for him to meet Adam.

While a great man, my uncle Joe was an acquired taste and had his fair share of quirks. He was opinionated, stubborn, well-traveled (he had practically been all over the world), frugal (that's putting it mildly), educated (especially in history), wickedly funny and sarcastic, and fiercely loyal to his friends, but primarily to his family (my mother in particular).

A self-proclaimed bachelor, it would only be later, right before he died, that we learned his truth. He came from a different generation where many didn't readily accept homosexuality. I sort of always knew, and honestly, it made no difference to me. It wouldn't have made a difference to my mother or father, but that was his cross to bear, not ours.

While Adam and I were in Grand Cayman, I convinced myself Adam would propose. The island setting would be excellent for a proposal, one we'd never forget. As each day went by and there was no proposal, I got more irritated.

"What's wrong?" he asked me one day.

Not wanting to blurt out, "When will you ask me to marry you?" I kept quiet and replied, "Nothing."

My parents picked us up at the airport in Miami and drove us back to their house. I couldn't wait to see my uncle, and as I predicted, he loved meeting Adam. But I couldn't shake the feeling that something seemed off with him. He didn't appear his usual fun, sarcastic self. In fact, he didn't want to spend time away from my parents' house besides going to the party. I let the feeling go for the time being.

When my father took Adam to play golf one afternoon, he asked my dad for my hand in marriage. I only know this because my mother couldn't keep this information to herself. "Adam and your father had a conversation today," she said with a huge smile.

"And that would have been about what?" I asked her.

Like I needed to ask. I wasn't upset with my mom at all. This explained why no proposal came in Grand Cayman. At least I wasn't wrong to think it was coming. But even though my father gave Adam his blessing and declared, "Yes, please take my daughter," the proposal didn't happen for another six weeks. Every day I asked myself, "Will this be the day?" But Adam had a plan that I, of course, ruined.

*   *   *

That suspicious feeling I got from my uncle Joe while we were all in Florida turned into a nightmare.

"Your uncle has advanced colon cancer," my mom called to tell me after we were home from Florida.

"I knew something was wrong," I said.

"It's pretty bad, and it appears they'll have to remove a lot of his colon."

My mom flew to St. Louis, where my uncle Joe lived. He didn't want her to come until he got home. A very stubborn man, but a fighter, too. He'd also traveled the world and loved sharing the journeys with his family. When Celia graduated high school, Uncle Joe and my grandfather took her to Spain as a graduation gift. They agreed to take me somewhere great when I graduated high school, too. We went to Costa Rica, and while it wasn't Europe, I still had a fantastic experience, even though we didn't always agree on what makes a good vacation.

"I can't believe you missed the sunset because you were washing your hair," he screamed at me one night.

"Please, Uncle Joe, it was just a sunset," I said.

My uncle reveled in the importance of enjoying the little things in life, like a sunset.

"To me, clean hair is more important than watching the sunset," I said.

I still loved him deeply even if his priorities were misplaced. He also enjoyed good food but didn't always eat healthy food.

"I'm so hungry, and my blood sugar is dropping. I'm just going to have a few chocolate croissants," he told us one time when we were visiting him in London.

"But we haven't had lunch yet," my mother said.

"It's just a little snack," he replied.

I'm sure his lifestyle led to colon cancer, but that made no difference now. It was just a setback, I told myself. I knew he'd come out just fine. He had way too much living left to do.

* * *

My apartment lease came up for renewal in September 2004, and I had to decide whether to renew or look for a new place to live. Always a plight for New Yorkers: stay put or find something better. While we weren't theoretically living together, Adam and I spent all our time together. He still had his place in Connecticut, but I wasn't too keen on moving away from Manhattan even if that meant more space.

Before he asked me to marry him, he wanted to know if I'd move in with him. My mind went back to something Melinda's father said of one of his daughters when they moved in with a boyfriend before marriage. "Why buy the cow when you can get the milk for free?" I went home to my mom and dad, asking what that meant. When they explained, I got it and vowed never to be the milk.

Would I now be the milk by saying yes to moving in with Adam before committing to marriage? I didn't want to be a cow either, but that would be the better option in this scenario.

"I'll consider moving in with you if we can talk about our future together. I mean, I'm not getting any younger. I'm about to turn forty," I told him.

One Friday afternoon, after searching apartments all over New York City and Connecticut for months, we decided to sign a lease for a larger apartment in my building. The following Saturday, we were out running errands, and as we walked out the front door, Adam started walking toward Central Park.

"Where are you going," I asked him.

"Let's walk through the park," he said.

"Are you kidding me right now? It's like one hundred degrees outside, and I'm sweating. Please, can't we take the air-conditioned bus?"

He agreed, not that I gave him a choice.

With no makeup or lipstick on (lipstick is always a must for a Southern woman no matter the situation, according to my mom) and my hair stuffed into a baseball hat, we trudged through the city, running our errands. It was a typical sweltering summer day in New York City. I despised these days living in the city.

After we got home, as I lay on the couch trying to cool off, Adam walked over and got down on one knee. I just stared at him.

"I think I know what will look great in our new apartment," he started. "This ring on your finger. Will you marry me?"

Was he kidding me right now? What? I'm not even sure I realized what was happening because my heart was racing, and I was so hot and filthy.

"Oh my gosh, did you just ask me to marry you?" I screamed.

"Yes. What do you think?"

I looked at myself and then at my unpolished fingernails and cracked cuticles and said, "Hold that thought. I want to run downstairs and get a manicure."

It would have been sacrilege to get engaged with unmanicured nails.

I grabbed my purse and ran out the door. I busted into the nail salon where I'd been going for years and told the owner, "I just got engaged, and my nails are a mess. Quick, I need the fastest manicure before he changes his mind."

I went back upstairs, opened the door, and said, "Now, please ask me again."

He did, and of course, I said yes. But what I wanted to say was, "What took you so long?" Poor Adam. Did he think it through who he was asking to marry him?

He'd made reservations for dinner at Café des Artistes, a famous restaurant down the street from my apartment he knew I'd always wanted to try.

"I didn't want to propose at the restaurant because the minute you learned that's where we were having dinner, you'd figure it out. I had to stay ten steps ahead of you because I can't hide anything from you," he said. "I wanted to propose in Central Park, but it was too hot for you."

Yep, I officially felt like an ass. But no matter because the proposal was perfect, and I now had freshly manicured nails to show off my beautiful engagement ring.

I couldn't believe it. Me—engaged. I never thought I'd see the day. I honestly thought that ship had sailed a long time ago. Who gets married for the first time at forty? But as happy as I felt, a big hole pierced my heart. I desperately wanted to share this news with Celia, the one person who would be the most excited for me.

When alone, I imagined my conversation with her: *"Celia, I'm engaged! You'd love Adam. He's a wonderful man who loves me a lot. Oh, and he cooks, so I don't ever have to. How great is that? Mama and Daddy are so excited, and they love Adam, too. Daddy is excited to have someone to play golf with him and talk politics. He's also bald like Daddy. I wish you were here to be my matron of honor because you're now married with several children. It would be the perfect day if you were here. But I know you'll be with me through all the planning and for the big day. Tell me I'm doing the right thing? I know I am, but I wish you were here to support me and be part of this journey. I knew this moment would be one of the hardest: getting married without you. The other moment will be if I have a child, but I'm just happy to get married at my advanced age. I love you and miss you every day."*

Chapter 24

I had the absurd idea I wanted us to get married in New York City. Having planned many client events in town, I knew different venue locations, whom to speak to, and what to ask. The only thing I didn't realize was when you used the word "wedding," the price automatically increases by fifty percent. We ultimately chose Florida for a mini-destination wedding for our family and friends.

I hadn't told Hannah about the engagement because she was out of town on business. When we finally connected, I screamed, "I'm engaged."

"Oh my gosh, Havey, that is so exciting. Have you picked a date?"

"Yes, Saturday, January 15, 2005."

"Oh no. I think I have a conflict," she said.

I started crying. How could I get married without Hannah? I wasn't marrying her, but I couldn't do this without her there. Hannah and I were the ultimate problem solvers, and there had to be a solution to this massive problem. And I had it.

I called Adam and said, "If the hotel has January 8, 2005, available, would you mind if we switched the date?"

I explained Hannah's conflict, and right away, he understood.

"You can't get married without Hannah," he said.

I called Hannah back.

"Would you mind if I got married on your anniversary?"

Hannah and her husband Dan's anniversary was January 8. It made sense because Hannah and I had shared so much; why wouldn't we share an anniversary, too?

She started screaming. "No way, you're serious? Of course I wouldn't mind, and we will both be there!"

Everything began to fall into place for our perfect wedding. And then life happened—again.

In October, three months before the wedding, Adam and I flew to Florida to meet with the vendors, and then we flew to Houston to buy my wedding gown. Before I arrived in Houston, I called the man in charge of the bridal division of Al's Formal Wear and asked for his help.

"Emil, I'm getting married, and I need a dress," I told him.

"I never thought I'd live to see this day," he said.

Neither did I.

When I worked at Al's Formal Wear, and we would participate in bridal fairs, Emil often asked me to try on a dress to see how it looked, and I always declined.

"First, I'm not a model," I told him. And then I added, "Besides, I don't want to jinx anything by trying on a bridal gown with no groom prospects."

We'd always get a good laugh. But now it was my turn to try on gowns for my wedding.

Melinda and Kay went with me to look at dresses, fitting since they were both like sisters. Before we got to the bridal store, I asked Melinda the big question.

"Will you be my matron of honor?"

Of course, she said yes.

"And you can choose whatever you want to wear," I said.

I thought she'd be thrilled compared to her wedding, where we all wore dropped waist fuchsia dresses with shoulder pads and matching dyed shoes. Oh, how I didn't miss 90s fashion styles.

Getting married at forty years old meant we were way beyond the pomp and circumstance of having a large bridal party. And while I would have loved to have returned the favor of making my friends wear tacky bridesmaid dresses in all colors of the rainbow, I passed. Instead, I just made sure Melinda stood right by my side.

They always say you know the dress when you see it, and I knew the minute I tried on the first gown I selected.

"You should try on a few more," Melinda said.

And I did, but I kept coming back to the first dress. The simple plain white strapless dress with no ornamentation and beautiful satin butter-like fabric spoke to me. I loved everything about it, especially the price. It was reasonable already, being off-the-rack and not a special-order gown. But add in the Emil "friends and family" discount, and I had the ultimate bargain. I think I paid more for alterations. With my dress selected, everything started to fall into place, and the countdown to the wedding had officially begun.

Unfortunately, things started going downhill with my uncle Joe's health in early December.

"I'm flying to St. Louis to get your uncle's affairs in order," my mother informed me.

I decided to meet her so I could say goodbye.

"You need to prepare yourself before you go inside because he's lost a lot of weight, and he doesn't look like he did when you saw him six months ago," my mother told me when I arrived at his condo.

I couldn't shake the déjà vu thought of my mother saying those exact words just before I walked into Celia's hospital room the day she died.

His face lit up when I saw him. "Judy, I'm so happy to see you," he cried.

I ran and threw my arms around him, ecstatic to see him.

"Let me see your engagement ring," he said.

I proudly held my hand out for him to see it.

"I'm so happy for you and Adam, and I just wish I could be there."

We both sat there and cried. I wanted him to be there, too. I was so tired of death and cancer. While mine wasn't the only family to be stricken with this insidious illness, it still hurt. My uncle didn't deserve this. Yes, he could have taken better care of himself, but being struck down in this harsh, brutal way made me so angry. But I had to pull it together. I didn't want to make him feel worse about things.

Instead, I turned the conversation into happy reminiscing. Over the next several days, we talked about the letters I wrote him as a young girl, always asking for money and begging him to visit me. He kept many of them, and we read them together.

"How about always signing my letters with 'your favorite niece' but then adding 'next to Celia' at the end?"

Celia and I had an extraordinary relationship with our uncle Joe. He never had children, so we were like his daughters and his nieces.

In addition to getting his affairs in order, the other big thing my mother had to handle was the funeral arrangements. My uncle had precise instructions when it came to cost and his friends.

"He wants to be buried in Wharton next to Mama and Daddy and fly these people to Texas for the funeral service," my mother explained.

"Boy, we spent a lot of money on your funeral," I jokingly said after returning from the funeral home.

"I hope you're kidding," he replied.

"Nope, we bought the most expensive package with the top-of-the-line casket and everything."

He just stared at me.

"You know I'm just messing with you," I finally told him.

"Not funny," he said.

Even at the very end, he remained one of the most frugal men I'd ever known. Later that evening, I sat next to him on his bed.

"Uncle Joe, can I ask you a favor?"

He looked at me and said, "Anything, Judy."

"When you see Celia, will you tell her I miss and love her every day?"

We both just cried. "I will, but I'm sure she knows that," he said.

"Are you afraid to die?" I asked.

"No, I'm not afraid. I'm just angry that it's happening now. I'm worried about leaving your mother and you, especially since you're getting married and starting a family soon. I'm just furious."

Then we talked about the importance of good friends in life, seeing how all of his dear friends had rallied around him in these final days.

"You are very blessed to have a good group of friends to lean on," he said.

He always loved my friends.

"Lifelong friendships are sometimes more important than family," he said.

So true, I thought.

"But even though I'm very fortunate to have good friends, family is important, too, and I'm so blessed to be your uncle."

We sat in silence until he fell asleep. The following day when the time came for me to leave, I wasn't sure I'd have the strength to say goodbye.

"Thank you for everything you ever did for me. I'm so happy you were my uncle, and I'll love you always. And don't worry, I'll do my best to take care of Mama," I told him through buckets of tears. I'm pretty sure I didn't stop crying until I got home to New York.

About a week after returning from St. Louis, I talked to my mom while I was at work. "Hang on, a call is coming through from St. Louis on the other line," she said.

When she returned, she started screaming, "He's gone, Judy. Uncle Joe died."

Life is filled with sorrow and joy, and sometimes these sentiments can collide at a moment's notice. While we all knew the possibility of my uncle dying close to the wedding date, after speaking with the rabbi, we decided not to cancel, no matter the timing. The rabbi explained, "In Judaism, we believe the joy of a wedding should continue even during tragedy because it's our sacred duty to celebrate marriage."

I once again found myself confronted with unthinkable grief, but just like life continued after Celia died, I knew it would continue again after my uncle's passing. But that didn't stop the supernova explosion of emotions I felt.

Chapter 25

My cell phone rang while I was standing at a bus stop on Madison Avenue. I looked at the number and didn't recognize it but decided to answer. "Hi, this is Devon with *The New York Times* Styles section," the voice on the other line sang.

OH-MY-GAWD, I thought to myself. On a dare, several weeks prior, I submitted our wedding information to the Styles section to see if they'd run the announcement. A wedding announcement in *The New York Times* Styles section was a coveted fête, and they let you know it, too.

But Devon's call wasn't to let me know we'd been selected. No. He called to get more information like copies of our diplomas and Adam's exact position at his company.

"I'm sorry, but I don't think I'll be able to send this information to you in time," I explained.

"Well, if you can't, I'm sorry to say we won't consider your wedding announcement for our section."

Seeing as minutes before this call, I had learned my favorite uncle had passed away, I'm pretty sure the last thing I cared about was *The New York Times*. That probably explained my obnoxious response to Devon.

"Wow, I work with *The New York Times* on behalf of clients seeking coverage in your paper. If fact-checkers of news stories were half as thorough as you are, I'd imagine there'd never be a need for retractions," I said.

Silence.

I ended with, "Well, Devon, thank you for your consideration. I guess my wedding won't be gracing the Styles section pages, but I'm certain it will still be an amazing event."

Yep, I probably could have handled that whole conversation a lot better. Oh well.

* * *

We arrived in Texas on Christmas Day, and the funeral took place the following day. Adam and I met my parents at the hotel.

"This is for you and Adam," my mom said as she handed me an envelope. "It's a wedding gift from your uncle."

I opened the card and started to cry. The card included a check for $5,000. "No," I said. "It's too much."

Of course, my frugal uncle would give us such a substantial gift after he died, and I couldn't tease him about parting with his money.

"He wanted to make sure you and Adam bought something special," she said.

We would later buy a beautiful China cabinet to store all our crystal, wedding gifts, and other sentimental knickknacks, many of which belonged to him. We flew home to New York the day after the funeral, and the countdown to the wedding began, albeit with the heaviest of hearts.

Adam and I touched down in Florida the Wednesday before the wedding.

"I knew I'd forget something," I told him. We'd bought a Lladró bride and groom figurine as our cake topper. But I realized I'd left it at home.

"I'll just find another one," I said.

Nothing could upset me this weekend after burying my uncle only a week before. It just didn't matter. I'd been around many overstressed brides, and I vowed not to be a bridezilla.

The rehearsal dinner took place on the Friday night before the wedding. There was so much love in the room, with many family members and friends there to celebrate with us, and it overwhelmed me. While my heart was heavy, missing my uncle and my sister, I knew they weren't far from me and were probably watching everything together from above.

* * *

Saturday, January 8, 2005. My wedding day! Melinda stayed by my side the entire day as we hung out in the bridal suite, drinking champagne while getting our hair and makeup done.

While the photographer took pictures of the wedding party under the chuppah, I heard someone yell from above, "Hey, Havey." I looked up to see Hannah and Dan coming in from the beach. "I love you so much," she screamed.

"I love you, and Happy Anniversary!"

It was perfect.

Butterflies filled my stomach as we got closer to showtime. It was not that I had cold feet about marrying Adam or getting married in general. I just couldn't believe this day—my wedding day—was happening.

We gathered in the bridal suite to sign the ketubah, the Jewish marriage certificate. Rabbi Fratello, our Italian-Jewish rabbi, explained the story of the ketubah.

"In ancient times, the ketubah was more like a bill of sale whereby the father would give their daughter in marriage to a suitor. Today, it's a little different," he said.

And out of my father's smart-ass mouth came, "Not really. I mean, I'm happy to sell you to the highest bidder."

I loved this sarcastic man. Like the night before, so much love filled the room. They always say you never remember details about your wedding because you're busy taking pictures and making sure everything goes well. And that's true, but I'll never forget all the special people in that room.

With everyone set, it came time for my parents to walk me down the aisle. As we turned the corner to start walking, I saw my cousins, Mark and Jay, running in front of us to sit down.

"Of course, you'd be late," I said to Mark.

"He forgot his hair gel," Jay said.

Mark shrugged, gave me sympathetic eyes, and said, "You look great."

Honestly, that made the evening even more perfect because it represented how my family never takes itself too seriously and always has fun.

Rabbi Fratello began the ceremony with prayers and an explanation of the Jewish wedding ceremony. We had a lot of non-Jews in the room. Two birds flew into the room and circled the chuppah at one point. I turned to my mother and father.

"It's Celia and Uncle Joe," I said.

I knew they'd give me a sign. And while there wasn't a dry eye in the room at the end of the service, everyone smiled and cheered with happiness when Adam finally stomped on the glass, and Rabbi Fratello declared, "Mazel tov to Mr. and Mrs. Adam Cohen!"

Married. I couldn't believe it, and I couldn't wait to start my life with Adam, even as nervous as I'd been all day. But first, we had a kick-ass party to attend to with two bands (one to play when the other took a break), an open bar, great food, two wedding cakes, and lots of love. I knew how happy my uncle and sister would have been if they'd been with us in person, even though I knew they were both with us in our hearts—and under the chuppah.

The following day, before we went downstairs to attend our good-bye brunch, my cell phone rang. It was my friend Karen from New York. She couldn't attend the wedding because of the recent death of her father.

"Hello, Mrs. Cohen," she said. "Or should I say Mrs. *New York Times* Styles section?"

I couldn't believe it. They ran our announcement in *The New York Times*. I guess Devon had appreciated my direct approach after all.

Chapter 26

Something isn't right. I kept telling myself this when flying home from a business trip to Dallas. I had a peculiar feeling in my stomach. With my period one week late, I didn't think much about it since I'd never been one to have a regular cycle. But this time, I felt different. I didn't know why; I just did.

I decided to consult everyone's favorite doctor, WebMD, the website people use to self-diagnose brain tumors, heart conditions, and every other disorder they're certain they have. I searched the site to find an ovulation calendar. Could I be pregnant? If anyone could tell me, it would be WebMD.

After a few calculations on the ovulation calendar, I saw the dates I would have been ripe for baby-making, and my stomach dropped. When Adam and I returned from St. Louis, where we helped my parents clean out my uncle Joe's condo, we were very excited to finally have some alone time. The emotions from the weekend were overwhelming, and oh, by the way, we were still newlyweds.

Adam and I had been cautious while we were dating, except once. I went almost two weeks past my normal cycle and convinced myself I was pregnant.

"You know I'll marry you," he told me as I was freaking out.

At thirty-nine, there was never a thought that I wouldn't have the baby if it turned out I was indeed pregnant—regardless of whether he would marry me or not. At that point in our relationship, we hadn't talked about getting married, much less having children.

We went to buy a pregnancy test at the drugstore that night. "How do you know which one to choose?" I asked after seeing twenty different brands. I just picked the one I always saw advertised on TV. Oh, the power of the brand. I went home and took the test.

It was one thing to pee in a cup at the doctor's office but peeing on a stick in your bathroom is another experience. I was surprised I even got any on the strip. We waited. Negative.

"Well, that's that," I said.

Strangely, I cried. Since we weren't trying to conceive, the fact that I wasn't pregnant turned out to be a letdown. The pregnancy kit came with two tests, so I decided to keep the second one just in case I needed it in the future.

"If you could choose between buying an apartment in New York City or having a baby, which would you want?" Adam asked me one night when we were walking in the city.

"I'd choose both," I told him.

I wanted a baby but also knew I'd be happy with whatever God's plan was. And since my entire life felt unplanned to this point, I never gave having a child much thought. Hey, I didn't think I'd ever get married, so I'd already defied the odds. Regardless of what the calendar said, I couldn't imagine being pregnant, no matter how I felt. I mean, seriously, at forty years old?

I came home from work, and Adam was standing in the kitchen, making one of his fabulous dinners.

"Hi, I'm home," I called out. "I'll be right out. I just need to pee."

I dug up the pregnancy test I'd been saving and locked myself in the bathroom. At first, I hesitated to take it but finally gave in. I read the directions, peed on the stick, and waited. For some reason, I read the instructions wrong. I thought it said two pink lines meant you weren't pregnant. After waiting three minutes, the strip showed two pink lines. I sat quietly by myself for a few minutes, feeling a little depressed. Oh well, we'd have to try again.

"This can't be right," I told myself. I'm not sure what prompted me to reread the directions, but this time I read two pink lines meant you *were* pregnant. Again, I sat quietly by myself to gather my thoughts. Could this be true? Was the test defective? Did it have an expiration date I didn't know about? Was I pregnant?

Instead of asking these questions to myself and having no one answer me, I walked out of the bathroom and started pacing around the room. How would I tell Adam? Would he be upset I got pregnant so soon? Again, I asked questions to no one, expecting someone to answer me.

I decided on the direct, "rip the Band-Aid off" approach.

"Adam, I need to show you something," I said after grabbing his hand and dragging him towards the bathroom.

Before he got to the door, he looked at me and said, "You're pregnant?"

My eyes said it all. We just stood there for a moment with smiles and tears, and then laughter and shock. We'd been married for about six weeks. Wow, that didn't take long at all. Talk about Fertile Myrtle!

After dinner, we went to the pharmacy to buy more pregnancy tests to be sure.

"Let's buy different brands just in case there's been a recall on one brand I didn't know about," I said.

All the new tests clearly showed two pink lines. Yep, we were pregnant.

"We haven't even ordered our wedding pictures, but we are having a baby."

Living in New York City, you get used to waiting in lines for restaurants, apartments, sample sales, and the latest culinary trends. Can you say Cronut? But who knew there were waiting lists for ob-gyns to confirm you're pregnant?

"Dr. Levine's first available appointment is in two weeks," the nurse said.

"Just to confirm I'm pregnant?" I asked.

How could I wait two weeks to confirm whether the six pregnancy tests I just took were accurate?

"I'll put you on our waiting list, and if someone cancels, I'll call you right away."

Why would anyone cancel one of these appointments more coveted than an appointment with a hair colorist? But I agreed to wait. I started to panic and desperately wanted my mother.

"She would know what to do," I told Adam.

"Yes, but don't you want to wait to tell them in person when we see them next weekend?" he replied.

I did. But I rarely kept secrets from my parents. Now an adult, I finally grew out of my rebellious days where I shared nothing with them.

"I just spoke to Dr. Saltzman, and she's squeezing you in tomorrow for a blood test," Adam told me when he called me at work the next day.

"That's the best news ever," I said.

After getting married, Dr. Saltzman, Adam's internist, became my doctor. Thankfully, we were having dinner guests that night, which would keep my mind off the pregnancy. The next day might confirm my life would soon change forever.

"I have to leave early this afternoon for a dentist appointment," I told my co-workers.

I hated lying to them. I just knew I'd get a cavity because of this tale. Adam met me at Dr. Saltzman's office.

"I didn't go to the bathroom yet if I need to pee in a cup," I proudly told the nurse.

"We're doing the blood work first," she snarked back.

"Oh, I hate needles passionately, so I just wanted you to know."

She looked at me with no expression. And boy, did I learn how much Adam freaked out about needles, too. More so than me.

"I will call every ob-gyn in our network to try and get you an appointment sooner than the one you have with Dr. Levine," Dr. Saltzman told me.

Unfortunately, she didn't have any luck either, and in fact, some told her it would be another month to see new patients. I always knew New York City to be a very competitive town. I guess this included amongst fertile women, too.

"I will get you an appointment with an ob-gyn, so don't worry," Dr. Saltzman assured me.

As I left the doctor's office, it started snowing. We were in February, so that was not unusual at all. But this snow felt different as it came down hard and fast. Later that evening, our phone rang.

"It's Anne from Dr. Levine's office," she said. "Are you able to come to our uptown office tomorrow morning? We've had a lot of cancellations from our patients in New Jersey and Connecticut because of the snowstorm."

At that very moment, I decided I loved snowstorms. While it was good news, I had to lie once again to my co-workers about why I wouldn't be there in the morning. Oh well, maybe it would snow so hard the office would close. Doubtful, but a good thought.

Before Dr. Levine came into the examination room, I had to meet with his nurse for her to take my vitals. "So you know, I hate needles passionately," I told her.

I felt that the more I explained this fact to anyone who listened, especially those holding the needles, the less it would hurt.

"Oh, you should be a fun patient," she replied. "How old are you?" she asked me while taking my vitals.

"I'm forty," I said.

With her mouth open, she replied, "What? That can't be possible. I thought you were in your late twenties, early thirties."

I had to remember to be very nice to her.

Dr. Levine entered the room with a med student, Phillip. I'm not sure who appeared more nervous about being in that room, Phillip, or me.

I looked at Phillip and said, "How old are you?" I kid you not, Phillip looked sixteen.

Dr. Levine started his examination and confirmed my uterus was soft, whatever that meant. For some reason, my nervousness turned into chatter.

"I just got married and didn't think I could get pregnant so fast," I babbled on.

"That's when it always happens when you're not trying," he responded. "When was your last period?" he asked.

"I think about January 19," I replied.

At the same time, without blinking, Dr. Levine and Phillip both said, "You're due October 26."

Wow, how did they know that, and so quickly?

They explained, "The way to determine a woman's pregnancy due date is to count backward three months from her last period and add seven days. It's not always accurate, but it's a good baseline."

I continued with a rapid round of questions.

"How much weight should I gain?"—twenty-five to thirty pounds. Yikes, that was a lot of weight.

"When can I get my hair colored?"—after twelve weeks. I thought we might need to negotiate that one.

"Can I eat sushi?"—No. Okay, I would give you that one if you could give me an earlier hair color date.

"Can I travel to Italy for my honeymoon in April?"—Yes, where are you going?

That question turned into a fifteen-minute conversation about Tuscany and where to go. Once the question-and-answer session of the appointment concluded, I then had the pleasure of another six vials of blood drawn, including the "Jew" test, as Dr. Levine called it—Tay Sachs.

After a very long morning, I called Adam once I got back to the office.

"You are going to be a father," I confirmed.

Even though he remained silent, I could feel his smile. In less than twenty-four hours, I had two doctors appointments for multiple examinations, a battery of blood tests, a scheduled sonogram, and other tests. All I wanted was my mother and a cheeseburger.

I secretly wondered if my child would say the same thing about wanting me one day. I wouldn't trade anything to see my parents' faces when they learned they'd soon be grandparents. They were robbed of this moment after my sister died and seeing how long it took for me to get my act together, this might be their only opportunity. Every time I thought about it, I'd get all choked up. But I knew my mother would understand my withholding this information.

Adam made a dinner reservation at one of our favorite restaurants, Balthazar, to celebrate the occasion.

"Here's to parenthood," we toasted—me with a ginger ale, of course.

"I just can't wrap my mind around the fact that we will be parents," I told Adam.

I prayed we would have a beautiful, healthy baby at the end of the pregnancy journey.

On our way home from dinner, we stopped at our neighborhood Barnes and Noble and bought the book *What to Expect When You're Expecting*. the bible for all new parents. As we stood in the checkout line, I started laughing.

"When Melinda was pregnant with Shelly, her first child, she wanted a copy of the book but wasn't feeling well enough to go to the store," I said. "She sent Steven and me to the bookstore to buy it, and when we got there, Steven told me to go buy it because he didn't want anyone to see him holding it. I said okay, but do you think it's okay for me, an unmarried woman with someone else's husband, to be seen buying it?"

I couldn't believe I was buying the book for myself all these years later.

When we got home, I started reading.

"Just getting a glimpse into pregnancy is enough to make me want to go into hiding for the next nine months," I said.

The following weekend, Adam and I traveled to Florida. I couldn't wait to get there and tell my parents. I could imagine their faces when we told them they were going to be grandparents. The ride from the airport to their house felt so long because I couldn't wait to share this news, and I had to pee. I didn't want to blurt it out in the car, but the anticipation overwhelmed me.

Once we got to the house, I quickly dropped our suitcases in the bedroom and joined everyone in the living room.

"Daddy, are we all up to date on payments from the wedding?" I asked.

"Yes, I think so," he replied.

Then I smiled and said, "Well, that's good because you will have to start putting money away for college."

My mother looked at me and then at Adam and my father and screamed, "You're pregnant."

This is precisely how I'd always envisioned this moment. Happy tears and smiling faces.

And then came the sarcastic retort from my father. "Well, that didn't take you long. You're just like your mother."

I wouldn't have expected anything less. His statement about me being like my mother referred to how she got pregnant on their honeymoon. They were married on November 25, 1956, and Celia arrived on August 17, 1957. However, our ages were the main differences between my mother and me: twenty-one and forty years old. Compared to her, I was a walking medical miracle. That was a generation or lifetime apart.

"How far along are you?" my mother asked.

"I'm about seven weeks along, so you can't tell anyone for another five weeks."

I mainly directed that statement at my father, often challenged in the secret-keeping category.

"Whether you have a boy or girl, I'll take them golfing, and we need to clean the old train set," my father proudly told us.

They were going to be the best grandparents ever. My child would be so loved and so fortunate to have them in their life. I couldn't believe my life right now. Adam and I were married and having a baby, and my parents were going to become grandparents. And then this thing called life happened—again.

* * *

Shortly after we came home from Florida, my parents were heading out on a cruise to Europe.

"Here's our email address for the cruise. If you need to get in touch with me for anything, I'll have access to this when we're docked at a port," my mother said.

I wasn't sure why I'd need to contact them, but I took it just in case. "Have a great time, and please don't buy too many tchotchkes for the baby."

But I knew she wouldn't listen to me.

I had an ultrasound around the ninth week of my pregnancy. I couldn't wait to see this little nugget, even though I knew, according to my book, there probably wouldn't be much to see at this point. When we got to the doctor's office, they directed us to the room for the ultrasound. As we eagerly waited for the technician to come in, I looked at Adam. "Are you ready for this?"

He smiled and said, "Well, there's no turning back now."

The technician came in. "Okay, let's take a look."

My heart started racing, and my palms were sweaty. I'd seen scenes like this on television and in movies hundreds of times, but I never believed I'd be the person lying on the table. And then the technician got quiet.

"Have you been sick lately?" he finally asked.

"No, why?" I said.

"There seems to be some fluid behind the neck, but I'm sure it's nothing."

My heart started racing again, and I felt like I was going to pass out.

"Fluid, what do you mean by that?" I asked.

He pointed to a discolored spot on the ultrasound, but I couldn't tell what I was looking at. "Let me get Dr. Levine," he said.

I grabbed Adam's hand and started to cry.

"Don't worry yet," he calmly said.

But how could I not worry? He just asked me if I had been sick and then said something didn't look right. This was precisely the time for me to worry.

We continued waiting for an eternity, and finally, Dr. Levine entered the room. "Get dressed and then meet me at my office across the hall where we can talk," he told us.

My legs were so shaky, I felt like I would faint. Adam held my hand and helped me walk across the hall.

"We're not sure, but there appears to be fluid behind the neck, which can indicate chromosomal issues," Dr. Levine explained.

I'm pretty sure I zoned out because I don't remember what else he said. All I heard was something could be wrong with my baby.

"We want to wait another week and have you come back for another ultrasound, so we can definitively say what we're looking at," he continued. "Until we fully understand what's going on, you will need to prepare yourself for the possibility that this baby might have a chromosomal issue like Down's Syndrome and ask yourself if this is something you can handle."

Feeling overwhelmed, I couldn't think of anything to ask him. I finally found my voice. "Dr. Levine, did I do something to cause this?"

He looked at me with sympathetic eyes and said, "Judy, you didn't do anything wrong. These things happen, and unfortunately, we don't always know why."

That explanation eerily sounded like so many other events in my life. The random act of violence with me and Celia dying sat at the top of the list. While I lived my life never wanting to play the victim card, I couldn't understand at this moment why these things kept happening to me.

After we left his office, I wanted to go home and cry. How would I get through the next week? Adam and I barely spoke as we made our way home.

Over the next several days, I read everything I could on the internet about chromosomal issues during pregnancy, and none of what I read looked good.

"I know it would be a huge challenge to bring a Down's baby into the world, but how could we ever decide not to?" I said to Adam.

"We just need to wait and see what we learn at our next appointment," he said.

He became my voice of reason.

At our appointment, they took us to the ultrasound room first. We had a different technician this time. She took several pictures then told me to get dressed and head back to the waiting room.

"Why didn't she say anything to us about what she saw?" I asked Adam.

"Maybe she wants to consult with Dr. Levine first," he said.

Dr. Levine brought us back to his office, and I knew from the look on his face he didn't have good news for us.

"I'm so sorry, but there's no heartbeat," he solemnly told us.

"Wait, what?" I asked. "I thought there was just a chromosomal issue. What do you mean there's no heartbeat?"

He grabbed my hand and said, "Judy, the baby died."

No stranger to death, but the revelation that a tiny baby—my tiny baby—that had been growing inside me just died, and I'd never get the chance to meet them or love them, that I couldn't grasp. Feeling total numbness, I stared into space as Dr. Levine kept talking. "We often see chromosomal issues in-utero with older moms," Dr. Levine explained.

And there he said what scared me the most, the "older moms" comment that hung over me like a heavy cloud.

"I knew it was my fault," I said.

"No, it's not," he said. "You're a perfectly healthy woman, and all I'm saying is sometimes women past the age of thirty-five have these things happen, but it doesn't mean you can't try again if you want."

Try again? Could I even do that knowing this could happen?

"We'll have to schedule a D&C, the procedure to remove the tissue," he said.

That comment hit me like a gut punch. Not only did I lose the baby, but now I had to have a procedure to remove it. I couldn't stop my tears and felt sick to my stomach, which explains why I threw up when we got home from the doctor's office.

"Are you going to get in touch with your parents to let them know?" Adam asked me.

They were still on their cruise, and suddenly I realized how important it was that my mother had given me her email address.

"I guess I'll write them an email, so they'll stop buying things for the baby," I said.

I sat down to write the email and couldn't stop crying. My tears were not just for me. They were also for my parents. It still felt like a massive loss at only ten weeks pregnant. And I couldn't stop thinking of how Dr. Levine kept referring to the baby now as "tissue." I realized he only meant it as a clinical term, but to me, I just lost a baby, not a bunch of cells.

I finished typing the email and hit send. I explained everything and assured my parents that I would be okay. At least physically. Their well-being concerned me more than my own. A day later, I got a response that said, "We are so sorry, and we love you both very much. We will see you when we get home." I'm sure my mother and father had more to say, but honestly, their words, albeit few, carried all the compassion I needed.

I scheduled the procedure for the following week. But before I left the office that night, I spoke with my co-workers.

"You don't know that I was pregnant. Unfortunately, I lost the baby, so tomorrow I have to have a procedure to remove it," I said.

I couldn't bring myself to call it tissue. I worked with all women, and there wasn't a dry eye in the room.

"We will hold down the fort for you, so don't worry about anything," they all told me.

I wasn't worried about the office. My concern centered on me and how I would move past this whole ordeal. I had to channel the inner strength that I knew existed from all the other times in my life I needed it. I had to tell myself, like always, ours is not to question the ultimate plan for our life. Funny, it still sounded like bullshit to me, even after all these years.

"If I could just get through this procedure with no IV or needles, I'd feel more relaxed," I told Adam.

My heart wouldn't stop racing, and I couldn't stop crying. How did this happen?

"We'll get through this, and then we'll be on our honeymoon in a few weeks," Adam sympathetically said.

Yes, our honeymoon. We decided not to take our honeymoon directly after the wedding and instead enjoy Italy and Switzerland in the spring. Before the pregnancy, I couldn't wait to get to Europe. I'd only been to England and France, so adding stamps from Italy and Switzerland to my passport excited me. I just prayed I'd stop crying by the time the flight took off.

"I need you to change into this robe, and I'll be back to start your IV," the nurse said to me.

Oh grand, the IV. My favorite thing ever.

"I have small veins, so please be careful," I pleaded—my forever disclaimer before getting stuck with a needle.

"Ouch," I cried when she made her first attempt.

"You have to keep still," she barked back at me.

"You're hurting me."

And I started to cry more. This hurt, and I wasn't just being a wimp for once. But were my tears because Nurse Ratched was jamming a thick needle in my arm like I was a human pin cushion, or because of the procedure? She finally hooked up the IV, and Adam and I sat quietly, waiting for my turn.

"I just wanted to see if you had any questions and check how you were doing before proceeding," said Dr. Levine.

"Well, now that the horrible nurse who gave me the IV is gone, I'm doing better," I replied.

"If you ever feel uncomfortable in a situation like this, always ask for the doctor to put the IV in."

Now he told me.

"How long will this take?" I asked.

"Not long," he said. "We'll let Adam know when we're done, and then he can wait with you until you feel strong enough to get up and go home."

I didn't think I'd ever feel strong again. I just wanted this whole ordeal to be over. To this day, every October 26, I mourn for a life I'll never meet or know and for what could have been.

I took the next couple of days off from work to recuperate. I didn't leave the apartment and barely left my bed.

"We'll come up to New York after we get home from our cruise," my mom wrote in an email.

"Thank you," I wrote back. "I need you."

And I did. I needed my mother more than I even imagined. I just knew her being with me would bring a sense of calm, and it did.

"Is it me, or is every woman on the Upper West Side of Manhattan pregnant?" I asked my mom while walking around the neighborhood some days later.

I swear I never noticed how many little kids, nannies, and pregnant women lived around me, but I guess I'd now become hyper-focused on this category of people.

"Geez, you can't walk a block without running the risk of being mowed down by a stroller," I said. "Maybe we should move."

Chapter 27

"Would you like champagne before we take off?" the flight attendant asked as we boarded our flight to Zurich. Adam had treated us with first-class tickets, and I could tell already the experience would be nothing short of spectacular.

"Champagne, yes, please," I replied.

Now that I wasn't pregnant, I would be drinking my way across Europe, and what better way to start than by indulging as we traveled across the pond. Not that alcohol would replace the void of what I'd just lost, but it could at least allow me to enjoy the many tastes of Europe I'd have missed if I were still pregnant. Of course, I would have gladly skipped alcoholic beverages in all of Europe to still be pregnant.

I ended up sleeping for much of the flight and woke up with about an hour left to go.

"Ladies and gentlemen, this is your captain speaking. We're starting our approach into Zurich," the pilot announced.

"I'm starving," I told Adam.

And as if on demand, the flight attendant came over with the most beautiful smelling pastries and coffee.

"You know you've ruined me for future air travel forever," I told Adam. "How on earth can I ever go back to coach? It's like another world behind the curtain."

At customs, the agent said, "Welcome to Switzerland. Are you here on business or pleasure?"

"Pleasure. We're on our honeymoon," I said.

I'm not sure why I felt the need to explain, but the agent smiled.

Because we'd taken an overnight flight, we arrived at the hotel in the morning, and I quickly fell asleep. Probably the worst thing I could have done, but my body was still healing.

Eventually, Adam woke me up. "Let's go explore Zurich and find good food," he said.

On our way, we stopped at the train station to buy our tickets to Florence for the next day.

"This is nothing like Penn Station," I told Adam. "It's too clean, and you don't have people begging you for money or food."

But everyone smoked. And as we walked from the station to the city center, we immediately found the equivalent of Fifth Avenue, Rodeo Drive, and Worth Avenue rolled up into one street.

"Naturally, we'd find this area to shop," I said.

Fortunately for Adam's wallet, everything closed around 5:00 p.m., and we were too late.

"It's like we're walking through a pile of money," I commented.

And like with Starbucks in New York City, a Swiss bank sat on every corner.

We stopped at a tapas bar for dinner. We sat a very long time. "What is taking so long for the food?" I asked.

"We're in Europe, and everything is slower here," he answered.

"But we're eating tapas, not a four-course meal."

Two and half hours later, feeling calmer and full, we finally left.

The following day we boarded our train to Florence. Like our flight, Adam had booked us first-class tickets. It felt like an Agatha Christie novel before anything terrible happened.

"This train is nothing like the Amtrak," I said.

We eventually made our way to the dining car, where we found tables with white cloths and napkins.

"Here's a glass of sparkling champagne. Would you like the linguine with tomato sauce or pesto?" the waiter asked as he took our order.

I opted for the tomato sauce, and hands down, it ranked as one of the best plates of pasta I'd ever tasted. I felt like licking the plate.

"It's now time for the beef course. Would you like the beef or pork tenderloin?" he asked.

"He's kidding, right?" I asked Adam.

He wasn't. It's customary for the pasta course to be the appetizer before the beef, chicken, or fish course. I politely passed, and the waiter looked annoyed.

"How on earth isn't everyone in Europe a thousand pounds with all this food?"

After exiting the train station through a cloud of smoke—everyone smoked in this country—we took a taxi to our hotel.

"Buongiorno, Mr. and Mrs. Cohen. We're so happy to have you join us," the hotel manager said as he greeted us.

With Florence as our base, the next several days were filled with endless shopping, glorious sightseeing, calorie-filled meals, and lots and lots of wine.

"Our motto for the trip is 'Ship It, Don't Schlep It'," I said to Adam whenever I found a must-have item.

The thought of carrying everything back to New York overwhelmed me. But we soon learned we could buy the wines at home, and shipping things would cost double what we originally paid.

"Let's take the train to Rome for the day," Adam suggested. "We can leave early in the morning and spend the entire day hitting the hot spots."

I couldn't wait for this spontaneous adventure. They say Rome wasn't built in a day, but Adam and I were determined to try and see as much of it as possible during that short time.

"We can find a hop-on, hop-off bus tour to take us all over," I said.

When we exited the train station to search for a tour bus, a man approached. We must have had "sucker tourist" stamped on our foreheads.

"You are looking for the best tour bus in Rome?" he asked in his thick Italian accent.

"Yes, but we'll just wait in this line," we told him.

"No, no, come with me. My tour has more stops, and we take you to better places," he said.

We hesitantly followed, and as we got further away from the station and started walking down a strange street, I said to Adam, "Let's get the hell out of here."

We quickly bolted and probably saved not only our money but our lives. We found the right bus and were off to explore Roma.

"We'll be stopping at St. Peter's Square, so take your time exploring," our guide said. "But please note that you will not be able to visit Michelangelo's Sistine Chapel because it's in use today. The conclave is meeting to elect a new pope."

Before our trip, Pope John Paul II had passed away, and the selection process for the new pope was underway. While we were disappointed not to see the famous chapel, it thrilled us that history was happening steps away.

"Can you imagine if white smoke comes out while we're here?" I said to Adam.

The Vatican and its history were unlike anything I'd ever experienced. After touring the Basilica, we went underground to see all the crypts where former popes were buried. We even saw Pope John Paul II's tomb.

"Wow, that was fast," I commented. "And I thought they buried Jews quickly."

I slept on the train the entire way back to Florence. Rome did not disappoint, and I couldn't wait to revisit its magic one day.

The next day we were off to Tuscany. Despite the rainy day, we enjoyed all the charm, character, shopping, food, and wine of the region, including San Gimignano, Siena, Greve, and the entire countryside. It was the perfect day.

As we drove up to our hotel, I asked Adam, "Why are so many church bells ringing? It's not even 6:00 p.m."

We had gotten used to hearing church bells every half hour, but these bells were clanging continuously.

He looked at me and said, "They picked a pope."

We quickly ran to our room and turned on the TV to see white smoke pouring out of the stack on top of the Sistine Chapel, and then they showed a shot of St. Peter's Square. But this time, the space that twenty-four hours earlier had sat practically empty was now filled with people celebrating the selection of the new pope.

"We'll always remember we were in Italy when a new pope was chosen," I said.

History in the making.

We decided to eat dinner at our hotel for our last night in Florence. An American couple sat next to us. We learned she was early in her pregnancy but planned this trip before they found out, like our situation just a month ago. It saddened me, but I didn't let it take away anything from our fantastic time in Italy.

"For one of the world's fashion capitals, this train station is filthy," I said as we changed trains from Milan to Lugano the next day.

Scattered with litter and with everyone smoking, the train station looked more like a homeless shelter—anything but fashionable. Once in Lugano, we wandered into the little village and started exploring. The town felt clean, and the people were all so friendly.

"When we retire, I'd like to move here and work in that little chocolate shop. I'll be fat and happy," I told Adam. "You can take pictures of tourists with the mountains in the background. It will be a wonderful life."

I sort of wasn't kidding. If Switzerland wasn't one of the most expensive places on the planet, I could see myself here. We stopped at a cheese shop and then a wine store and picked up a variety of yummy treats for our dinner.

"We've been eating at so many nice restaurants, I'd like to just feast on wine, cheese, and chocolate tonight," I said—the perfect meal in an ideal setting.

*   *   *

Our honeymoon was officially over, at least the trip portion. It felt good to be home and start the next phase of our lives. I had thought it would be difficult to enjoy myself on the trip because of the physical and emotional toll of losing the baby. I had moments of sadness, like meeting the woman at the hotel in her early stages of pregnancy, but I couldn't stop living. If my past experiences of loss and sadness taught me anything, it's that life goes on. And what better way to live than by eating and drinking across Europe?

Even though this vacation helped keep my mind off losing the baby, I couldn't stop obsessing about trying to get pregnant again. I truly wanted a baby, and while my life felt blessed with Adam, I couldn't move past wanting a child. But would I even be able to get pregnant again? And if I did, would I be faced with the same fate?

Chapter 28

Reality quickly set in after Adam and I returned from our fabulous European honeymoon. Every month, I'd remind myself how far along I would have been if I were still pregnant. Such an unhealthy habit, but I couldn't help it. Why did this happen to me?

My mind drifted back to all the bad things that had happened in my life. But then I realized how pathetic I sounded. I had my health, a wonderful husband, a job I loved, and great family and friends who loved me, regardless of whether I had a baby. I needed to end my pity party of one, and fast.

"We're driving up to Virginia and Washington, D.C. this August. Why don't you and Adam meet us?" my mom suggested.

We still had vacation days since neither of us ever used all our days. This sounded like a great getaway to end the summer.

My mom and I spent one afternoon shopping in historical Williamsburg while my dad and Adam golfed.

"Oh, how far along are you?" the saleslady asked me as my mom and I browsed through a store.

I stood in silence, but my mother filled the void. "She's not pregnant, and you should think before speaking," she snapped back.

We walked out of the store.

"Don't let that bother you. She doesn't have any manners," my mom said.

I looked down at my clothes to see if I looked pregnant. I didn't. Ironically, I weighed the least I had in years. Why would she think I was pregnant?

A few weeks after Adam and I got home from the week with my parents, I found out I was pregnant again. We couldn't believe it.

"I guess I lost track of my cycles," I told Adam.

"As Dr. Levine said, it always happens when you're not thinking about it."

Even though the thought of being pregnant again thrilled me, I couldn't get as excited as I did the last time. Would this pregnancy end, too? I knew I had to erase those negative thoughts from my mind and start thinking positively, but I couldn't shake the feeling that something terrible would happen.

At the end of September 2005, I had plans to travel to Miami and speak at a conference, but Hurricane Rita had other plans. This hurricane caused significant damage to Cuba and South Florida, and because of it, the travel conference in Miami was canceled.

"It's probably for the best because I'm not feeling great," I told Adam.

I had the worst stomach cramps and couldn't get off the sofa.

"Maybe you have a stomach virus," Adam said.

"It's either that or something is wrong with the baby," I replied.

I got up to use the bathroom, and I got my answer.

"Adam, you need to call Dr. Levine's office for me. I think I'm miscarrying," I cried.

And that's precisely what happened, right there in my bathroom. Fast but painful—physically and emotionally. I'd never seen so much blood.

"Dr. Levine wants to speak to you," Adam said.

"It happened again," I told him.

I hadn't even had a chance to get an ultrasound.

"Try and save as much of the tissue as you can and come to my office," he told me.

That word again: tissue. I got a Ziplock bag and did as Dr. Levine instructed.

There is no way to adequately describe the heartache of miscarriage. I'm certainly not the only woman to have suffered a miscarriage, and I wouldn't be the last, but it still hurt.

"Why did this happen again?" I asked Dr. Levine when we got to his office. "Is there something wrong with me?"

He once again tried to put things in perspective. "Judy, we don't know why some women miscarry and others don't. Childbirth is a miraculous wonder. But you don't have an issue getting pregnant."

"Oh well, if it's meant to be, it will be," I said.

I felt so defeated.

As the months passed, I tried to keep my mind off getting pregnant, babies, and all things related to motherhood. I had so many blessings, but I desperately wanted a child. This pregnancy journey thus far taught me that I shouldn't get upset over things I couldn't control. I had learned that when Celia died, but as I was younger, it made no sense to me at the time. While I understood the words, in theory, the in-practice part is where I struggled.

"Do you want to go to Paris this weekend for our first anniversary?" Adam asked when he called me at my office.

"Yes, when do we leave!" I screamed.

We had just returned to work after the holiday break and our first anniversary was the following weekend. To surprise me, Adam booked a long weekend in Paris. The spontaneity was just what I needed.

I was lucky enough to see Italy, Switzerland, and soon, Paris, in less than a year. Even though I'd suffered two pregnancy losses, I knew I had to keep living. This was fast becoming a familiar mantra after so many losses in my life. I couldn't think of a better way to do just that than jet-setting off to Paris. I knew a trip to Paris wouldn't erase the sadness of this recent pregnancy loss, but it was still what the doctor ordered to keep my mind off it.

As Audrey Hepburn's character Sabrina says, "Paris is always a good idea." Even when it's freezing in January. The frigid temperatures made this adventure even more memorable.

"Let's take another hop-on, hop-off bus, so we don't miss a thing," I said. "We can just wear blankets with our coats and winter gear to keep warm."

We were fast becoming hop-on, hop-off bus enthusiasts because it was the best way to see everything. We layered on clothing and sat on top of the bus where we could see everything: the Eiffel Tower, Champs de Élysées, Arc de Triomphe, The Louvre, etc.

"When my parents were in Paris, they went to the Moulin Rouge. We can't miss can-can dancing," I said.

Even though it was super touristy and cheesy, we had a fabulous time. We sat with another couple; the wife spoke a little English, and the husband spoke none.

"I speak a little French, so we should be fine," Adam said.

Of course, most of Adam's French came from cooking terms, but it all worked out.

The costumes and dancers were magnificent. I never wanted to leave, except for all the cigarette smoke. I guess Europe didn't get the U.S. memo that said smoking will kill you, and you're no longer allowed to partake in the activity anywhere. But even that didn't ruin the trip.

The food tasted just as I'd imagined: buttery pastries, creamy cheeses, fabulous French cuisine, and delicious champagne.

"Again, how isn't everyone in Europe morbidly obese?" I asked.

"Because the Europeans believe in portion control, and you don't get the pasta troughs like at the all-you-can-eat buffets in the states," Adam said.

How true. Americans certainly know how to indulge in food. But the French, they know how to prepare it. On our final night, Adam made a reservation at Le George, the famous restaurant inside the Four Seasons Hotel. The lobby still had its magnificent Christmas decorations displayed. There were giant gold ornaments and twinkly lights everywhere.

"I feel like we're in a storybook," I told Adam.

When we walked into the restaurant, I noticed only six or seven tables inside. "Are we sure we're in the right place?" I asked.

"Yes, they have limited seating, so guests can relax and enjoy their meals," he explained.

And this wasn't just any meal; it was a magical culinary experience.

"Bonsoir Monsieur et Madame. Welcome to Le George. Will you have our tasting menu this evening?" the waiter asked us.

We said yes, and the marathon meal began.

"Each portion will have a wine pairing," our waiter explained.

We indulged in pâté, tartare, sea bass, lobster spaghetti, and veal. Then came what looked like dessert.

"This is to cleanse your palate for the dessert course," he explained.

I thought I'd explode but kept going. I felt like Mr. Creosote in Monty Python's *The Meaning of Life* at the end of his meal.

"I'm glad portions are small, but they add up," I said. "I don't think I'll need to eat for a week."

The dessert cart came out, and I almost started crying. "It's just too beautiful to eat," I said.

The most glorious pastries and cakes I've ever seen filled the trays. They almost looked fake. After about two and a half hours, we finished the meal, and even though I'd eaten more food than I ever thought possible, I floated out of the restaurant.

"That was the most amazing experience I've ever had. I didn't want it to end," I said. "Can we come back for our second anniversary, too?"

Regardless of where our lives took us after the weekend, we would always be able to say with certainty that we didn't stop living and that "we'll always have Paris."

Chapter 29

A month after Adam and I got home from our glorious last-minute anniversary getaway to Paris, I found out I was pregnant again.

"I want to be happy about this, but I'm worried it will have the same ending," I told Adam. "But I'm hopeful."

And I was, or at least I wanted to believe that.

I scheduled a sonogram with Dr. Levine, and this time, he would be the one performing it. I had no idea how far along this pregnancy was, but my best guess was about eight weeks. As I lay on the examination table watching Dr. Levine, I noticed a puzzled look pass over his face. He kept squinting and staring at the monitor.

"What's wrong, or do I even want to know?" I asked him.

"It appears you have a blighted ovum," he said.

"Does that mean I lost another baby?" I asked

"No, it means there is no baby," he said. "There's a sac, and your body thinks it's pregnant, but a baby never formed."

I sat up and tried to process what he said.

"So let me get this straight. I have the pregnancy hormone in my body, I have the sac where a baby should be, but I have no baby?"

He nodded yes.

"Well, where did it go?" I asked.

"A blighted ovum is a miscarriage that occurs very early in pregnancy," he explained. "The fertilized egg cannot develop into an embryo after it has attached itself to the uterine wall."

I just shook my head. "You're telling me that in less than a year, I've lost one baby to a chromosomal issue, one baby to God knows what, and one baby who was never there, yet there's nothing wrong with me, and these losses are anomalies?"

His response didn't matter because no one would be able to convince me I wasn't responsible for all of this. It reminded me of how my mom felt when Celia got cancer and died. It wasn't my mom's fault, but no one could convince her it had nothing to do with her. Both scenarios were preposterous, but my thinking was beyond rational.

"Unfortunately, I have to perform a D&C to remove the sac," Dr. Levine informed me.

With that announcement, the floodgates opened, and I broke down into a pool of tears. A few days later, I found myself in a familiar unwelcome setting.

"You realize we were in this same spot almost a year ago?" I told Adam while waiting for Dr. Levine.

"And we'll get through this, too," he said.

I felt very fortunate to have him by my side. As hard as these traumas were for me, I'm sure he felt so helpless.

"I wonder if that nasty nurse is here and if she'd remember me," I jokingly said.

And like clockwork, she walked up. "Oh, I'm sorry to see you again under these circumstances," she said.

"Thank you," I replied.

"Just change into this gown, and I'll be back to put in your IV," she said.

Uh, not so fast.

"Dr. Levine said he'd put in my IV when I got to the OR."

She stared at me and snarked, "Okay, but Dr. Levine isn't as good as I am."

I begged to differ.

A few weeks after the procedure, I made an appointment to talk to Dr. Levine about options.

"I'm forty-one years old, so what are the chances of having a baby now?" I asked him.

"Well, we won't put you out to pasture just yet at forty-one, but the percentages do decrease as you get older," he said.

"What about IVF?" I asked.

"Judy, as your doctor, I will help guide you with any decision you make, so if you and Adam think IVF is the path you want to explore, I'm here to help," he said. "But what I'll tell you is that it could take years and what you typically see and hear about, when it comes to this treatment, are only the successes. Maybe you should give your body a rest and see what happens."

So that's what I decided to do.

While I knew IVF proved successful for many women, and you certainly always heard about it, you didn't hear much about the emotional toll of it not working and the amount of time it would take.

I told myself, you know what, I have an amazing life with or without a child, and I'm going to start living it.

I went home that afternoon and told Adam about my conversation with Dr. Levine.

"I think I'd like to hire a personal trainer," I said.

We both belonged to Equinox Fitness at the time, and while I liked to work out, I needed accountability and guidance from someone who would kick my ass.

"I have the perfect person in mind for you, so let me check her availability, and if she's free, I'll have her call you," the guy at Equinox told me.

My phone rang that night.

"Hey, this is Jenny," she said. "I hear you're interested in hiring a personal trainer. Let's get going."

Jenny became more than a personal trainer to me. She became my cheerleader and confidante. She was a wild child and the youngest of several kids, raised in a very conservative, religious family in Minnesota.

"I had to escape conformity," she told me. It wasn't that she didn't love her family and all her siblings and fifty plus nieces and nephews; she simply wanted more in her life. She also had the wildest hair, and you never knew what color it would be from week to week.

"Have you ever worked out with a personal trainer?" she asked me.

I hadn't.

"Honestly, they sort of scare me," I told her. "I've had a pretty crappy past year with getting pregnant three times and no baby to show for it, and I'm ready to just focus on me."

"Okay, but do you still want to have a baby?" she asked.

And there it was, the question I'd been avoiding answering aloud. Yes, I wanted a child, but the thought of another pregnancy loss petrified me. Forgetting the physical toll these three pregnancies had on my body, the emotional weight overwhelmed me more.

"Yes, I do. But that's not in my control anymore," I said. "However, my body is in my control, and only I can make sure it's healthy and in the best shape possible. So let's make it happen."

The third pregnancy loss reminded me that there are so few things we can control in our lives. And when you find something totally in your power—like creating a healthy body and mind—it helps you heal and understand. Now was the time for me to change course. I could either curl up in a ball and say life isn't fair and act like a victim, or I could concentrate on living. This time the choice was in my complete control.

After our first training session, I thought I'd die.

"I think I'm going to throw up," I told her.

"Good, it means it's working," she replied.

Was she kidding me? After that first workout session, my body started adapting, and I no longer felt the need to toss my cookies after each training.

I had so much fun training with Jenny. She pushed me harder than I'd ever imagined I could go. Our sessions were filled with squats, burpees, lunges, kettlebells, cardio, gossip, and laughter. Beyond training, we became friends, finding time to hang out between sessions.

When I started traveling more for work, our training sessions became less frequent.

"Don't worry, I'm still working out," I'd always remind her.

It had been almost a year since my last pregnancy loss, so I felt pretty vulnerable.

"I made it an entire year without getting pregnant and losing a baby," I said.

A morbid statement, but I needed to say it aloud.

Chapter 30

In early March 2007, I realized I had missed my period. "No, I can't be pregnant," I thought. "Could I be?"

On the way home from work, I stopped to buy a pregnancy kit and quickly went upstairs to take the test.

Adam wasn't home from work yet, and I'd be meeting him in another apartment within our building to see if we should rent it. Our lease was going to come up for renewal in a few months, and we wanted more space.

Such a New York thing to do, staying in the same building since moving anywhere is a nightmare, but add in all the rules and regulations with a New York City apartment building, and your stress level increases exponentially. The new unit sat on a higher floor with a better view and had three bedrooms and three bathrooms, unthinkable in New York City terms. I took the test and couldn't believe it. Two pink lines: pregnant. I thought, "Here we go again." Dr. Levine was right when he said my problems had nothing to do with getting pregnant.

I met Adam at the apartment and walked in, quickly looked around, and, in rapid response, said, "It's great. Let's take it. We'll need the space now that I'm pregnant."

The apartment was empty, so my words echoed as they hung in the air.

"Did you hear me? I said I'm pregnant," I said again when I thought maybe he missed it.

"I did hear you, and oh my goodness. Really?" he replied.

"I guess Dr. Levine was right. It will happen when you stop trying."

Sure, I'd stopped thinking about it, but did I stop trying? Who knows?

"I have a good feeling about this pregnancy; I don't know why, but I just do," I said. "The universe can't be cruel to us again, can it?"

Only time would tell, but I was pregnant for now, and we were signing a new lease on a larger apartment that would hopefully be home to the three of us by the end of the year.

"Let's go out to dinner and toast our new apartment and future," Adam said.

"Yes, that sounds like a great idea. No negative thoughts, only positive ones. Everything is going to be great," I said—and prayed.

A few days later, I met with Dr. Levine.

"I told you just to give your body a rest and let it happen," he said.

I got up on the examination table, and before he started the sonogram, I said, "Listen, please don't tell me anything, especially if it's bad news. I don't think I can take it."

He started the exam and looked at me and then at Adam, and then he motioned for Adam to come over to the monitor. He started pointing out to Adam different things on the monitor, and they were exchanging words and talking low.

"Hey, what are you two talking about over there? Why aren't you telling me anything?" I asked.

"You said not to say anything to you," Dr. Levine responded.

"And you believed me?"

He laughed.

"Well, everything looks good," he said.

"So there's a sac and a baby in the sac?" I asked.

"Yes, it all seems to be in order right now. Based on your last cycle, you should be due around November twenty-third."

I couldn't stop smiling even though I had nervous butterflies in my stomach.

Although thrilled to be pregnant, I couldn't let myself get as excited as I did the first or even the second time I found out, which made me sad.

"I need to let you and Adam know that I'm stepping away from obstetrics and will only be focusing on gynecology," Dr. Levine said. "But you'll be in good hands with other doctors in the practice."

Certainly, unwelcome news to me.

"Did I wear you down?" I asked. "How will I ever get through this pregnancy without you?"

"You'll do just fine, and I'll be a phone call away," he assured me.

I seriously couldn't imagine going through this experience without Dr. Levine. He had become my rock throughout the whole journey.

"I'll hold you to that," I said.

After work, I had a training session scheduled with Jenny and decided to tell her the news that night. I wasn't twelve weeks yet, but I needed to let Jenny know, so she'd take it easy on me.

"You ready to get to it?" she asked when I walked up to her.

"Yes, but first, I want to talk to you about my program," I replied.

"Is there something you don't like that we're doing?" she asked.

"Well, yes, everything," I joked. "But there's nothing wrong. I just thought you should tweak it for a pregnant woman."

It took a minute, but she figured it out and began to whoop and holler.

"Stop screaming. I'm not ready to announce it yet," I told her.

She couldn't stop screaming.

"I spoke to my doctor about working out, and he said I could if I don't get crazy. And then I told him that might be difficult with you since you're crazy," I joked.

"Girl, I've got you. I will create the best program for you to follow throughout your pregnancy, and I'll be right by your side. This is going to be so awesome."

The months following my pregnancy revelation weren't always rosy. Still, for me, I took every day of morning sickness, heartburn, belly kicks, and endless peeing as a blessing and badge of honor. I was so thrilled to be finally experiencing pregnancy. I never took anything for granted. Yes, I had momentary lapses when I'd look in the mirror and scream, "I'm so fat, and nothing fits me." But that was all part of the process.

Before each doctor's appointment, I'd hold my breath, wondering if this would be the day the other shoe dropped, and I'd be told something was wrong. But that day never happened. I don't remember when I finally conceded that maybe everything would be okay, but I did. And once I came to that realization, I started to relax and enjoy the wild hormonal ride.

"Because of your history and age, we recommend you have a CVS, chorionic villus sampling, to see if your baby has a genetic or chromosomal condition," the new Dr. Levine told me.

"How exactly does that work, and can it cause me to miscarry?" I asked.

I had heard all sorts of pros and cons about these tests. Honestly, I understood the rationale of the tests, but at this point, for me, what else could go wrong?

"While there is a slightly higher percentage of miscarriage with the CVS test versus an amniocentesis test, it's proven more accurate for diagnosing issues in women of your age," he explained. "As for how they administer it, you sure you want to hear about that right now?"

He must have noticed the look of panic on my face.

"Yes, get it over with," I said.

"A thin needle is inserted into the uterus to remove a sample of chorionic villus cells from the placenta. These cells contain a baby's genetic information," he explained.

"The only way to get those cells is with a needle?" I asked. "There's no other way?"

He nodded.

Adam went with me for the test.

"Are you going to be able to handle watching this needle go in my stomach?" I asked him. It was no secret that when it came to needles, he was more of a wimp than me. "I don't need you passing out."

He assured me he'd be okay.

Before performing the test, the doctor introduced himself to us in the treatment room. "I understand you're a little nervous about this test. Don't worry; I've done hundreds and hundreds of them, so I know what I'm doing. The doctor that's only performed a few of these is who you need to worry about," he laughed.

While slightly comforted by his words and resume, I couldn't move past the fact that he looked like an absentminded professor with white messy hair and glasses that hung down his nose.

"He reminds me of Christopher Lloyd's character from *Back to the Future*," I told Adam. Maybe this would give me a focal point to stare at while he was jamming the needle into my belly.

"Okay, I'm getting ready to start, but have you been watching *American Idol*?" he asked.

Okay, random, but I played along. "Yes, I love Simon so much. He cracks me up," I said.

"Yes, he makes the show. I think this season has some good contenders, but you never know. Oh, and I'm done."

Wait, what? "You're done?" I asked him. "I didn't even know you started."

He laughed and said, "That was my goal. You can get up now and get dressed."

Wow. I loved this man, giant mess of white hair and all.

A couple of days after the CVS procedure, the doctor called. "Good news; there are no chromosomal abnormalities, and everything looks great."

I started crying.

"These are happy tears," I assured him.

"I understand," he replied.

"Do you want to learn the sex of the baby, or will this be a surprise?"

"I think I'd like you to tell me," I said.

"You think, or you know?" he asked.

"I know. And for the record, I think I'm having a boy."

He paused and said, "You are correct. Congratulations, you're having a boy."

I just sat in my chair and smiled—a boy. I was going to be a boy mom.

"Oh, thank God," I said.

"Why do you say that?" he asked.

"Because if I were having a girl, my mom would win," I told him. "She said her ultimate wish for me would be that I one day had a little girl who was exactly like me, and honestly, I was a huge pain in the ass."

He laughed, and I kept crying tears of joy. Not because I was having a boy but because I was on my way to having what appeared to be a healthy child.

I got off the phone with the doctor and called Adam. "Do you want to know what we're having?" I asked. "Because I can always keep it from you if you want to be surprised."

He didn't.

"We're having a boy!"

He kept silent, but I could feel his smile through the phone. We decided to keep the gender news to ourselves, except for my parents. I loved to listen to all the speculation by friends, family, and total strangers over the following months as to what we were having. I loved how people *just knew*. I should have started a betting pool.

The following six months were filled with excitement, panic, stress, worry, happiness, terror, and anticipation. And being pregnant in New York City, well, that just added a whole new layer of emotion. Crowded trains, subways, and pushy people on the streets brought the most stress. But occasionally, I would meet someone with basic manners. One evening, as I got on the crowded bus to come home from work, there were no seats. I grabbed a pole and decided to hang on.

"Excuse me, would you like to sit down?" a man standing next to me asked.

"Yes, but there is no place for me to sit," I told him.

"Oh, I'll get you a seat. My wife's been pregnant three times, so I'm no stranger to kicking people out of their seats."

He then proceeded to kick a young guy out of his seat so I could sit down. And to think they say chivalry is dead.

Another time I experienced the best of people in New York City was when I got off the bus near my office. I fell in the middle of Fifth Avenue, right in front of St. Patrick's Cathedral. More like I bounced in the middle of the street. I guess I lost my footing getting off the bus and splat, there I sat, in the middle of the road. Several people came to my aid to help me up.

"I'm fine, thank you," I assured them. "I'm more embarrassed than anything."

But by the time I got to the office, I didn't feel the baby kicking as he had been all morning.

"I need to come in to check to see if the baby is okay," I explained to the nurse, giving her all the details of what had just happened.

I got an appointment and came in.

"Everything is fine," the nurse said as she pointed to the ultrasound. "It looks like your little guy was just taking a nap."

A rush of relief fell over me. I couldn't even imagine if my klutziness had caused him any harm. From that moment, I knew my little guy was tough.

"I think we should take one last vacation before the baby is born, a babymoon," I told Adam.

I had read a lot about couples taking these trips before having a baby since who knew when they'd ever be able to take a trip together again.

"What do you think about going to Anguilla?" he asked.

The beach sounded great to me, so we booked tickets and a hotel in Anguilla. Neither of us had ever been to this part of the Caribbean and were excited about the adventure. However, I hadn't factored in having to wear a bathing suit.

"I guess I never thought about putting on a bathing suit while pregnant. I'm going to look like a beached whale," I told Adam.

"You're pregnant, not fat," he said.

"So I'll be a pregnant beached whale."

For four glorious days, we explored the island, sunbathed on the beach, and took advantage of all the great culinary treats. Even though I still felt like a Beluga whale, I didn't mind the staff's extra care and attention.

Soon, we were back in New York for the final months of my pregnancy. My parents had gone on another cruise and were docking at the Bayonne, New Jersey port. They had several hours before their flight left to go back to Florida, so I picked them up, and we went to buy more things for the baby.

"Your father is having way too much fun trying out the rocking chairs," my mother said, pointing.

He looked so cute, too. So happy. I may have been the one carrying the baby, but this child belonged to the entire family. Sharing this journey with my parents meant so much to me. They were robbed of this experience with Celia's passing and my pregnancy losses.

I then took them to a doctor's appointment to see an ultrasound.

"I can't believe we're looking at our grandchild," my father said through his tears.

There wasn't a dry eye in the room.

I finally made it to November, known as the "get this baby out of me" month. There isn't a pregnant woman alive who isn't ready to give birth in her last month of pregnancy. Why would I be different?

I was so proud that I continued exercising regularly with Jenny throughout my pregnancy.

"You'll be back at it in no time once this baby is born," Jenny said. "You're such a rock star, and now you're even stronger than before you got pregnant." And then she added, "Just try and not have a C-section."

At my weekly check-in with the doctor the day before Thanksgiving, I prayed there'd be progress.

"Can you please give me good news?" I asked the doctor.

"Well, if you want me to tell you you're starting to dilate, I will, but you're not," he said.

How can this be?

Thanksgiving came and went, and no baby.

The following day, my dad and Adam went to pick up the crib while my mother and I walked around the neighborhood. The freezing temperatures outside didn't help, so we stopped at a Starbucks to get a hot chocolate.

"Maybe the hot chocolate will start things moving," I said to my mother.

But it didn't.

After dinner, anxious and tired, I went to sleep early. The next day my parents went shopping, and Adam and I stayed home to work on the baby's room.

"We can at least put the crib together," he said.

"After I get something to eat," I smiled.

I went into the kitchen to get some cheese. Not paying attention to how I sliced the cheese, I felt a sting on my finger.

"Uh, Adam, I need you to come here, but don't get angry."

He walked into the kitchen and saw my hand covered in blood. "What happened?" he screamed.

"As I was slicing cheese with this knife, I couldn't figure out why it was so difficult to cut and kept pushing down on it.

Then I realized that I wasn't slicing the cheese; I was cutting my finger."

Honestly, as gross as it appeared and how painful it was, I welcomed the diversion from stressing out over the baby being late. That night, I went to bed early again. But this time, I woke up around 1:30 a.m. because I had to pee.

Washing my hands, I noticed water all over the floor.

"How on earth did I get all this water on the floor" I asked myself. It didn't make sense; the sink was dry. Where did the water come from? And then it hit me. My water broke.

"Adam, wake up," I said. "My water broke. We have to call the doctor."

We got the doctor on the phone, and he told us to go to the hospital.

"Okay, but can I please take a shower and wash my hair before we leave?" I asked him.

I didn't know the next time I'd be able to take a full shower. This reminded me of my Uncle Joe and washing my hair during the sunset in Costa Rica. At least I remained consistent with my hair priorities. I knew he'd laugh if he were here. When we were ready to go to the hospital, I woke up my mother.

"My water broke, and we're on the way to the hospital. We'll call you when we know anything."

"Are you sure you don't want us to come with you?" she asked.

"Not yet. Get some sleep, and I'll call you soon, Grammy."

She decided to be called Grammy, which Celia and I had called her mom. Except I couldn't pronounce Grammy and opted for Mammy. Not a good thing by today's standards, but acceptable in the 1960s.

Adam and I got to the hospital around 2:30 a.m., with all the labor and delivery rooms strangely occupied. We were told on our hospital tour that there were ten labor and delivery rooms. I jokingly asked how often they were filled simultaneously. "Rarely," the woman had replied.

She failed to add "unless there is a full moon." It turned out the moon was full. An old wives' tale says that since the moon's gravitational pull is strong enough to influence the tides, it's also strong enough to affect a woman's body—like if she's pregnant and nearing her due date. While this theory is not based on natural science, it could explain why every labor and delivery room had a pregnant woman waiting to give birth and several more expectant moms in the waiting room that night.

"I hope I don't have the baby while sitting here," I said to Adam.

"Hi there, are you here to have a baby tonight?" a nurse asked me.

"I sure hope so. Aren't all these women here to do the same thing?"

They were, but she explained some would go home because of a false alarm. I truly hoped I wouldn't be going home.

"Well, the good news is you'll have a baby soon," the nurse said after examining me.

"Was that a question?" I asked.

"No, but several women thought their water broke when they only peed themselves, so we sent them home. Not you. You're here to stay for the duration. Let's set you up in this room for the time being, and if you need to use the bathroom, here's a pan. It will be easier since you'll be hooked up to an IV," the nurse explained.

We sat in the little room for what felt like hours.

At one point, Adam said, "This chair is so uncomfortable. It's killing my back."

I rolled my eyes at him.

"Really, you're uncomfortable? I'm sitting with my ass on a bedpan, ready to birth a baby, but you're uncomfortable? Please, tell me more. In fact, please call my mom and tell her exactly how to get to the hospital, and then you go home, take a shower, and get some sleep. You can come back later with my dad."

I loved him, but I needed my mother at that moment, not him complaining about an uncomfortable chair.

My mom walked into the room an hour later, and I started to cry. "I want to get in a room and out of this closet," I said.

My tears made the baby's heartbeat go up, and all these bells and alarms started ringing. Several nurses ran into the room.

"What's wrong," I cried.

"Everything is okay. It puts pressure on the umbilical cord when you move around, taking oxygen away from the baby. You need to try and lie still."

Oh sure, no problem, I thought.

Finally, after about eight hours in the small room, they moved me into one of the labor and delivery rooms. This massive room felt so much better.

The doctor came in and explained everything. "Your water did indeed break, but all the amniotic fluid released, and now none is protecting the baby. But because you're not yet dilated, we will have to give you some medicine to try and push things along."

The next several hours were spent poking, prodding, and shoving things inside me to try and start my labor. But nothing seemed to be working. The oxygen through my nose hurt, so I kept pulling it out, and each time I did, another alarm bell would sound.

"You have to keep oxygen flowing, so it will get to your baby," the nurse explained.

I started to panic.

My dad and Adam finally joined us.

"Why are you always on the phone?" my dad said when he saw me.

"I'm not on the phone, Daddy. I'm hooked up to oxygen."

He felt terrible for making fun of me. "I'm so sorry," he said.

And, of course, that made me cry.

"How much longer will this take?" I kept asking nurses as they came in and out of my room.

Patience has never been one of my strengths, so this ordeal tested my limits. Several more hours passed, and I finally felt something.

"I think I just had a contraction," I said.

"This is good news. Will you be getting an epidural?" the doctor asked.

"Like that's a question? If you could knock me out and wake me up when the kid turns sixteen, I'd appreciate it more," I said.

Everyone got a good laugh, but they didn't realize my seriousness. I couldn't even endure a little labor pain. How would I ever handle motherhood?

"We'll send the anesthesiologist to administer the epidural," he said.

I looked up right as a smoking hot doctor walked into my room: the George Clooney of anesthesiology. "Hi there, I'm here to administer your epidural," he said.

"Okay, great, anything you need to do is fine," I said. I'm sure he was used to this reaction, but he didn't let on.

No one prepares you for how painful a procedure the epidural is, but I swear I barely felt it as I concentrated on the doctor's face. They probably got the best-looking doctor in the hospital to give the fat pregnant women epidurals on purpose. And that strategy worked fine for me.

Within minutes, I felt nothing below my waist. A weird sensation, but it didn't bother me at all.

Several more hours passed, and my mom and dad were fading fast. But they weren't as tired as me. "This baby will never come out of me," I cried.

"Judy, what is your birth plan if you cannot have the baby naturally?" the doctor asked me.

"Birth plan? You're kidding, right? My birth plan is for you to get this baby out of me however you need. This is not my area of expertise, so I'll look to you for what to do next."

He explained that many women come in with a strict birth plan and instructions not to deviate from it.

"Respectfully, I'm not those women, Doctor. You do what you need to do."

At about 10:00 p.m., my parents were ready to return to the apartment. The doctor stopped them as Adam was getting up to help them find a taxi.

"It's not serious yet, but if she doesn't start to move in the next couple of minutes, we will have to perform a C-section. I would hate to wait much longer, so it becomes an emergency. If you can hold on, you'll be grandparents within the hour."

Then the doctor turned to me. "Judy, we will have to perform a C-section as the baby's umbilical cord is too short, and he's not getting enough oxygen. We don't want to wait much longer and have this be a more serious situation," he explained.

"Please promise me you'll get him out perfectly," I cried.

"I'll do my very best, and soon, you'll meet your baby."

A few minutes later, Dr. George Clooney walked back into my room to give me more epidural.

"Will you be in the OR with me?" I sweetly asked him.

He smiled and said, "Yes, I'll be there—with your husband."

Oh, right—my husband.

Before they wheeled me into the OR, my mom and dad walked up to the side of my bed.

"Remember what I told you about C-section babies?" my mom asked.

"Yes, they have perfect heads."

Celia and I were C-section babies. I kissed my parents goodbye.

"I'll see you soon, Grammy and Papa."

Adam met me in the OR as they put a big curtain at my waist, blocking my view of anything on the other side. Not that I could see anything since I had to lay flat on my back with my arms spread out to either side. Adam sat next to my head and gave me the play-by-play.

"What are they doing?" I asked.

"They're preparing the area."

C-sections are no joke. What they don't tell you is that it is major surgery. They cut so far down the abdominal muscle that it takes several weeks to heal. Of course, I kept hearing Jenny when she said to me, "Whatever happens, try not to have a C-section, or your recovery will be that much longer."

Oh well, not in my control, I thought. Like so many events in my life where I felt helpless and not in control: my attack, my parents getting sick, Celia dying, the three pregnancy losses, why wouldn't this experience bring more of the same to me?

"Okay, Judy, you'll feel a little pressure, but we're almost there," the doctor said.

And then, at 10:55 p.m., after more than twenty hours of labor, the doctor said, "It's a boy!"

But I didn't hear anything.

"Why don't I hear anything?" I screamed.

And right as I spoke, the most glorious sound I'd ever heard filled the room; my baby was crying. I couldn't see anything, still flat on my back, but I asked, "Adam, is he cute?"

"Oh yes, he is," he said.

"Does he have ten fingers and ten toes?" I prayed.

"Yes, he does."

Oh good. All the harmful things I had put in my body through the years hadn't hurt him, I thought. And a few minutes later, Adam walked over to me, holding our son in a blanket, and put his little face right up to mine. I looked directly into his big blue eyes and said, "Hello, you."

I looked back at Adam and said, "Now, what do we do?"

So many emotions flooded me. Could I do this? I mean, I'm the one who wanted to be a mother, but what if I failed? And why was I thinking about all of this now? And oh, how I wished Celia were there with me at that moment.

Chapter 31

It took a while to stitch me up, and once the doctor finished, they wheeled me into the recovery room. My mom and dad were waiting for me, along with Adam.

"I did it," I said to my parents.

They couldn't speak. And they didn't need to. I knew everything they wanted to say without ever hearing one word.

"Oh my gosh," I finally said. "Happy Anniversary! I'm so glad the baby was born before midnight because I didn't have time to buy you a present."

November 25 is my parents' wedding anniversary, and I was sure this gift topped all the others I'd ever given them, including the homemade cards of macaroni and glitter.

"By the way," I said. "Would you mind if we named the baby after Papa and called him Jack?"

Once again, I rendered my mother speechless. "That would be so wonderful," she finally said.

Next to my father, my grandfather represented the most important male figure in my life and getting the chance to honor him by naming my son Jack meant everything to me.

His middle name is Aaron, named for Adam's mom. Her name was Gail, but we didn't like any "G" boy names.

"How about an 'A' name," Adam asked. "Technically, Gail is a derivative of Abigail, so it still works."

We chose Aaron. Once we selected the name, I laughed to myself. My son would be a handsome man and probably attract many beautiful women, some Jewish and some not. If he grew up to marry a non-tribe member, my little gift to her would be her name, Mrs. Jacob "Jack" Aaron Cohen. I win.

A few minutes after I got to recovery, they wheeled in Jack.

"He's perfect," my mom said.

And he was, all seven pounds four ounces of him.

"Adam, I need your phone," I said.

"Who are you calling at this hour?" my father asked.

"You'll see," I said. "We had a boy, and his name is Jack," I told Kay and Fred when they picked up the phone. "I know it's late, but I thought you'd want to know."

They, of course, did.

"Oh, and I need to ask you something," I continued. "Will you both be Jack's godparents?"

After a brief silence, they said, "We'd be honored."

The circle of life was now complete. My son was named after my grandfather and Adam's mother, and his godparents would be the other people in my life who had always been there for me through every twist and turn. Jack was a very blessed little boy. But even with all the joy and love surrounding me, I couldn't shake my sadness as I wished for Celia's presence. She never strayed far from my thoughts, even all these years later.

At around 2:00 a.m., almost twenty-four hours since I had arrived at the hospital, they finally brought me to my room. I said goodnight to Adam and my parents as the nurse took Jack to the nursery.

"Why can't he come sleep in the room with me?" I asked the nurse.

"Because you just had a C-section, and we need you to get some rest. We'll bring him back to you in a few hours," she explained.

I already felt guilty. That didn't take long, I thought.

Being hooked up to loud machines, I didn't get any sleep.

A few hours later, another nurse came to my room to help me use the bathroom.

"I can't get out of bed," I told her.

"Well, if you don't try, I will have to put a catheter in you," she said.

And like magic, I got out of bed. It was beyond painful but probably nowhere near what a catheter would feel like.

"When will you bring Jack to me?" I asked.

"Soon, dear, you need your rest," she said.

"I need my baby."

I kept thinking about baby cubs and puppies and their feelings if their moms neglected them. Finally, after several hours, they wheeled Jack to my side.

"It's time to feed the baby," she practically sang as she entered my room.

Right about that time, Adam and my parents came back with lunch.

"Are you going to try breastfeeding?" the nurse asked.

"I guess," I said. I hadn't thought much about it. But I did like the idea of my boobs shrinking because of it. They were the size of watermelons.

I tried, and nothing. And then I tried some more and nothing.

"I guess I don't know what I'm doing," I said.

"Don't worry, we'll have someone come in and help you, but in the meantime, here's some formula to feed him."

A few minutes after Jack ate, and less than an hour since Adam and my parents arrived, Hannah waltzed into the room.

"Hi, everyone! Oh, hey, Judy, you look great. Now, give me that baby."

And before I had any real bonding time holding Jack, Hannah held him in her arms. But I didn't care. With three daughters, she knew what to do more than I did. Hannah and I were like sisters, so naturally, she'd be the first one at my side.

For the rest of the day, I desperately tried to get someone to perform a simple blood test on Jack to determine whether he was a hemophiliac.

"I can't leave the hospital without knowing this information, especially since we have his bris scheduled for a week from today," I explained.

"We know, but there's been a lot of emergencies, and we're getting someone to you as soon as possible."

Later that evening, after everyone had left, Jenny came to the hospital.

"We did it," I told her.

"We? You did it," she said.

"Technically, yes, but emotionally I'd never have been able to do it without you."

She cried hearing me say that.

"And, sorry about the C-section."

She smiled and said, "It's okay. We'll have to train harder when you're ready to come back."

No one came for the blood test the next day, and I started getting anxious.

"We'll send someone as soon as possible," they told us.

In the meantime, I celebrated that I had finally started breastfeeding, or at least I thought that's what I was doing.

"When's the last time you fed him?" the nurse asked.

"An hour ago. Why?" I replied.

"Well, his lips are dry, which means he's dehydrated," she said.

It turns out I did it all wrong. I started to cry. "Did I just starve my baby?"

She assured me I didn't and handed me more formula.

"Just keep trying," she said. "You'll get it eventually."

I finally got up and went for a walk around the floor with my dad. "Are you okay," he asked.

"Yes, are you okay?"

He appeared so overwhelmed with joy and happiness.

"A grandson, can you handle it?" He just smiled and nodded as he held onto my arm.

Later that evening, after Adam and my parents left, I walked downstairs to the nursery to see Jack. When I got there, I gasped. Of the dozen babies, at least eight of them were huge. I mean gigantic heads and bodies. Jack appeared to be the smallest of the bunch. The average-sized baby in that room had to be at least ten pounds, with some tipping the scales at twelve.

"What did these mothers eat?" I asked.

"We typically get one or two babies over ten pounds, so this is not normal," she explained.

I thought about the full moon.

The following day we were still waiting for someone to come and take Jack's blood. Finally, around midday, they came to get him.

"I can't watch," I said.

"We'll take him to another room and bring him back," they told us.

"Mama, please go with him," I said.

And she followed behind.

They came back not long after. "He was a real trooper, more so than his parents," my mother said.

"How long will it take to determine whether or not he has hemophilia?" I asked.

"We hope to let you know tomorrow before you're discharged from the hospital," the nurse said.

I had one more night in the hospital where I could ring the call button.

"Oh my gosh, after tonight, we'll be on our own," I told Adam.

Reality had finally hit me, knowing we'd be going home with Jack the next day.

The following day as we waited to be discharged, we still didn't have the test results from Jack's blood test.

"I thought we'd have the results by now. Can you please check again?" I asked.

"The results aren't back yet, but they promised to call you at home with them," the nurse said. That wasn't the answer I wanted to hear.

"His clothes are way too big," I told Adam.

My mom bought a ginormous "coming home" outfit that could have fit three Jacks. But he looked so cute.

"Do you know how to get the car seat installed in the backseat?" I asked.

"Yes, but I just want to ensure it's secure," Adam said.

I crawled into the backseat and sat next to Jack. As we drove away from the hospital, another car cut us off, and Adam jammed on the brakes.

"I hope this isn't an omen for our parenting to come," I said.

When we got inside the apartment, I put Jack's car seat on top of the coffee table, and he stayed there for several hours sleeping. I think the four of us just stared at him the entire time.

"Are you going to keep trying to breastfeed?" my mother asked me.

"Yes, I've called a lactation specialist, and she's coming over later to help me," I said.

Of course, the doctor never called with the test results, and I started to panic and get angry. "I'll call first thing in the morning, but for now, I need sleep," I said.

Having my mother help me with Jack meant so much to me. I knew this wouldn't be forever, so I took full advantage while I had her.

A few hours later, the lactation specialist came to the apartment.

"I just can't get him to latch on," I told her.

"Don't worry, dear, these things happen," she replied.

Nothing seemed to work after several attempts to place Jack's tiny mouth on my engorged nipple.

Finally, she said, "Sometimes, a mother's milk just doesn't come in, and a baby can sense there's nothing there, so they don't try."

Wow, I thought. I've already failed as a mother.

After she left the apartment, my dad asked how it went.

"Oh, it went great," I said. "I just spent two-hundred dollars to have a strange woman feel me up and then tell me my milk never came in."

Only in New York City.

The following day, I called the doctor's office to let them know I needed the results as soon as possible because I had Jack's bris scheduled for Monday and wanted to make sure it would be okay to have one. Finally, a few hours later, the phone rang.

"Based on Jack's blood work, he does have hemophilia. You'll need to find a hematologist and make an appointment to assess his levels," the doctor explained.

"Do you have any recommendations for me?" I asked.

"I'm sorry, I don't."

What?

Here I sat, on a Friday afternoon, and I needed to find a hematologist to determine if I should cancel the bris and the celebration scheduled for Monday. And more challenging, hematology isn't a common field of study. I mean, it's not like I could pick the first name in the phone book to call.

Once again, the universe was testing my strength. While I'd known there would be a possibility that Jack would be diagnosed with hemophilia, it didn't make the confirmation any easier to hear. Regardless of my anger and frustration with how long it took to get the results, I realized it was no longer about me. It was all about my baby.

Before Jack's birth, Adam and I met with a pediatrician, and although she'd not yet met Jack, I thought maybe she could give me a referral. She gave me the name of a pediatric hematologist/oncologist at Mount Sinai Hospital, Dr. Ann Hurlet.

"I had a baby last Sunday night and just found out he has hemophilia, and I need to make an appointment to see a hematologist, and my pediatrician gave me Dr. Hurlet's name.

Also, I'm a little panicked because I have a bris scheduled for Monday, and I need to know if I should reschedule it," I babbled on without taking a breath.

"I'll have Dr. Hurlet call you back," she calmly said. "I'd cancel the bris, and Dr. Hurlet can help you determine when to reschedule."

I let out a huge breath I didn't even know I was holding.

Next, I called the mohel, who would perform the circumcision.

"I just found out my son has hemophilia, so I need to cancel his bris for Monday," I told him.

"I would have appreciated a little more advance notice," he snarled.

And then I started crying. I apologized and hung up.

I wasn't sure if my tears and anger were directed at the hospital for waiting so long to take Jack's blood or the mohel who had just yelled at me. Either way, I sat there and tried to breathe. It made me think about conversations with my client Al during our 9/11 meltdown. "Sometimes you just need to breathe," we'd tell each other.

A few hours later, the phone rang. "Hi, this is Dr. Hurlet," a woman with a very thick European accent said when I picked up. I explained the whole situation, including my father having hemophilia.

"Is your father still alive?" she asked.

"Yes, he's with me now."

Then she brought me peace.

"I'll make an appointment for you on Monday at 9:00 a.m. Bring Jack and your father to see me, and I'll run bloodwork and speak to your father. I want you to relax because everything is going to be just fine. Also, once we determine the severity of Jack's hemophilia, we can decide when to have his bris, and I'll give you the name of one of the best doctors in the city to perform it."

My hormones surely had something to do with my reaction, but I couldn't stop crying. Dr. Hurlet was an angel sent to me. I secretly wondered if Celia had anything to do with her appearance.

The following Monday morning, in the cold air, we bundled Jack's tiny body into his large clothes, and Adam drove all of us across Central Park to Mount Sinai Hospital.

Dr. Hurlet, it turns out, wasn't just a specialist doctor. She was the head of Pediatric Hematology/Oncology for all of Mount Sinai Hospital. I couldn't believe someone of her stature had taken the time to speak to me on a Friday at 5:00 p.m., not knowing Jack or me but treating us as if she'd known us for years.

We spent several hours meeting with Dr. Hurlet and different staff members.

"Because your father has hemophilia, you automatically have the gene because he passed it on to you, but it didn't necessarily mean you'd pass it on to Jack. There was a fifty-fifty chance you would," she said.

I'd always been an overachiever.

"I can't watch them sticking, Jack," I told my mom as the nurse tried to draw his blood. "You and Adam just go in the other room, and I'll stay with him."

My mother remained so calm. After her own cancer experience and watching her daughter die, nothing rattled her.

After meeting with my father, and based on Jack's blood tests, Dr. Hurlet determined Jack had hemophilia A, the same as my dad.

"Fortunately, like your father, his case is mild."

Hopefully, in addition to hemophilia, he'd get the tall gene and grow into a six-foot-four man like my father.

But even though Jack's case was mild, it still upset my father. "I feel so awful that he has this condition because of me," my dad said.

His words and declaration gave me déjà vu. I remembered my mom's feelings of guilt regarding Celia's cancer.

I tried to comfort him by saying, "It means he'll be just like you, and that's an excellent thing in my book."

And then I kissed his cheek. I loved my father deeply and respected him even more. I couldn't think of a better person for Jack to take after than him, hemophilia or not.

Even though I was strong for my father, I was having a meltdown on the inside. Being a new mother is overwhelming enough without finding out your newborn has a bleeding disorder.

But I just put the whole thing into perspective. Life could always be worse. Jack was a beautiful, healthy little boy with a hereditary condition. And like every challenging experience I'd had in my life, I would find the strength to handle this one. I had no choice.

Dr. Hurlet gave me the name of one of the best doctors in the city who performed circumcisions. We rescheduled Jack's bris for that Thursday and would have clotting medicine on standby if we needed it for the procedure.

That Thursday, once again, we bundled Jack up for another drive across Central Park, this time to Dr. Jeffery Mazlin's office. Dr. Mazlin, a prominent Upper East Side ob-gyn, also performed bris ceremonies in his office. And he made us all feel so welcome.

Jack must have sensed something terrible was about to happen because he started to scream when we walked into the office.

"This is normal," Dr. Mazlin explained. "I'm just going to let him suck on this wine-soaked gauze to relax him."

Wow, what an unexpected but welcome relief.

"This is one of the oldest tricks in the book," he explained.

I'd make a note of that trick for sure.

Dr. Mazlin then said several prayers, including giving Jack his Hebrew name, Yakov Arun, and then he said a few words about Jack being named for my grandfather and Adam's mother.

"There is no way I'll be able to watch this," I told my mother.

When Dr. Mazlin began, I took my mother's hand and squeezed it so tight I think there are still ring indentation marks to this day. Thankfully the wine did its job, and while Jack did cry out at first, he quickly fell asleep and stayed that way for hours.

Fortunately, there were no bleeding incidents. And while it wasn't the bris celebration we had planned (the adage of making plans and God laughs coming back into play), I felt so blessed having my parents with us.

We drove my parents to the airport ten days later, and that's when reality kicked in. While I'd had my fair share of life challenges up to this point, none seemed as big as motherhood. But as they say, be careful what you ask for.

Epilogue

As we drove away from the airport, Jack started crying, his tears flowing harder than mine. And the louder he screamed, the more inept I felt as a mother.

"Jack knows we have no idea what we're doing," I said to Adam.

And that sentiment proved true over the following days when he started melting down every night at 6:00 p.m.

"Why is he crying, and why did you leave me?" I whined to my mom over the phone when he wouldn't stop. "Every night at the same time, he starts crying for hours. His diaper isn't wet. He's not hungry. He's not tired. What is wrong with him? I've tried calming him by walking back and forth around the apartment, cradling him in my arms, but nothing's working."

Why did I feel so helpless and vulnerable when things felt out of control? Sure, I'd experienced life events in the past that I had no control over, with my attack and sister's death at the top of the list. I mean, he was just a tiny baby. I could do this, right? I needed to relax and pull it together.

After countless calls to the pediatrician, my mother, Melinda, and Hannah, the consensus on what ailed Jack was colic.

"Some babies get colic, and others don't," the doctor explained.

"Let me get this straight," I said. "Jack starts crying every night, about 6:00 p.m., and doesn't stop until close to midnight, and the explanation is some babies have this and others don't?"

I quickly decided colic must be a five-letter word for "we don't know."

Fortunately, we had no shortage of people giving us advice.

"Change his formula; he probably just has gas." "Put his carrier on top of the washing machine. The motion will lull him to sleep." "Walk him around the block until he falls asleep." We tried it all, except putting him on the washing machine; living in an apartment, ours was stackable. Nothing worked.

Miraculously, about three months into our colic nightmare, it disappeared.

"It's 8:00 p.m., and Jack hasn't melted down—yet. I think it's over," I told my mom.

It was the best night ever. The sleepless nights that accompany new parenthood can only be described as slow torture. You tell yourself it's all good, and you can function on minimal sleep each night as long as your baby is okay. But it's all a lie.

When my maternity leave ended, I found myself in a sleep-deprived fog every day. It remains unclear how I got dressed and out the door each morning.

"Is the baby sleeping through the night?" many a stranger asked.

"How do you know I have a new baby? Do my eyes give it away, or is it the spit-up on my clothes?" I'd respond to such a ridiculous question.

The truth was even once Jack started sleeping in two to three-hour blocks of time, I'd still sit in his room and stare at him. Most nights, when I didn't hold him in my arms, rocking him gently in the chair, I would fall asleep on the hard apartment floor next to his crib. I couldn't help it.

I had longed for this child for many years and through several losses. The thought of anything happening to him became my constant fear. I knew it wasn't healthy, but that's how life had conditioned me.

When I finally felt things were going well, I would wait for the other shoe to drop, holding on to that whole "make plans and life gets in the way" line of thinking, which unfortunately began haunting me from a young age. But I told myself: That's victim thinking, and I've never thought of myself that way. Not after I was attacked and not after my sister died, and I wouldn't start now.

It's important to note that these revelations came to me after years of therapy that I continue today. It can be hard to ask for help, especially when your life feels like one traumatic event after another. But for me, psychological support became one more tool to support me through my journey.

Jack's birth represented so much more to me than a relationship between a mother and her new baby. It meant I finally had permission to live my life—just as Celia had always hoped for me.

In the years following my sister's death, I never pictured myself having an everyday life that included marriage and children—much less happiness and joy. But this time, God had another path for me to follow. And I had my very own guardian angel to watch over me, too.

Once Jack started sleeping longer through the night and showing his great little personality more and more, I began to relax and breathe, or as much as a new mother can.

I knew the days, months, and years ahead would present their challenges—some happy and others sad—but I finally understood that all the life planning, sleepless nights, and helpless feelings don't matter.

What matters is living your best life every day despite whatever obstacle gets in your way. What matters is understanding life doesn't always go as planned, but you don't stop living. What matters is what you do with your life, however long it lasts. Because in terms of universal time, we're only here for a moment.

Understanding these ideas is how I find the strength to withstand the sorrow of unimaginable grief. It's how I go on living. And with this thinking, I keep the promises I made to Celia all those years ago: to celebrate the good times, like the birth of my son; accept the bad times, even when they don't make sense; and never stop living. Because I know Celia wouldn't have had it any other way.

Photo Captions

1. Daddy and his girls.
   My 1st and Celia's 8th birthday.
   Celia and me in the matching red dresses.

2. With my Papa.
   Papa celebrating my 3rd & Celia's 10th birthday.
   Looking happy on the first day of 1st Grade.

3. Mama and her girls.
   My family in the 1970s.
   Dressed up with Celia for a family outing.

4. With Celia, at the Grand Canyon.
   With my cousins, Kay and Fred.
   Celebrating Celia's graduation from UT.

5. Backstage with Vanilla Ice.
   At a private concert with Sir Elton John.
   Hanging out with Donny Osmond.

6. With Adam, after the perfect wedding.
   With Jack, my greatest accomplishment.
   My parents, to whom I owe everything.

Acknowledgements

Writing this book has been a lifelong dream that I never would have fulfilled without the help of so many people who told me I could do it.

To my mother—you are my strength, role model, and best friend. I know you always tell me not to "thank you" for being my mom, but since I never listen to you anyway, why start now? Everything I am begins with you, and no matter where we are in our lives, it will always be you and me against the world.

To my father—your belief in me even when I didn't believe in myself and always saying I could do anything if I wanted to have carried me through life. You are with me every day and always in my heart.

To Adam—thank you for being my last "first date" and not getting mad that I ruined your perfect proposal. You are my sounding board, financial advisor, editor, and partner who always supports my zany ideas. I love you.

To my incredible son, Jack—you complete me and give me purpose. No matter where the road takes you, I will always be there to cheer you on without embarrassing you (too much!) and forever love you more. You are my greatest accomplishment.

To Fred—thank you for being the big brother I never had. I can't imagine my life without your guidance, sarcasm, and great lessons on mastering the art of talking on the telephone. Love you!

To Kay—thank you for being ready for your first family crisis. I'm not sure I would have gotten through it—or my life without you. I love you.

To Leslie, Mark, Jay, and Nancy—you will always be more than my 3rd cousins once removed. Thank you for always making me feel like your big sister. I love you all.

To my spirit sister and BFF, Melinda—thank you for telling me my story matters and encouraging me to share it with others. Your friendship is one of my greatest gifts.

To my soul sister and partner in crime, Hannah—you helped me find light in what felt like a very dark world. I can't think of anyone I'd want to scam through life more than with you, and I'll always be your biggest fan.

To Helen—thank you for literally pulling me off the ledge and not firing me days after you hired me. Your confidence in me helped me to fulfill so many dreams.

To Dana—thank you for giving me the space to always be my true self.

To Jenny—thank you for putting my broken spirit back together and pushing me to limits I never knew I could reach.

To my brilliant writing coach and editor, Amy—I'm so fortunate to have been paired with you for this project. Thank you for holding my hand throughout the process and confirming I was writing a book!

To my fantastic editor, Shasta—you made my words sing! Thank you for keeping my story accurate to my vision through your meticulous editing and thoughtful suggestions.

To my talented book cover designer, Laura—thank you for capturing the book's essence with your beautiful artistry. You nailed it!

To Jenna and the entire team at One Lit Place, I knew I'd found my home from the very first phone call. Your unwavering support and kindness in answering all my questions—and I mean all of them—confirmed that I made the right choice in working with you. Thank you!